# WOMEN
# AT HOME IN
# VICTORIAN
# AMERICA

# WOMEN AT HOME IN VICTORIAN AMERICA

## A SOCIAL HISTORY

*Ellen M. Plante*

☑®
Facts On File, Inc.

Women at Home in Victorian America: A Social History

Facts On File, Inc.
11 Penn Plaza
New York NY 10001

**Library of Congress Cataloging-in-Publication Data**

Plante, Ellen M.
Women at home in Victorian America : a social history / by Ellen M. Plante
p.   cm.
Includes bibliographical references and index.
ISBN 0-8160-3392-7
1. Middle class women—United States—History—19th century.
2. Middle class women—United States—Social conditions.   I. Title.
HQ1418.P53   1997
305.4'0973—dc21                    97-1417

Facts On File books are available at special discounts when purchased in bulk quantities for businesses, associations, institutions or sales promotions. Please call our Special Sales Department in New York at (212) 967-8800 or (800) 322-8755.

Look for Facts On File on the World Wide Web at http://www.factsonfile.com

Text design by Cathy Rincon
Layout by Robert Yaffe
Cover design by Semadar Megged
Illustrations are from the collection of the author unless otherwise noted.

Printed in the United States of America

MP FOF 10 9 8 7 6 5 4 3 2

This book is printed on acid-free paper.

For my daughter,

Kelly,

that she may better appreciate

the women

who came before us.

# CONTENTS

# INTRODUCTION

While the years 1837 through 1901 are commonly referred to as the Victorian era by historians, the culture and customs of this fast-changing, romantic period actually lingered in America until the outbreak of the First World War in 1914.

Named in honor of Queen Victoria of Great Britain, who was loved at home and abroad, these 19th- and early 20th-century decades in America were marked by rapid change, growing industrialization and tragedy as well as triumph.

In 1837 when the Victorian period officially began there were 26 states in the Union and Martin Van Buren was the eighth president. By the 1840s railroad travel had become a reality and women were being granted their first university degrees. The sewing machine had been invented and had far-reaching impact on labor done at home.

The midcentury period saw literary giants publish notable works such as Nathaniel Hawthorne's *The Scarlet Letter* and Harriet Beecher Stowe's *Uncle Tom's Cabin.* Architectural styles reflecting the popularity of the Greek Revival home remained steady, while the Gothic style had become the new darling of home or "cottage" design books. Inside the home, the coal and/or woodburning stove had revolutionized the manner in which cooking was done.

During the 1860s Americans fought the horrendous battles of the Civil War (1861–1865), and the 13th Amendment was ratified, putting an end to slavery. During this decade of bloodshed and tears President Lincoln was assassinated. The industrial revolution was pushing full steam ahead, with an increasing number of manufactured goods being turned out for household use. Parlor and bedroom suites with matching pieces of furniture in the latest style filled the rooms of middle-class homes.

The 1870s saw bicycles manufactured and the light bulb and phonograph introduced by Edison. America's centennial celebration captured the imagination of 38 states in 1876. Charles Eastlake's book *Hints on Household Taste* became the standard by which middle-class homes were decorated.

The Statue of Liberty was dedicated during the 1880s, suffragists formed the National Equal Rights Party and the box camera became a huge success. The quintessential Victorian home design, the Queen Anne style, became a hallmark of the Gilded Age.

By the time the 1890s rolled around, there were 44 states in the Union, Wyoming had granted women the right to vote and Henry Ford had built his first automobile. The World Exhibition opened in Chicago in 1893, drawing visitors from around the world. Before the turn of the century, boxed foods such as Jell-O and canned soups and meats were filling grocers' shelves.

The early years of the new century brought air flight, the establishment of the Ford Motor Company and General Motors Corporation, the introduction of Arts and Crafts furniture and accessories for home decoration, and the popular bungalow architectural style. Department stores had become a consumer mecca.

To say this was a century of change seems an understatement. In an era marked by so many and varied changes, home was revered as a safe haven from the uncertainty of a transforming world. And at the very center of this refuge and glorified domestic sphere was the Victorian woman.

Who exactly were the women at home in Victorian America? What were their life experiences? How did 19th-century customs and culture shape their lives? And what, we may ask, of their homes, their family life, their pastimes and domestic chores? These are some of the questions explored in the pages that follow. To be sure, the vast majority of women at home during the Victorian era were of the growing middle class. They were married to businessmen, preachers, farmers, small plantation owners, doctors, teachers, lawyers, artisans and entrepreneurs. For the most part, these women resided in growing cities, towns, villages and rural areas across the Northeast and throughout the South. Their sisters who forged West lived by different standards out of necessity as they struggled to fulfill the most basic human needs of food and shelter. This is not their story, for the lives of pioneering women, especially during the early and mid-Victorian periods, differed dramatically from what we have come to recognize as genteel Victorian culture.

This then is a look at middle-class women who took up residence as "the angel in the house." They were expected to live their lives comforting work-weary husbands, devoting themselves to molding young children into moral, upright citizens and fashioning homes that were at once a retreat from the outside world and a material as well as cultural inventory of refinement, social standing, intellect and honor.

These women were of a middle class that was unquestionably religious—equating gentility and morality with the high road to the pearly gates of heaven. Since women were regarded as the more sentimental sex, they were thought the ideal candidate for harnessing man's coarse nature and, of course, for child rearing. These virtuous middle-class women of the 19th century were trained to their lot in life from an early age, and the strict code of etiquette surrounding courtship eventually propelled the majority of them into matrimony. Once they became mistress of a house, Victorian wives were expected to start a family and establish and maintain a peaceful, comforting home. This was the stage on which they played out their lives, and child rearing along with the emotional bonds of family relationships were the focus of much of their energy.

In the home itself—the domestic altar—specific spaces were given over to "public" and "private" activities, and home decoration had the power to present the family in a positive light. Material culture was all-important in an era of heightened symbolism.

Maintaining the home in antebellum America was at the very least a challenge and more often an unending series of tedious tasks. In the North the bulk of the housework was carried out by the mistress with the help of one or more domestic servants, while on small plantations and Southern farms, slave labor created its own unique set of responsibilities and tasks for Victorian women. During the late 1800s the end of slavery, growing industrialization that lured would-be domestics into factory jobs, and increased consumerism forever altered how and by whom domestic chores were done. With the advent of packaged foods and such household appliances as the ice box and gas stove, middle-class women were introduced to "scientific" ways to run their household with limited or no help at all.

Symbolic and ritualistic, deportment was all-important for women and could be a way of gaining entry into polite middle-class Victorian society. Familiarity with the strict code of etiquette was vital to good social standing.

To be "accomplished" during the Victorian era included the ability to create handiwork: to sew, do needlepoint and make ornamental crafts that decorated the home. Mastering a musical instrument, singing with a melodic voice and speaking foreign languages were desirable skills, but not nearly so important as continuing serious self-education and performing good deeds. Spare time was best spent reading or performing charitable works, provided they did not interfere with duties at home.

In her old age the Victorian woman received the comfort of family until her dying day. Still, she often experienced financial hardship if widowed and had to rely on the generosity of her children—especially the eldest daughter—to meet her needs.

While there were members of the Victorian upper class only a generation or two removed from the 18th-century gentry who were trained for their elevated station in life, the aspiring masses were in need of instruction. Much of the information presented in the following pages has been culled from the printed guides that answered this need. For example, small "behavior" books included series of lectures that were helpful in guiding young women on their proper course in life. Deportment or etiquette manuals provided much-needed information on how to be a member of polite society. Household manuals advised the middle-class Victorian woman on everything from home decoration and cookery to caring for the sick and dealing with servants. By the late 19th century, all-purpose social compendiums combined at-a-glance useful knowledge with instructions on letter writing, etiquette, mourning practices and information on then-popular culture. In addition to these various how-to books, leading magazines such as *Godey's Lady's Book* kept middle-class women up to date on fashion trends, cooking techniques, home decoration, crafts and more, and provided entertainment in the form of sentimental short stories, which reflected and reinforced the mores of the day.

Clearly many authors used such instructional books to express personal views, whether on the evil of hard drink, disapproval of women pursuing equal rights, or some other notable—but disagreeable—trend of the day. Such manuals did, however, present generally accepted guidelines and directives for proper behavior, dress, hygiene, child rearing, family relationships, home decoration, entertaining and domestic work. Given the massive popularity of these manuals, we can assume the Victorian middle class was highly interested in learning—and living—what the advice givers recommended. With this in mind, I have called upon these old tomes to help paint a portrait of typical middle-class life. In addition, vintage advertisements, trade cards, magazines and catalogs have been useful in examining the abundant material culture of the Victorian era and chronicling the growth of Victorian consumerism.

In his pioneering 1972 compilation, *Midcentury America: Life in the 1850s*, Carl Bode wrote, "In any struggle to present the average in American life, the odds are against us. It is not the average that survives. The average is taken for granted more often than not; no newspaper reports it, no artist pictures it. For that matter, no historian chronicles it; he is seldom interested in our daily doings."[1] Fortunately that has changed. Today there is a steadily growing interest in women's history, especially as it pertains to everyday life. Thanks to historians such as Harvey Green, whose landmark 1983 study *The Light of the Home: An Intimate View of the Lives of Women in Victorian America* explores the domestic lives of women in Northeast America between 1870 and 1910, and Catherine Clinton, author of *The Plantation Mistress: Woman's World in the Old South*, which looks at the lives of white women of the plantation society in the antebellum South, we can better appreciate what women's lives were really like during the 19th century. In addition, the work of people such as Kenneth L. Ames, author of *Death in the Dining Room and Other Tales of Victorian Culture*, presents us with a look at the material culture of bygone days.

It is my sincere hope that readers will take from the pages of this book a clearer understanding of the Victorian woman's joys and sorrows, a glimpse of her private, family and public lives, as well as a better appreciation for the material culture that helped define her very existence. She was a woman who often sacrificed hopes and dreams, ambitions, talents and desires to devote herself fully—as expected—to home, family and ultimately the good of the world at large.

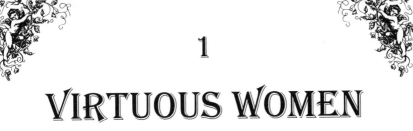

# 1

# VIRTUOUS WOMEN

Man for the field and woman for the hearth:
Man for the sword and for the needle she:
Man with the head and woman with the heart:
Man to command and woman to obey;
All else confusion.

—"The Princess" (1849) by Alfred, Lord Tennyson

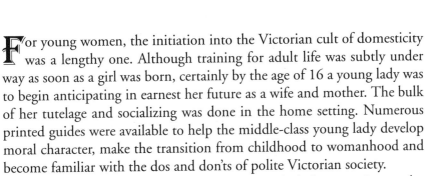

For young women, the initiation into the Victorian cult of domesticity was a lengthy one. Although training for adult life was subtly under way as soon as a girl was born, certainly by the age of 16 a young lady was to begin anticipating in earnest her future as a wife and mother. The bulk of her tutelage and socializing was done in the home setting. Numerous printed guides were available to help the middle-class young lady develop moral character, make the transition from childhood to womanhood and become familiar with the dos and don'ts of polite Victorian society.

In most instances, courtship rituals ultimately led to marriage and a woman's role as wife. Courting, often sentimental and quite romantic, included choosing a partner one loved while keeping in mind the more practical qualities that would assure spending a lifetime with a devoted and proper husband. A flirtatious man, a gambler or a drinker, while often charming and attentive, was a poor choice for a mate.

Etiquette dictated the manner in which courtship was pursued and a marriage proposal extended. The social whirl surrounding the engagement, actual marriage ceremony and reception were grand events indeed.

Once settled into her role as wife, the Victorian woman's primary responsibility was to provide a cheerful, loving and comfortable home for her husband and the children she would soon have—an oasis of peace and morality in a bustling, noisy and rapidly industrializing society.

# ADVICE TO YOUNG LADIES

From the time she was a mere infant until she married and established a home of her own, the Victorian woman, regardless of whether she lived in the North or the South, was schooled in becoming a "virtuous" being. During childhood she carried out her apprenticeship in the nursery, where she routinely played with dolls and miniature replicas of the Victorian home. Each room in her dollhouse was outfitted to mirror the real thing, and at a young and tender age the girl child became acquainted with the kitchen and its various appointments as well as the furniture and decorative aspects of the house as a whole. In contrast, her brother was occupied with rough and tumble toys like rocking horses or perhaps toy soldiers.

As she grew older a young girl was expected to devote time to the practice of sewing, needlepoint and knitting. She also assumed greater responsibility within the domestic circle of the home, and her developing character was of the utmost importance. To guide her, instruct her and encourage her on the road to moral righteousness, advice manuals became increasingly popular. Written for every segment of the middle-class population during the 19th century, these manuals followed women through every phase of their life. For example, during the late 1800s, Mrs. Mary Wood-Allen, M.D., and Mrs. Emma F. A. Drake, M.D., coauthored a number of books for females, including *What a Young Girl Ought to Know, What a Young Woman Ought to Know, What a Young Wife Ought to Know* and *What a Woman of 45 Ought to Know.*

According to John F. Kasson, "reading for general knowledge was one important sign of cultivation, but the immense economic and social changes that began in the early nineteenth century also created a vast new market for more specific instruction."[1] Toward this end, the ever-increasing numbers of advice manuals and deportment books being printed jumped from 28 published during the 1830s to 38 published in the 1850s. During the last 30 years

*This illustration entitled "Young Women,"*
*from the 1883 book* The Voyage of Life,
*depicts either the pursuit of "self-culture" through reading*
*to increase knowledge, or perhaps reading the Scripture,*
*also an important daily activity for young women.*

VIRTUOUS WOMEN
3

of the 19th century an average of 50 etiquette books per decade were written and published by a variety of authors, including ministers, popular fiction writers, notable icons of polite society, teachers and magazine editors.[2]

Regarding advice to young women, the majority of such manuals focused on the importance of religion in their daily life, the special value of time, acquiring useful knowledge, the moral obligation toward industry (a category that covered useful skills and accomplishments), good manners, sisterly virtues, cultivating friendship, maintaining a cheerful disposition, the art of conversation, benevolence, self-control and perseverance. After all, an industrious young woman with a cheerful disposition, love of God, and impeccable manners would make a good and fitting wife and the ideal mother. In short, she would be well suited to fulfill her predetermined role and ultimately act as a moral guardian of society and its future generations. Addressing this issue in the preface to his 1851 book *The Young Lady's Counsellor*, clergyman Daniel Wise drew an explicit connection between the future success of democratic America, whose "institutions depend on the virtue of the people," and the morality of its mothers. "Maternal influence, acting on the infant mind in its first stage of impressibility, stamps an almost ineffaceable image of good or evil upon it," Wise claimed, insisting that by fostering "the loftiest and holiest traits of mind and heart" in its young women, the nation could ensure the extension of such traits in the children they would bear.[3]

Exactly what then was the young Victorian woman taught? Teaching itself was instilled as her natural vocation. In schools, yes, but more importantly in the home setting. By her example, wisdom and caring she would someday teach within the confines of that all-important space—her own domestic sphere. Superficial tendencies and self-indulgence had no place in the life of a proper young woman—intelligence and virtue were the key to a happy future. With this in mind, girls were made to understand the value of time. Thus, in *Letters To Young Ladies*, 1854, Mrs. L. H. Sigourney advised her readers to "[c]onsider every day . . . as a sacred gift," and, on a more concrete level, to follow a strict schedule: "The assigning of daily duty to particular hours, helps to ensure its performance. The system must often yield to circumstances, and be subject to interruptions, yet by keeping its general features steadily in view, more will be accomplished, and to better purpose than by desultory effort."[4]

Ideally a young woman was to divide her day between self-culture (her duty to God and duty toward her own self-improvement) and her duty to others. For example, it was strongly recommended that upon rising in the morning she devote time to prayer, meditation and/or reading the Scripture. Religion was of paramount importance to middle-class Victorians. However, during the first three decades of the 19th century, Protestantism and the growing movement toward gentility clashed, engaging in what the social historian Richard L. Bushman described as a struggle between faith and worldliness.[5] By the mid-1830s, however, this conflict was reconciling and the refined middle-class Victorian was indeed considered a good and moral Christian. Bushman notes: "Refinement was less and less experienced as an artificial imposition, at war with the natural person hidden behind the masquerade of fashionable dress. Refinement was a personal quality like courage or kindness, ingrained in one's character and among the most admirable of the virtues."[6] As evidence of this, the vast majority of instructional manuals published for young women during the Victorian age had strong religious overtones, clearly conveying the fact that to be genteel was to be Christian and vice versa. In addition, the home was considered the ideal center of worship among those of the Protestant faith.[7] Prayer and devotion attained an honored place in the Victorian household. Asserting that "[r]eligion need not be disjoined from the innocent pleasures of life," Mrs. Sigourney adjured that it be given "a place by the hearth-stone, and in the walk among the flowers, where heart answers to heart. Let it have a part in the music that cheers the domestick circle, and in the fond intercourse of sisterly and fraternal love."[8]

Regarding a young woman's duty toward herself, she was to allow time to maintain good health, improve her mind through study and perform hands-on work of a domestic nature. Her relationships with others, such as parents, siblings, friends and teachers, would help mold her character by developing feelings of affection, kindness and charity.

Improving one's intellect during the early Victorian period was often accomplished through formal education at a boarding school as well as through home study. Private academies for girls were especially popular in the South. By the mid-19th century, common schools (the equivalent of modern-day grammar schools) were found throughout the Northeast and additional education was obtained via preparatory schools, private academies or religious institutions. After the Civil War educational opportunities for young women increased with the growth of the public high-school system, the establishment of numerous private female colleges and the admission of women into various state colleges. In *The Victorian Homefront*, Louise L. Stevenson notes that "by 1872, 97 colleges and universities admitted women, and by 1880 women represented one-third of all college

*Training children, especially daughters,*
*in musical accomplishments was an important*
*part of developing a genteel character.*
*This illustration from the 1882 book*
Our Deportment *shows mother and daughter*
*around the piano.*

and university students in the United States."[9] As the century progressed, a college education was considered an asset for the young women who would go on to raise the future children of America, as well as a way to provide the required training for those who sought employment in teaching, nursing and other professions before they entered into marriage.

Regarding home study, reading a variety of books was highly recommended to cultivate familiarity with the literary world. Young women were advised to keep a daily journal, which would not only enhance penmanship but would provide an abbreviated version of studies that could be reviewed at leisure. Self-culture, or "solid learning" as one authority referred to it, followed a logical order with the absolutely necessary (such as religion, philosophy and history) taking top priority, followed by useful knowledge or accomplishments and, lastly, that which was thought purely ornamental.[10]

Educating young women during the early 1800s was often limited to the basic knowledge required to run a household. The more fortunate also learned to read and write. By the dawn of the Victorian era increasing wealth among the upper class and growing middle class focused attention on female intellect and accomplishments as mundane household chores were increasingly performed by domestic servants. To be well educated suddenly referred to the ability to speak French, sing with a pleasant voice and master an instrument. Such studies, however, were insufficient when it came to the harsh realities of an industrializing society and by the late 1840s it became fashionable for female students to pursue studies in logic, mathematics, geography, history, the Scriptures and ancient languages. Letter writing and penmanship also became increasingly important and some combination of the above courses was thought the ideal education for a young lady during the antebellum years. In the South especially, mathematics was vitally important for the young woman who would someday have to keep records on a plantation, and familiarity with the ornamental arts helped promote the famed Southern hospitality.

In his 1848 manual *The Sphere and Duties of Woman*, George W. Burnap wrote:

*I place the education of domestic duties first, as essential and indispensable. No woman is educated who is not equal to the successful management of a family. A woman ought to know all the details of house affairs. She ought to know how every thing is preserved and kept in order. She ought to know how every thing is cooked that is an article of food, how every thing is cut out, made and mended, that is worn, and what is the ordinary cost and consumption of the various articles of domestic use. The duties of nurse she must learn at some period of her life by the stern constraint of necessity, and the sooner they are learned the better.*[11]

This same author regarded accomplishments such as singing, dancing or drawing as delightful ways of entertaining and enjoying society but considered them appropriate only to youth. The cultivation of the mind, on the other hand, would see a woman through all the years of her life, and when too old to sing or dance, she would still be able to draw others around her in the parlor and entertain via conversation. Burnap advised that "the great entertainments of all ages are reading, conversation and thought. If our existence, especially after middle life, is not enriched by these, it becomes meagre and dull indeed."[12] Burnap's advice is typical of many such authors who worried that the study and practice of domestic skills would be set aside for the more attractive arts and studies. Mothers as well as daughters were constantly being reminded that they must teach—and learn—those domestic skills so vital to maintaining a happy household. Once this priority was met the advice givers gave their blessing to the pursuit of other interests.

Education was also discussed in then-popular periodicals such as *Godey's Lady's Book*, whose editor, Sarah J. Hale, contributed an 1855 editorial that added to Burnap's prescription for female education an awareness of women's vast potential for society as a whole. Asserting that "professional studies" should be opened to interested women, Hale went on to call for a more broadly based education even for those who were not considering a profession: "But, especially, in everything that enters into the qualifications of the citizen, and the intelligent member of society, they should be equal to men. We can never progress rapidly towards that state of mental, moral, and physical equality, which forms a part of the very idea of an immortal republic, while one-half of the race, and that half wielding—as all must perceive—a most powerful influence over the common destiny, are held in the chains of inferiority, either by total neglect, or a pusillanimous unfitness of education."[13]

Advice to young ladies also centered on relationships with others, especially family members. Love and devotion were the keys to a happy home life and a basis upon which strong moral character was molded. A daughter was to offer peace, affection and joy to members of her household. For the mother, a daughter grew to be a companion and someone to assist with household cares and obligations. To the father, a daughter was to be dutiful and loving. Ideally she developed a strong bond with siblings of the same sex and was generous and self-sacrificing toward brothers. In the

South, sisters often grew to be the best of friends, since the isolation of prosperous farms or small plantations limited social activity. In short, a good daughter offered sympathy and support to all family members and was always polite. A selfish, whiny or rude daughter, on the other hand, was a curse to the family, disrupting their daily lives and causing constant misery.

An eldest daughter, because of her position in the family, assumed more responsibility toward parents and siblings than those children born after her. She was to set a good example for younger children and frequently assumed the role of teacher within the domestic circle. This, of course, was considered good training for her future role as a wife and mother.

Specific instructions dealing with the relationship between a daughter and her parents and daughter and siblings were offered in *The Young Lady's Counsellor*. Regarding deportment toward parents, Daniel Wise wrote:

*You should study to anticipate and obey their slightest wishes; address them in tones and words of respectful affection; never disgrace yourself by uttering an unkind word to either of them; make them your confidants; keep nothing secret, especially from your mother; consult them concerning your plans, studies, amusements, and friends; relieve your mother as much as possible, by rendering her assistance in household labors to the very limit of your ability; never permit yourself to be disagreeable or resentful to your brothers and sisters, and study to find your own pleasure in promoting the happiness of the family circle.*

Wise continued, counseling young women regarding their behavior toward siblings: "Be unselfish and attentive. Exert yourself to please them. Encourage them in their studies and amusements. Gently check any wrong manifestation of character, both in them and in yourself. By these means, you will wind cords of enduring affection round their hearts. They will love you, and they will also love home for your sake."[14]

Just as religion, morality, death and true love were the subjects of numerous short stories appearing in popular 19th-century women's magazines, so too did devotion to one's family provide abundant subject material. For example, a short story by Virginia DeForrest, entitled "Anna, or Cottage Devotion," appeared in the September 1855 issue of *Godey's Lady's Book*. This was the story of Anna, a beautiful young farmer's daughter who spent most of her time caring for her blind younger sister. A handsome young city man entered Anna's life and after they grew to know each other, the young man professed his love. He told Anna he must return to the city and asked her to elope with him, knowing full well Anna's father would never

*The epitome of decorum, this attractive young*
*woman from the late Victorian era*
*reflects her careful attention to dress,*
*modest jewelry and sensible good taste.*

consent to the marriage. Anna finally agreed to meet the young man late one evening and run off to Boston with him. Upon returning to her home to pack her belongings, Anna's family had their usual evening prayers and her father read from the Bible. He ended their devotions by reciting the fourth commandment: "Honor thy father and thy mother, that thy days may be long upon the land which the Lord thy God giveth thee." Anna's father of course knew of her plan to leave, for he'd overheard the young couple talking in the meadow. After everyone retired for the evening Anna prayed for the strength to make the right decision. As the night wore on the young man waited in the meadow well past the appointed hour of the planned meeting. When he finally gave up and returned to his room at a nearby inn, a note from Anna awaited him:

*Dear Edwin:*

*Could one who forsook her first duty, that to her parents, fulfill the holy duties the name of wife would bring? I dare not come: it has cost me much to write this, but I feel I am doing right, and that strengthens me. Win my father's consent, and I am yours.*

*Anna*

Of course Anna's father had been right to dislike the young man, for he'd decided that winning the father's consent wasn't "worth the trouble" and left town. By making the right decision and being a dutiful daughter Anna was spared a future of certain sorrow. In the end the family discovered the young man had, in fact, been in serious trouble with the law and had no moral character whatsoever.[15]

Yet another subject on which young Victorian women were widely advised was social self-culture. This grew increasingly important as the century progressed and, as previously noted, deportment or etiquette manuals appeared in growing numbers from the 1870s through the turn of the century. Good manners both in public and in the home were equated with good character, and young ladies were offered advice and instruction on everything from the art of polite conversation and table etiquette to correspondence or letter writing, gift giving, proper dress, chaperonage and personal beauty. For example, the 1907 book *Correct Social Usage: A Course of Instruction in Good Form, Style and Deportment by Eighteen Distinguished Authors* told readers:

> *Instruction on points of etiquette is every bit as necessary as instruction in any branch of learning which tends to broaden the mind. For every age and for every condition good manners provide helpful equipment. For the young woman, the thought is full of meaning. Whether millionaire's daughter or busy working girl, a knowledge of correct social usage is essential. A charm of manner, a ready fluency in expressing courteous phrases, a grace of gesture, an ease of movement and the dignity of thorough self-possession—these constitute a chain armor which will equip any woman for social conflicts.*[16]

While the importance of mastering social skills was driven home again and again in passages such as the above, young women also had to be attuned to changes in social regulations. Fashions changed and old customs became obsolete. Up-to-date etiquette manuals proved helpful in this regard, and so too did the popular periodicals.

Although schools and education for young women improved throughout the Victorian era and on into the Edwardian era—with notable starts and stops—it was still expected that a woman's proper role was as a wife and mother; the "angel of the house" ministering to her family's physical, moral and emotional well-being. As a result, the concept of virtuous womanhood remained paramount to a young lady's training throughout the 19th century. It is important to note, however, that during the antebellum period, "virtue" was interpreted differently by Northerners and Southerners. In *The Plantation Mistress*, Catherine Clinton notes that "by the 1830s celebrations of women had shifted perceptibly along regional lines. Virtue was the most prized feminine characteristic throughout the United States, but in the North, female virtue was synonymous with industriousness and epitomized by the 'frugal housewife,' while in the South, the plantation aristocracy celebrated virtue in the cult of chastity." Clinton also notes that this served as a power ploy for elite Southern men in retaining their stronghold as the ruling force in a slave society.[17]

Serious business, this process of growing up during the Victorian era. Lest it become too weighted down with duties and endeavors toward womanhood, young girls were reminded that it was indeed a beautiful time in their lives, enriched by many enjoyments and opportunities that would prepare them for "the great work of life."[18]

Make no mistake, however; not all young ladies blindly accepted their intended fate. As the following poem from an 1881 issue of *Scribner's Monthly Magazine* clearly conveys, many a Victorian maiden had doubts about her position in life and the limited future:

I want—I don't know what I want; I'm tired of everything;
I'd like to be a queen or something—no, a bearded king,
With iron crown and wolfish eyes and manners fierce and bold,
Or else a plumed highwayman, or a paladin of old.
We girls are such poor creatures, slaves to circumstance and fate.
Denied the warrior's glory and the conqueror's splendid state.

# COURTSHIP AND MARRIAGE

The advice books written for young ladies during the 1840s and 1850s extolled the virtues of marriage in mythical fashion. Not only was the Victorian daughter told that marriage would improve her character (by giving her higher aims and a more dignified position in society) but that "the grand essentials to happiness in this life are something to do, something to love, and something to hope for."[19] Marriage, most conveniently, would fulfill all three of these needs. That is not to say that a young woman could only find happiness in wedded bliss, for she was warned that it was far better to remain single than to accept an offer of marriage from someone unsuitable and thereby suffer a lifetime of regret and despair. With this in mind, during the mid-19th-century Victorian women were cautioned that true love was based upon mutual esteem and affection and not on the silly notions of love often presented in then popular works of fiction. For example, in *The Young Lady's Counsellor* Wise cautioned:

> Many young ladies indulge in very nonsensical opinions, or, I should rather say, notions, concerning love. They foolishly fancy themselves bound to be "smitten," to "fall in love," to be "love-sick" with almost every silly idler who wears a fashionable coat, is tolerably good-looking, and pays them particular attention. Reason, judgment, deliberation, according to their fancies, have nothing to do with love. Hence, they yield to their feeling, and give their company to young men, regardless of warning advice. Their lovers use flattering words, and, like silly moths fluttering round the fatal lamp, they allow themselves to be charmed into certain misery.[20]

# Marriage License.

—State of—                    —County of—

The people of the State of ........................................, to any person legally authorized to solemnize Marriage, **GREETING:** You are hereby authorized to join in the holy bonds of Matrimony, and to celebrate the rites and ceremonies of Marriage, between Mr. ......................................., and M......................................................., according to the usual custom and laws of the State of ....................................................., and you are required to return this license to me within thirty days, from the celebration of such Marriage, with a Certificate of the same, appended thereto, and signed by you, under the penalty of One Hundred Dollars.

**Witness**................................................................................................, Clerk of our said Court and the Seal thereof, at his office, in ................................................, in said County, this day of......................................, A. D., ............187....

Seal.

County Clerk.

State of..........................................., } S.S.       I, ........................................
.................................County. }           a........., hereby certify that on the..............................day of......................, 187...., I joined in Marriage, Mr. ..............................., and M......................................................, agreeable to the authority given in the above License, and the customs and laws of this State. Given under my hand and seal, this...........................day of....................., A. D., 187....

SEAL.

*The sentimental and romantic Victorian era had far-reaching impact on the material culture surrounding love, courtship and marriage. This marriage license from the 1888 Hill's Manual of Social and Business Forms features a charming script and romantic embellishments.*

Rather, young women were to keep a level head and study a young man's character, his words and actions. Ideally he was to be industrious, intelligent, energetic, thoughtful and economical. Wise further recommended that a young woman should call upon her parents to check into his background and discover if he'd been a good son and devoted brother.

How, then, did a young woman meet decent suitors, court and finally take the ultimate step into marriage and wedded bliss? For a young girl in the North, socializing actually began by the time she was 16 or 18, depending upon popular practice, and she was allowed to attend dances, elegant balls, theater performances, concerts, operas and picnics where she had the opportunity to mingle with the opposite sex. During the late 1800s it was common practice to pay calls with one's mother and to receive visitors at home—albeit their stay was to be brief. In contrast, for eligible young plantation women of the South, their social circle was sometimes limited to extended family members and, as a result, courtship and marriage between cousins was not unusual.

While the Victorian parlor was the setting for much of the social interaction between couples during the early and mid-Victorian periods, by the late 1800s new sports such as tennis, bicycling and golf allowed courting couples to move outdoors and away from Mother's watchful eye.

Regarding the etiquette of courtship, occasionally a young man would seek the approval of parents before courting their daughter. This undoubtedly prevented problems in some instances. Lee M. Edwards has noted that "mutual affection rather than income was the usual foundation for marriage, though parental approval could be problematic if a son's or daughter's choice of a future mate did not measure up."[21] While mutual affection was the deciding factor for the majority of marriages, there were exceptions to this, especially in the South before the Civil War when monetary riches or land holdings were the driving force behind a number of unions.

Parents, especially a girl's mother, were to be familiar with all the gentlemen callers a daughter received. If parents found any one man in particular not to their liking, every effort was made to remove him from the daughter's social circle. Failing at this attempt, parents were advised to try introducing the daughter to someone more desirable or, if necessary, to send the young woman on a journey or extended visit to put distance between the couple.

Keeping company with a gentleman of good character was important, but so too were other considerations. Before a young couple developed deep affections for one another, they were to keep in mind that they should not become involved with someone who was not their social equal. According to the 1888 edition of *Hill's Manual of Social and Business Forms:* "If there be a difference either way [in social position], let the husband be superior to the wife. It is difficult for a wife to love and honor a person whom she is compelled to look down upon."[22] It was also hoped that young couples would become involved with someone of the same religion and someone with similar tastes, likes and dislikes. Several writers also commented on the desirable physical characteristics of a young couple with an eye toward marriage. For example, *Hill's Manual* recommended the union of physically dissimilar partners, at least in part, so that their offspring should "balance out" the parents' more extreme features.

> *Those who are neither very tall nor very short, whose eyes are neither very black nor very blue, whose hair is neither very black nor very red—the mixed types—may marry those who are quite similar in form, complexion and temperament to themselves. Bright red hair and a florid complexion indicate an excitable temperament. Such should marry the jet-black hair and the brunette type. The gray, blue, black or hazel eyes should not marry those of the same color. Where the color is very pronounced, the union should be with those of a decidedly different color. The very corpulent should unite with the thin and spare, and the short, thick-set should choose a different constitution. The thin, bony, wiry, prominent-featured, Roman-nosed, cold-blooded individual, should marry the round-featured, warm-hearted and emotional. Thus the cool should unite with warmth and susceptibility. The extremely irritable and nervous should unite with the lymphatic, the slow and the quiet. Thus the stolid will be prompted by the nervous companion, while the excitable will be quieted by the gentleness of the less nervous.*[23]

We might wonder today just how closely Victorians actually followed this advice in regard to physical attributes, but the experts were adamant that such considerations would contribute to a "safe" marriage: one in which a proper balance was maintained between husband and wife.[24]

Although the strict formality of 19th-century etiquette dictated close adherence to the letter of the law regarding courtship practices, the sentimental and romantic spirit of the Victorian era was evident in all matters pertaining to love. Young women were expected to be flirtatious. Their language spoke of "beaus," "ardent lovers" or "suitors," and young men offered their "attentions" to or "courted" that special young lady. If deep "affections" blossomed between the couple, a proposal might be made and they were then "betrothed."

Coy and subtle (or not so subtle) messages could be conveyed between young women and men via the well-orchestrated movement of a lady's handheld fan or by the popular language of flowers. Whether a single blossom or a bouquet, presenting flowers or greenery offered an opportunity to exchange unspoken messages, reveal true feelings or nurture affections. During the 1880s and 1890s most etiquette manuals contained a chapter devoted to this form of expression and many a young couple was well versed in the sentiment attached to myriad flowerage. For example, the 1882 edition of *Our Deportment or the Manners, Conduct and Dress of the Most Refined Society* by John H. Young, told readers: "There is a sentiment attached to flowers, and this sentiment has been expressed in language by giving names to various flowers, shrubs and plants. These names constitute a language, which may be made the medium of pleasant and amusing interchange of thought between men and women. A bouquet of flowers and leaves may be selected and arranged so as to express much depth of feeling—to be truly a poem."[25] While a young woman's bouquet could imply several thoughts or emotions, feelings were also communicated by giving a single flower. One popular social guide offered the following example of a conversation conducted through the language of flowers:

The gentleman presents a Red Rose—"I love you."
The lady admits a partial reciprocation of the sentiment by returning a Purple Pansy—"You occupy my thoughts."
The gentleman presses his suit still further by an Everlasting Pea—"Wilt thou go with me?"
The lady replies by a Daisy, in which she says—"I will think of it."
The gentleman, in his enthusiasm, plucks and presents a Shepherd's Purse—"I offer you my all."
The lady, doubtingly, returns a sprig of Laurel—"Words, though sweet, may deceive."
The gentleman still affirms his declaration by a sprig of Heliotrope—"I adore you."
The lady admits a tenderness of sentiment by the Zinnia—"I mourn your absence."[26]

During the 1890s practicing the language of flowers could also provide amusement and entertainment for young couples at social gatherings. For example, *The Home Manual*, prepared by Mrs. John A. Logan, recommended that a pleasant diversion on a summer evening could be achieved by devoting an hour or so to "floral conversation." The hostess had large bouquets of assorted flowers scattered about as tabletop decorations and from these guests could select a blossom to communicate with their companion or loved one.[27]

Expressing sentiment through the language of flowers was a charmingly tender act that spoke volumes about the romantic nature of the Victorians. The following is a select listing of flowers we are familiar with today and the meanings attached to them over a century ago:

*Cabbage Rose—Ambassador of love*
*Deep Red Rose—Bashful love*
*Day Lily—Coquetry*
*Daffodil—Chivalry, Regard*
*Sweet Pea—Departure*
*Yellow Carnation—Disdain*
*Ivy—Friendship*
*Blue Violet—Faithfulness*
*Geranium—Gentility*
*Ivy Geranium—I engage you for the next dance*
*Mistletoe—I surmount all obstacles*
*White Rose—I am worthy of you*
*Iris—My compliments*
*White Lilac—Purity*
*Orange Blossom—Your purity equals your loveliness*

—Manners, Culture and Dress of The Best American Society
Richard A. Wells, 1891

Romantic (though prim and proper) love letters were written during the 19th century, and etiquette governed their exchange and to an extent their content. Generally young men initiated such correspondence and young ladies returned a reply. The sending of love letters was to be approved by one's parents, and they were to be carefully written with an eye toward perfection. An improper expression or misspelled word could cause disaster in the form of ridicule. Love letters were to be guardedly composed and ladies especially were cautioned to maintain their dignity when putting their feelings on paper. Above all else, letters were to honestly express the author's intentions and were to be held in strict confidence by both parties. In the case of a broken engagement (mutually agreed upon by both parties), all love letters and other mementos of the "dead love" were to be returned.

For what purpose were Victorian love letters exchanged? The 1888 edition of *Hill's Manual* offered examples of letters and replies written to request permission to call on a young lady, to invite a young woman on a public outing, to hint at love at first sight, to say good-bye before starting on a journey, to offer a proposal of marriage or to express a change of feelings. The following sample letters present an offer of marriage and a favorable reply to a proposal. Both are extracted from *Hill's Manual* and offer "acceptable" correspondence.

*248 _____ St., Dec. 10, 18__*

*Dearest Bertha:*

*I have intended, oh, how many times! when we have been together, to put the simple question which I intended this note shall ask; but, although apparently a very easy matter to ask the hand in marriage of one I so deeply love as yourself, it is no easy task. I therefore write what I have never found courage in my heart to speak. Dearest, will you bestow upon me the great happiness of permitting me to call you mine? If I have spoken this too boldly, you will forgive; but I fondly hope that you will not be indifferent to my appeal. I trust, if you answer this in the affirmative, that you will never regret doing so. Anxiously awaiting your answer, I remain,*

*Yours Affectionately,*
*Harlan Dempster*

*367 _____ St., Dec. 10, 18__*

*Dear Sir:*

*Your proposal is quite unexpected to me, but it is made with such candor and frankness that I can take no offense. I cannot, in this note, give you a definite reply. Marriage is a very serious matter; and, while I regard you with the greatest favor, I desire to consult my near relatives, and consider the subject myself carefully for a few days, ere I give you a final answer. I think I can assure you, however, that you may **hope**.*

*Very Sincerely,*
*Fannie Kimball*

Affections were also offered during courtship via small gifts or tokens of regard. Valentine's Day provided the perfect opportunity to give that special someone a beautiful, often intricate, lacy and embellished card expressing love, sentimental feelings or admiration. At other times a thoughtful young man might present sweets, a volume of touching poetry or of course flowers, which a young lady could accept only after securing the approval of her parents. Gift exchange was often reserved for the engaged couple.

In reciprocating, a proper young woman never offered too personal a gift, but rather select gifts in kind—tasty edibles or perhaps a book. If, however, a couple was engaged, gifts of a more lasting nature might be exchanged. A young man might present his fiancée with an attractive silk or satin fan trimmed with lace and an ivory handle, a delicate handkerchief, a pretty box for gloves or perhaps a piece of jewelry such as a pendant or earrings. A young lady might pour heart and soul into creating a piece of needlework or knitting a scarf for her future husband as a loving gift for a birthday or other special occasion.

Victorian deportment assigned a young woman a passive role in the game of love. She was never to presume to declare her love for a young man, revealing her true feelings only if and when a marriage proposal was offered. According to one expert on such matters, "this trial of a woman's patience is often very hard to bear."[28] A gentleman on the other hand was permitted to reveal his true feelings. Richard A. Wells notes in his etiquette manual: "In this he has great advantage over the lady. Being refused, he may go elsewhere to seek a mate, if he be in the humor; try his fortune again, and maybe be the lucky drawer of a princely prize."[29]

It was of course expected that no respectable young woman would allow a gentleman to pay her too much attention unless she was seriously interested in him. To "trifle with his affections" would not only lead him to false assumptions but would give others the impression she was "spoken for." Likewise, no true gentleman would pay excessive visits to or shower constant attention upon a lady whom he was not considering for marriage. Such Victorian sensibilities lingered throughout the early 20th century until the outbreak of the First World War.

Regarding paying misleading attentions, a reader's letter to Mrs. Stickney, Parks, author of the "Girls' Affairs" column in the June 1912 issue of *The Ladies Home Journal,* related the following:

*My trouble is about a young man with whom I have been going for more than a year. He has told me that he loves me, and his actions have gone far to prove it by devotion. For more than four months he has called from three to four nights a week. We have spoken of marriage, but it was only in an indefinite way. My family think we are engaged, although I have never told them that we are. Why he does not ask me frankly to marry him I do not know. I have thought our relation to one another will have to be changed but I do not know how to tell him so. Should I let things go on until he finally asks me to marry him, or what should I do?*

Mrs. Parks responded to the reader as follows:

*Your mistake was made in the beginning of your friendship. You should not have allowed the young man to absorb your time and attention to the exclusion of other friends; neither should you have admitted your love for him unless he asked you in marriage. Being on such intimate terms I think you must take matters into your own hands and very kindly and frankly tell him that he must not expect to monopolize you. Speak plainly and say that your relatives and friends believe you to be engaged, and that you are unwilling to "sail under false colors." If he is a manly young man he will appreciate the wisdom of what you say, and will perceive the injustice he has done you.*[30]

Throughout the 19th century young women were advised not to marry until they reached the age of at least 21, or even better, 23. According to the experts, their physical development, mind and moral character required this time to "ripen." Ideally a young man would be 25 years old before he sought a wife. By this age he would have established himself in some form of employment and be better able to judge the qualities in a woman that would make her a proper wife. For the most part this was quite typical in the North, but in the South, especially during the antebellum period, girls often married at an earlier age.

After a marriage proposal was made, whether face to face or in the form of a love letter, and accepted, the next course of action was to secure the approval of the young woman's family. According to one noted authority, "in presenting his suit to them [the parents] he should remember that it is not from the sentimental but the practical side that they will regard the affair. Therefore, after describing the state of his affections in as calm a manner as possible, and perhaps hinting that their daughter is not indifferent to him, let him at once frankly, without waiting to be questioned, give an account of his pecuniary resources and his general prospects in life, in

*The January 1856 Godey's Lady's Book*
*featured this color fashion plate in which*
*the bride's attire is described as follows:*
*"The bride is, of course, the principle [sic]*
*figure in the group, around which all the rest centre.*
*Dress of white silk, with three lace flounces,*
*the upper one falling directly from the waist;*
*lace to correspond is also gathered in a slight fullness*
*over the corsage, and falls over the open sleeve.*
*Bouquets, wreath, and cordon of white roses,*
*orange-flowers, and jassamine, with light foliage:*
*veil of thulle, wide and full."*

order that the parents may judge whether he can properly provide for a wife and possible family."[31]

Assuming all went well in the young man's interview with the family, the couple became officially "betrothed." Evidently time was of the essence because it was strongly suggested this period of engagement be brief, otherwise the couple would discover each other's imperfections and become disillusioned, possibly breaking off their engagement.

As a token of his pledge it was customary in polite society for a young man to give his fiancée an engagement gift. The engagement ring became quite popular during the early Victorian period, in the 1840s these were usually bands with a symbolic heart design or hands entwined with a heart. Styles, of course, were subject to change and the engagement rings commonly presented during the second half of the 19th century were embellished with diamonds, pearls and/or rubies. The diamond ring eventually became the ultimate symbol of betrothal, although often only the well to do could afford diamonds. During the late Victorian era many a middle-class young woman received an engagement ring with a stone other than a diamond, or a family heirloom was placed upon her finger. Simple gold bands were also frequently used as engagement rings.

The engaged couple's behavior was subject to the same intense scrutiny it received prior to their betrothal. While it was now permissible for a young man to call every evening if he was available to do so, his visits were not to be too lengthy and he was never to press for romantic signs of affection. By the same token, no respectable young lady would allow her reputation to be compromised by being overly demonstrative, for again, what if the engagement should be broken?

Popular 19th-century etiquette manuals stated that it was a lady's privilege to set the wedding date. Whether the ceremony took place in the morning or evening, it was held on a Sunday or weekday, Saturday being an unpopular choice for a wedding since it was associated with bad luck. Once the wedding date had been set, the weeks leading up to the event were a flurry of activity. The intended bride was entertained by her fiancé's family, she had to arrange for a wedding gown to be made, prepare a trousseau, see to the distribution of wedding cards, pay last visits or social calls before the marriage took place (this was customary during the late 1800s) and help with preparations for the wedding.

While clothing styles changed throughout the 19th century, it remained widely accepted during most of the Victorian era that the bridal costume should be entirely white. The 1877 edition of *The Ladies' and Gentlemen's*

*Etiquette: A Complete Manual of the Manners and Dress of American Society,* by Mrs. E. B. Duffey, noted the following regarding the bride's outfit:

> *Her dress may be of silk heavily corded, moire antique, brocade, satin or plain silk, of lace, merino, alpaca, crape, lawn or muslin. Her veil may be of lace, tulle or illusion, but it must be long and full. It may or may not descend over the face. The dress is high and the arms are covered. No jewelry is worn save diamonds or pearls. Slippers of white satin and gloves of kid complete the dress. The flowers of the bridal wreath and bouquet must be orange blossoms, either natural or artificial, or other white flowers.*[32]

The white bridal outfit was symbolic of purity and the wedding veil became popular after Queen Victoria was married in one. The use of orange blossoms in the headpiece or bouquet, an old European custom, symbolized both purity and fertility.

By the end of the century simplified styles and fashions resulted in brides marrying in plainer but attractive dresses that could be worn again, and colored bridal outfits were not unheard of. A colored wedding dress (navy blue or brown were the most common colors) with a matching hat could also be used as the bride's going-away dress. This was a practical alternative to an often costly investment.

Changing fashions and the bride's own taste allowed some leeway in wedding apparel. For example, the fashion pages of the February 1885 issue of *Godey's Lady's Book* reported on the latest trends by telling readers:

> *The form of weddings varies with the whim of the contracting parties, but a morning wedding, where the gentlemen wear frock coats, and the ladies demi-toilettes, is considered most elegant. Eleven o'clock is the most popular hour, but the service and reception is always by gas or candle light, the latter being the "swellest." Floral decorations at weddings are carried to excess. Brides are still arrayed in white, with liberal adornments of silver brocade, etc., but a new English idea is a dress of flaming red. A widow, at her second marriage, is never permitted to wear white, and is usually expected to appear in a very pronounced costume of some distinct order. A turquoise blue velvet, embroidered in gold, was a recent robe worn by a lady at her second wedding. Very gorgeous, oriental looking gowns of plush, with tinsel embroidery, are now fashionable.*[33]

*This photo from the late Victorian era features
a bride wearing a more practical colored dress
(perhaps brown) that could conveniently be worn again.
Note the customary orange-blossom corsage,
a symbol of purity and fertility.*

Ideally the trousseau a bride assembled prior to her wedding included all undergarments and clothing she would require for a period of at least two years. This was a daunting task, given the assorted morning dresses, carriage dresses, walking suits, evening dresses and traveling dresses the new bride would require. By the 1880s advice givers were calling for simplified trousseaus or doing away with them altogether, as many an anxious bride became a physical wreck worrying over the making of her clothing. After all, wasn't her present wardrobe perfectly suitable for entrance into married life?

During the late 19th century the rules governing acceptable behavior in polite society required the bride-to-be to pay visits, along with her mother, to those she wished to retain in her social circle once she was a married woman. If a visit was impossible she was to present a calling card with the letters P.P.C. (*pour prendre congé*, which translates from the French as "to take leave") engraved on the right side.

A fine white note paper was used for wedding cards, which were generally ornate in the early Victorian era but somewhat simpler during the late 19th century. The wedding card included the names of the bride and groom and the date, time and location of the wedding ceremony. Marriages often took place at the bride's home or in her church. The accompanying reception card (if indeed a reception was to be held after the ceremony) conveyed the time and location of the reception. According to one advice giver, "After the marriage invitations are issued the fiancée does not appear in public. It is also de rigueur at morning weddings, that she does not see the bridegroom on the wedding-day until they meet at the altar."[34]

After the wedding ceremony a reception was commonly held at the home of the bride's parents and a refreshment table bedecked with flowers offered cake and wine. Often a breakfast or dinner reception was held, depending upon the hour of the ceremony. In the South, where family and friends might travel some distance to attend a wedding, the home was elaborately decorated and a large, sumptuous feast prepared.

During the late Victorian era it was customary, following the wedding or reception, for the bride and groom to embark on their "bridal tour" or honeymoon, during which they were "exempt from all claims of society."[35] With travel vastly improved during the late 1800s, thanks to the railroad, many young couples chose to honeymoon at popular resort areas or tourist attractions such as Niagara Falls, New York; Atlantic City or Cape May, New Jersey; Lake George, New York; Newport, Rhode Island; Newport News, Virginia; or Saratoga Springs, New York.

Thus the young Victorian woman had arrived at her appointed position—she was a wife, a future mother and guardian of the home. Undauntedly she was to fulfill the obligations of her role until the end of her days.

# THE DUTIFUL WIFE

During the early Victorian period newlyweds retired to their new home directly following the wedding ceremony and celebration. Later in the century, upon returning from the "bridal tour" a young couple took up residence in their house or apartment, and etiquette dictated they make available certain hours to receive calls from members of their social circle. "At-home" cards were distributed or had been distributed with the wedding cards so that friends and acquaintances would know when they were expected to visit. An informal reception was usually held at the couple's home on a designated evening or two and guests extended their best wishes and shared in wedding cake and wine. In addition, family and members of the wedding party often hosted dinner parties in honor of the young couple, and they were of course expected to reciprocate unless their means were quite limited.

If a bridal portrait was done, it was routinely taken after the honeymoon. Advances in photographic equipment and technique made the bridal portrait a popular commemorative among the middle class from the late 1860s through the end of the century.

After dealing with the more public aspects of being a newlywed, a woman was to turn her attention to homemaking and being a dutiful wife. Her role was idealistically portrayed in 19th-century novels, short stories and even advice manuals as the pinnacle of her very existence. Her home was equated with a "kingdom" and she a "queen," cherishing her duties of governing all beneath her roof. In reality her life more often than not took a far different course. As pointed out in *Victorian Women: A Documentary Account of Women's Lives in Nineteenth Century England, France, and the United States*, 1981,

> *Once married, nineteenth century women found their personal lives beset with contradictions. On the one hand, the idea of the 'angel in the house' called for a selfless, dependent creature who pleased and fascinated her hus-*

*This illustration from the 1883 book* The Voyage of Life *conveys the woman's devotion to her husband. As a dutiful wife, the Victorian middle-class mistress strove to please her mate and assure him a happy, comfortable home.*

*band and devoted herself to him without reserve. On the other hand, the re-*
*alities of coping with a household . . . required sustained strength, skill, and*
*creativity. To add further confusion, the marriage vows, reflecting the ideal*
*of romantic love, evoked the image of loving partnership and mutual trust,*
*yet the woman entered a 'partnership' in which she had none of the legal*
*and economic rights enjoyed by her spouse.*[36]

What were the responsibilities of the dutiful wife toward her new husband? According to most of the advice manuals her greatest responsibilities were making a happy home and doing her best to please her new mate. *Hill's Manual* told wives, "Whatever have been the cares of the day, greet your husband with a smile when he returns. Make your personal appearance just as beautiful as possible. Let him enter rooms so attractive and sunny that all the recollections of his home, when away from the same, shall attract him back."[37] In addition to creating a happy home, being thrifty was important and women were warned to avoid being overly ambitious in decorating their new homes. Rather, their own handiwork could be used to embellish the home and make it attractive for little cost. What husband wouldn't be pleased with a wife who could carefully manage the household money?

Regarding her conduct, a wife was never to reserve her best nature for guests or appearances in public but to shower her smiles, witty conversation and kind attention on her husband always. She was to be very mindful of her behavior in front of him, never giving him reason to lower his own moral standards by resorting to foul language or harsh words. She was to be virtuous and complacent and avoid arguments or domestic disputes at all cost. In addition, no loving and devoted wife would ever discuss personal matters regarding her husband's faults with others.

Constant devotion to husband and hearth was also thought important, and many advice manuals and magazine articles warned wives of the danger in devoting too much time to "society work." Such activities left matters at home unattended, or worse, a husband home alone. A dutiful wife was to seek her husband's approval before participating in any outside cause—he was after all her first priority.

An even more basic piece of advice offered to young wives reminds us of Fanny Fern's (Sara Parton's) 1853 quote: "The way to a man's heart is through his stomach." For example *Collier's Cyclopedia of Social and Commercial Information* told readers:

*Not the least useful piece of advice—homely though it be—that we can offer to newly-married ladies, is to remind them that husbands are men, and that men must eat. We can tell them, moreover, that men attach no small importance to this very essential operation, and that a very effectual way to keep them in good humor, as well as good condition, is for wives to study their husbands' peculiar likes and dislikes in this matter. Let the wife try, therefore, if she have not already done so, to get up a little knowledge of the art of ordering dinner, to say the least of it. Moreover, if in addition she should acquire some practical knowledge of cookery, she will find ample reward in the gratification it will be the means of affording her husband.*[38]

The authors of advice manuals also offered guidance in regard to how spouses should treat each other. One well-noted book offered the following suggestions for the etiquette between husbands and wives:

*Let the rebuke be preceded by a kiss.*
*Do not require a request to be repeated.*
*Never should both be angry at the same time.*
*Never neglect the other, for all the world beside.*
*Let each strive to always accommodate the other.*
*Let the angry word be answered only with a kiss.*
*Bestow your warmest sympathies in each other's trials.*
*Make your criticism in the most loving manner possible.*
*Make no display of the sacrifices you make for each other.*
*Never make a remark calculated to bring ridicule upon the other.*
*Never deceive; confidence, once lost, can never be wholly regained.*
*Always use the most gentle and loving words when addressing each other.*
*Let each study what pleasure can be bestowed upon the other during the day.*
*Always leave home with a tender good-bye and loving words.*[39]

Inspirational portraits of the dutiful wife appeared in numerous British and American novels and short stories in popular Victorian periodicals. Jenni Calder has noted the centrality of social and domestic institutions, particularly marriage, to the Victorian novel.[40] One such story, "The Other Side—A Tale of Buttons," appeared in the July 1855 issue of *Godey's Lady's Book*. Author Lucy Ellen Guernsey wrote a charming tale about a preacher and his bride of six months, Christina. Although the preacher was a kind and loving husband, he often berated his new wife over small things such as a tack out of place on the carpet or a button missing from his shirt. As he made his rounds visiting the sick one day, everyone inquired after his

*Properly entitled "A Wife's Devotion," this 1896 illustration from*
The Glory of Woman or, Love, Marriage & Maternity
*shows the loving wife providing comfort for her husband. She was the good
influence that gave him direction in the fast-changing Victorian world.*

VIRTUOUS WOMEN

lovely wife, commenting that she did not seem so cheerful or spirited as in weeks past. Indeed, after giving it thought the preacher realized his parishioners were right. The story continued: "He thought, indeed, that it was a pity he should be so sensitive, and he wished he had not such a love for order and symmetry, for then he should not be so often annoyed by the disorderly habits of other people." The preacher rushed home to speak with his wife and discover if this was truly the cause of her unhappiness. Christina admitted it was so but told him, "It is neither a grateful nor a gracious office for a wife to reprove her husband, or a woman her pastor. But, if you are not angry, I am glad that I have told you all that was in my heart; for, indeed, my dear, it has been a sad aching heart this long time." Christina then went on to explain she had every intention of keeping her household affairs in order but had, on occasion, been called from her duties to help a neighbor. In the end the whole matter was resolved with "a warm embrace and a fervent kiss, and though there were not many words spoken there was a light in the eyes of both husband and wife which showed the understanding was perfect between them."[41]

The dutiful wife was also subject to a nobler calling—as a great civilizer of man. For many years Victorian culture paid tribute to the middle-class wife by deeming her the good influence and life's anchor that kept a husband from roving, gave him direction in the world and provided him with an orderly life. In short, she civilized him and empowered him to civilize the world at large. She did this through love, providing a comfortable home and peaceful setting to which he could retreat each day. The advice givers went so far as to declare man was no more than a barbarian if left to himself without woman's influence.[42]

For the dutiful wife, what about the romantic notion of love? On the one hand, Victorian women were told that love would grow through their married years provided their high moral character kept their husbands on a straight and narrow path. Like tending a garden, they were to cultivate their marriage with affection, kindness and constant care. Such deep abiding love would in fact make the matron even more lovely than the young, blushing bride. In *What a Young Woman Ought to Know*, Mary Wood-Allen, M.D., wrote: "Love would not so often fail if wives knew the secret of retaining it, and that is not by sacrifice of principle, nor by tearful reproaches and upbraidings, but by being true to the highest impulses, and while having the good common sense that can make all reasonable allowance for fallibility, still permits no lowering of moral standards."[43]

In contrast, some advice givers spoke of love being like a caged bird, requiring constant attention or suffering certain death. "Wooing and courting" could revive a lost love but a couple was advised to look instead to friendship, "that good dear cousin to love," which is actually the main ingredient of marriage. According to one expert, "It [friendship] is not so intense and poetical and magnetic as love, but is more stable and enduring, does more work, bears more burdens, exacts less and gives more, and on the whole does immensely more for the home and family."[44] So while the bloom of young, romantic love was expected to fade, the dutiful Victorian wife could look for friendship with her husband to sustain their relationship and shelter the home.

In the antebellum South it was more than love or friendship that sustained a marriage, for there were both economic and political factors that entered into a union—especially on slave-holding plantations or farms. While many Northerners looked to growing industries for their source of income, Southerners participated primarily in agribusinesses for their livelihood. Husband and wife were bound together by the land they lived on, worked on and depended upon for valuable cash crops. Anne Firor Scott points out that women played a vital yet secondary role in plantation life, noting that "[w]omen, like slaves, were an intrinsic part of the patriarchal dream."[45] Indeed, Southern wives were considered a political asset during the unrest over slavery issues in the 1850s and 1860s. Portrayed as the epitome of gentility and hospitality, an ideology promoted by Southern men, their lives were actually quite different. In *Tara Revisited: Women, War, & The Plantation Legend*, Catherine Clinton writes: "Women did not inhabit mythical estates but lived instead on productive working plantations where routines were grueling. Cotton was king, white men ruled, and both white women and slaves served the same master."[46]

By nature of her virtue it would seem the responsibility for the marriage was solely in the wife's hands. To a great extent this was true, but 19th-century advice manuals were quick to dispense words of wisdom for the husband as well. It is interesting to note that the advice offered to the man frequently had more to do with social appearance and correct behavior for his social standing as a married individual than with the intricacies of a loving relationship. Appearances were all-important for middle-class Victorians, both inside and outside the home. With this in mind, no proper young husband would allow his wife to go to church unescorted. This was unseemly and his absence spoke volumes about his lack of gentility.

On the subject of monetary issues, husbands were advised to be honest with their wives about their salary or income so women could plan accordingly regarding household expenses. While the husband was seen as the ruler of the house, the wife managed all that went on inside the home and therefore required a weekly or monthly allowance. The husband was advised, by all means, to give it to her. If need be he could offer his wife advice on running household affairs or handling money, but he was never to interfere unless absolutely necessary. The domestic sphere was her domain, but he was to be mindful not to treat her like a domestic servant. Also, a husband was never to make comparisons between his new bride and his mother but rather to show confidence in her abilities and encourage her in her important new duties.

Being attentive and kind to a wife was imperative and according to the social experts arguments were to be avoided. For example, Richard A. Wells wrote: "If small disputes arise, and your wife has not sufficient good sense to yield her opinion; nay, even if she seems determined to have her own way do not get angry; rather be silent and let the matter rest. An opportunity will soon occur of speaking affectionately, yet decidedly, on the subject, and much good will be effected. Master your own temper and you will soon master your wife's."[47] One would think the husband was dealing with a petulant child from the tone of Wells's advice, but then again, the Victorian husband was considered the lord and master of the house.

Lastly, every married man who wished a happy home was to consider his wife "the light of his domestic circle, and to permit no clouds, however small, to obscure the region in which she presides."[48]

As a young girl the Victorian woman was schooled in developing her moral character and learning self-control as well as self-sacrifice. As an eligible young lady she experienced firsthand the intimate workings of 19th-century etiquette and deportment and tested the waters of true love. As a wife, she was instantly transformed into the ultimate virtuous being and, ready or not, assumed responsibility for the world both inside and outside her door.

# 2

# THE VICTORIAN HOME

My son—thou wilt dream the world is fair,
And thy spirit will sigh to roam,
And thou *must* go;—but never, when there,
Forget the light of home.

—Sarah J. Hale

Idealized and romanticized throughout much of the 19th century, the
Victorian middle-class home was a bastion of morality, comfort and
refinement, guarding the family against the dark or seamy side of an
industrializing world. Like a magic elixir or potent tonic, "home" replenished the spirit of the work-weary husband and protected the innocence of
children.

At the center of the home—the very heart and soul of the home—was
the wife and mother. Glorified at the pulpit and in printed pages as the
"high priestess of the home," the Victorian woman was the gatekeeper to
all that was good and beautiful in the world.

Her kingdom, the middle-class home, was much more than a mere
shelter for family life; the building itself was often Grecian-inspired during
the early Victorian period and then later echoed religious symbolism in style

or adornment. By the late 19th century, architectural embellishment flaunted the excesses of the romantic gilded age.

The clearly defined spaces within the home were designated public and private spheres with the more public areas, such as the front hall, parlor and dining room, situated at the front of the home while private spaces and work centers were typically at the rear, upstairs, or, as in the South, located in separate outer buildings.

The manner in which the home was decorated ideally reflected gentility and social standing, hinted at worldliness and presented the family as upright, moral citizens. Rooms were usually gender specific: the parlor was considered "her" domain while the dining room (and library if one has included) displayed masculine overtones. Decorating the home was an integral part of the cult of domesticity and a responsibility Victorian women did not take lightly. In an era marked by heightened symbolism, something as seemingly small as crocheting antimacassars for the parlor chairs actually spoke volumes about the mistress of the middle-class home.

# THE HIGH PRIESTESS OF THE HOME

Historians have noted that the ideology of "Republican Motherhood" emerged during the late 18th century after the American Revolution had been fought. Women indirectly aided the cause for freedom by boycotting British goods with high tariffs (thus allowing politics to enter the home setting), and once the war had been won, patriotic men viewed women as the future mothers of the new republic. As the role of mother took on newfound importance, home was viewed in relation to the world at large. Long before the dawn of the Victorian era, home and motherhood were being celebrated in popular songs, poetry and literature.

By the 1830s sentimentality regarding the home focused strong interest on children and the manner in which they were raised. No longer considered miniature adults to be dealt with sternly (as in the Colonial era), children were increasingly perceived as innocent beings in need of nurturing love and tender care. Republican Motherhood adopted these views and practices to raise good citizens that were the embodiment of growing middle-class gentility and virtue.

Marriage too was increasingly viewed as a loving bond rather than a relationship based on economic gain, property or increasing farm labor

Vol. CXI.        Number 662.

# ✳ Godey's ✳
# Lady's Book and Magazine.

### Philadelphia, August, 1885.

A WOMAN'S VOICE.

NOT in the swaying of the summer trees,
　When evening breezes sing their vesper
　　hymn;
Not in the minstrel's mighty symphonies,
　Nor ripples breaking on the river's brim,
Is earth's best music; these may move
　awhile
　High thoughts in happy hearts, and carking
　cares beguile;

But even as the swallow's silken wings,
　Skimming the water of the sleeping lake,
Stir the still silver with a hundred rings—
　So doth one sound the sleeping spirit wake
To brave the danger and to bear the harm,
A low gentle voice,—dear woman's chiefest
　charm.

EDWIN ARNOLD.

*Women and the domestic sphere were celebrated in books and periodicals throughout the 19th century. This frontispiece from the August 1885* Godey's Lady's Book *pays tribute to women with sentimental poetry and a beautiful illustration of a young woman.*

through children. However, as noted in the previous chapter, there were exceptions to this.

The concepts of Republican Motherhood and the cultural fixation with gentility and virtuous women had a strong foothold in antebellum America, both North and South, but while women in the North achieved a certain measure of recognition and even elevated status for their efforts, Southern women who were bound to the slave culture did not.[1]

As evidence of their elevated status during the pre–Civil War years, women in general gained full control of their households and were wholly responsible for all day-to-day activities, caring for children, dealing with the help (whether domestic servants or slaves), home decoration and entertaining. The rigid boundaries of their role, however, confined them to the home and to a private life, which excluded them from dealings of a political or (except as consumers) economic nature. While Northern women were able to compensate to a degree by building a support system of friendships, benevolent societies, literary clubs and so on, Southern women were often isolated in rural areas that allowed few visits to town and little, if any, companionship with other women in similar situations—except through letters. Also, for the Southern mistress to leave the confines of home in order to travel to town or a nearby plantation or farm required a chaperon to secure her safety, and chaperons were seldom available.[2]

During the mid-19th century, advice manuals, short stories in popular magazines, novels and poetry continued to reinforce the concept of woman as the "light of the home" in elevated and glowing terms. Should the middle-class Victorian mistress begin to question her role or have doubts about her destiny, she could turn to any number of sources for a reminder about her right and proper place. For example, in her 1848 *The Young Lady's Guide to Knowledge and Virtue*, Anna Fergurson wrote:

> *Let what will be said of the pleasures of society, there is after all, "no place like home." How beautiful are the relationships of home! How exquisitely touching to the feelings! All are linked to each other by the most intimate and endearing ties; a power like that of electricity seems to run through the family group. And as home is that place which has the strongest ties upon the feelings, so it is the place in which woman has the power of exerting her influence in the greatest degree. This is her true and proper station; the duties of home are peculiarly hers; and let it not be thought that, in assigning home as the appropriate sphere for action, we are assigning her a mean and ignoble part. It is, in truth, far otherwise. The sphere of her operation may*

*be a limited one; but as many rivers make up the ocean's waters, so the con-*
*junction of many homes makes up the world; and therefore, in performing*
*her duties at home, she is performing her part in the world at large.*[3]

Daniel Wise voiced similar sentiments but carried them even further:

*Her place is not on life's great battle-fields. Man belongs there. Woman*
*must abide in the peaceful sanctuaries of home, and walk in the noiseless*
*vales of private life. There she must dwell, beside the secret springs of public*
*virtue. There she must smile upon the husband. There she must rear the*
*Christian patriot and statesman, the self-denying philanthropist and the*
*obedient citizen. There, in a word, she must form the character of the*
*world, and determine the destiny of her race. Surely she is not degraded by*
*filling such a sphere. Nor would she be elevated, if, forsaking it, she should*
*go forth into the highways of society, and jostle, with her brothers for the*
*offices and honors of public life. Fame she might occasionally gain, but it*
*would be at the price of her womanly influence.*[4]

Wise was clearly an advocate of the concept of "Republican Motherhood"
and warned women they would relinquish this noble calling if attempts
were made to establish a life "outside" the home.

Others viewed the female predicament in broader terms. For example,
a published declaration of objectives was prepared by Mrs. E. Oakes Smith
circa 1851 and entitled "Woman and her Needs." In her controversial
manifesto Smith wrote:

*It is often said, "A womans' world is in her affections, her empire is home."*
*This is only in part true, and true only to a part of the sex. There is a large*
*class to whom the affections hold a very subordinate part—women who*
*find it irksome to sustain the relations of wife and mother, and who would*
*never have assumed them, but because public opinion has made it desir-*
*able, and the unequal action of labor necessary.*

Smith's declaration also faulted men for confining women to such a narrow
sphere when "the lions [men] have written the books, and having persisted
in making that part of our character which brings us in relation to
themselves the prominent subject of comment, they have ignored our other
attributes. Let it be understood, I do not disparage the home affections, the
circle of home duties. I only wish to assert that we must not be limited to

these; that we must and ought to be true to the talents committed to our keeping."[5]

To be sure there were many notable women who did not follow the path of the stereotypical middle-class Victorian woman, but rather combined family life with moderately successful careers as novelists, poets, artists, etc. Harriet Beecher Stowe, the author of *Uncle Tom's Cabin*, is among the most notable of these but there were certainly many others. While it was considered inappropriate for the middle-class wife to actually work for wages outside the home, writing was a permissible outlet for creativity and one which often added to the family coffers.

Although the 19th-century advice givers were saluting domestic endeavors and dispensing encouraging words about women's proper place, many of them voiced concerns over women (and their daughters) striking the proper balance between gentility and industry. As the growing middle class saw their financial resources increase, many women in the North were able to hire one or more domestic servants to assume responsibility for mundane (and rigorous) chores throughout the house. This allowed them extra time to devote to family, home decoration, ornamental needlework and socializing. Women, however, were cautioned to avoid overspending on home accessories and to maintain an active role in domestic undertakings rather than aspiring to a life of leisure. Catharine E. Beecher, 19th-century domestic science authority, expressed her concerns about such matters in the 1869 publication, *The American Woman's Home*, which she coauthored with her sister, Harriet Beecher Stowe. The sisters declared:

> *And, the higher civilization has advanced, the more have children been trained to feel that to labor . . . is disgraceful, and to be made the portion of a degraded class. Children . . . grow up with the feeling that servants are to work for them, and they themselves are not to work. To the minds of most children and servants, "to be a lady," is almost synonymous with "to be waited on, and do no work." It is the earnest desire of the authors of this volume to make plain the falsity of this growing popular feeling, and to show how much happier and more efficient family life will become when it is strengthened, sustained, and adorned by family work.[6]*

Striking the proper balance between industry and leisurely pursuits was also a common theme in popular Victorian fiction. A two-part story that appeared in the January and February 1867 issues of *Godey's Lady's Book* compared two homes and the families that occupied them. "Entirely at

Home" by Marion Harland (author of the *Common Sense in the Household* series of domestic and recipe books) was the story of two sisters who leave their warm, loving home in the country for an extended visit with friends in the city. Regarding their own home, the elder sister recalled: "We kept but two servants—a man to till the garden and take care of the cows and horses, and a woman to cook, wash, and iron. The lighter work of the chambers [bedrooms] and drawing-room was performed by the quick, willing hands of my sister and myself, our mother acting as directress and general supervisor. Our parlors were cheerful, airy, and even elegant. Neither books, music, nor pictures were wanting to give them at once a refined, yet home-like expression." In contrast, the home the girls visited in the city had a well-appointed but dreary parlor, which displayed "the absurd fashion of darkening drawing-rooms to Cimmerian gloom." The city home was indeed a showplace, but cold in that it lacked family warmth and spirit, its members always flitting to and fro to social engagements. The elder sister wrote of their visit: "Mother and daughter were amiable, selfish butterflies, making their own pleasure the chief end and aim of existence, and regarding the rest of the universe as mere accessories to the attainment of this object."[7]

After the Civil War advice givers became concerned that the elevated status of women was threatened by rising industrialism, new forms of entertainment, travel and massive reconstruction in the South. Thus, in *The American Woman's Home* Beecher and Stowe expressed their concerns that the "high priestess" was slipping from her exalted domestic altar as the outside world garnered increased attention: "It is the aim of this volume to elevate both the honor and the remuneration of all employments that sustain the many difficult and varied duties of the family state, and thus to render each department of woman's profession as much desired and re-spected as are the most honored professions of men."[8] Obviously the Beecher sisters felt strongly that woman's contibution in the home was every bit as important to the economy as man's work away from the home and therefore domestic undertakings should rightfully be looked on as a profes-sion.[9]

While such sentiments undoubtedly helped many middle-class women persevere in their role as a Victorian wife and mother, in all likelihood there were few men who viewed a woman's role at home as a "profession." Men did, however, continue to hail the home as woman's proper place through the dawn of the 20th century. Even as the concept of Republican Mother-hood lost significance during the late 1800s with more structured school systems, the ideology of virtuous womanhood persisted. According to Sheila M. Rothman, in *Woman's Proper Place*, this concept of virtuous womanhood continued to link women to the home, since job opportunities and social activities were limited to activities consistent with caring, nurturing behavior.[10] In other words, nursing was acceptable employment since being a caregiver suited the ideology. Entering a restaurant unescorted, on the other hand, would jeopardize a woman's moral reputation.

Household manuals, behavior books and etiquette books published during the 1870s and 1880s continued to reinforce the ideal of the virtuous woman, metaphorically comparing her role and her home to that of a higher kingdom. For example, in 1882 John H. Young told readers: "Home is the woman's kingdom, and there she reigns supreme."[11] Likewise, the 1883 book *The Heart of the World: or Home and Its Wide Work* by G. S. Weaver stated: "The woman is the priestess of home, and puts herself into it and its affairs and conditions. Her talents and tastes have given her a natural ordination to this holy office."[12]

By the 1890s there was an obvious change in the language of such instructional texts. Household manuals during the last decade of the century and the early 1900s were devoid of sentimental overtones regarding the home, and the nature of housework and etiquette books cut to the facts without lengthy homilies on woman's role at home. Such changes were due in part to a shift in ideology—the virtuous woman was no longer the focus of the home; children were. In addition, increased availability of material goods, packaged foods, household appliances or tools, and professional services realigned the manner in which cooking, cleaning and general household chores were done. Home lost much of its romantic appeal as "scientific" methods became popular.

As the new century approached, higher education for women was viewed in terms of how it could best benefit children in the home. The "profession" of high priestess was replaced during the early 1900s by a new profession called "educated motherhood," which placed emphasis on child development.[13] In addition, as Erna Olafson Hellerstein et al. point out in *Victorian Women: A Documentary Account of Women's Lives in Nineteenth-Century England, France, and the United States*, women slowly began to reliquish power in the home with the advent of professional medical services and advice from scientific authorities on child rearing and home management.[14] In contrast to the homey advice books that dominated the market during most of the Victorian era, the household guides published during the early 1900s were very clinical and geared toward home management as a "business" (with the kitchen as a great "laboratory") and child rearing as the modern new science.

The ideology and customs that shaped the life of the middle-class Victorian mistress at home are only a portion—albeit a significant portion —of the culture that defined who she was. Material culture—the home she lived in as well as the furnishings and accessories she chose for that home, also conveyed a great deal about her life.

## VICTORIAN HOUSES AND HOME SPACES

There is no question that the majority of middle-class Victorian women played out their lives in the home. The two were explicitly linked—domestic goddess and her domain. What was her home like? Both inside and out, the middle-class home paid tribute to genteel 19th-century culture.

Architectural styles in vogue during the Victorian era varied from the symmetrical lines of the Greek Revival–home and increasing numbers of urban row houses to the eclecticism of the late 19th-century Queen Anne–house and the marked simplicity of the Arts and Crafts inspired bungalow.

During the late 1830s, new home construction resulted in a landscape dotted with Greek Revival–style buildings (popular from the 1820s through the 1850s). Especially in the South, where this Grecian-inspired style was at its most elaborate, these buildings were often bedecked with Greek temple porticos or with porches having impressive Ionic or Doric columns. Throughout the rest of the country simplified or vernacular versions of the Greek Revival–home were frequently dressed with main entryways sporting heavy cornices and pilasters flanking the front door.

While the Greek Revival–style embodied subtle beauty and the spirit of democracy that patriotic Americans identified with, it wasn't long before the romance associated with the Victorian era and advances in industry sparked a craze for architectural embellishment. Inspired by medieval Europe, Gothic Revival–style "cottages," characterized by asymmetrical forms, arched windows and decorative bargeboard facades, were popularized by architect Andrew Jackson Downing in his 1850 book, *The Architecture of Country Houses*. This Gothic revival in architecture combined religious symbolism (arched windows reminiscent of old European cathedrals) with gingerbread trim and, at the same time, stressed the importance of harmony with the natural surroundings. Victorian Gothic–style homes

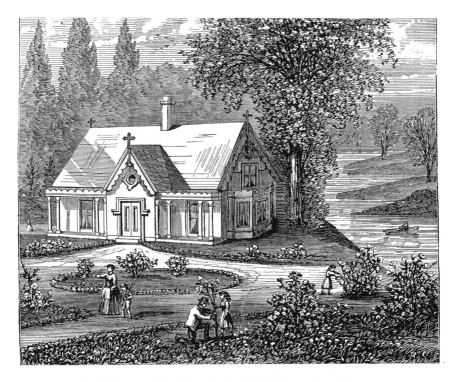

*The "Christian House" as described by Catharine Beecher and
Harriet Beecher Stowe in* The American Woman's Home
*(and, later, the updated* New Housekeeper's Manual *by
Catharine Beecher). The architectural style of this ideal
Victorian home is Gothic Revival, and the grounds are landscaped
with trees, flowers and gardens in order that all members
of the family may work for the common good.*

were built primarily in rural areas throughout the Northeast between the 1840s and the mid-1870s, but a variation on the Gothic style, Victorian Steamboat Gothic, could be found in the South during the same period.

The middle-class Victorian home ideally combined beauty (as it related to God and nature) with a sense of morality (found in a homey setting).[15] In the second chapter of *The American Woman's Home*, entitled "A Christian House," the Beecher sisters actually provided a specific plan (complete with illustration) for translating such eternal attributes into architectural reality. They defined a "Christian house" as "a house contrived for the express purpose of enabling every member of a family to labor with the hands for the common good, and by modes at once healthful, economical, and tasteful."[16] The modern scholar Colleen McDannell, commenting on the sisters' vision of a home as a concrete statement of abstract values, notes "how the creators of Victorian American culture . . . emphasized that the *house itself* shaped the character of its inhabitants," that "[h]ousing design, rather than being merely a matter of taste, provided the means by which good family life could be accomplished."[17] Whether "home" was a working man's cottage, a prosperous farmhouse, a city row house or an elaborate villa, it was considered an expression of its owners' spiritual condition as well as their aesthetic taste.

By the 1850s an increasing number of people were moving to the cities, and suburbs began to spring up around growing urban areas. City row houses, or town houses, were built in the Italianate style all across the country between the 1840s and the 1880s, and many middle-class families favored this classical yet romantic architectural style for single-family dwellings as well. The square Italianate style often featured arched windows and a low-gabled roof having eaves adorned with brackets. Unlike Greek Revival–style homes, Italianate houses were usually painted in earth tones rather than white to blend harmoniously with the surrounding landscape.

During the last quarter of the 19th century Queen Anne–style homes—the quintessential Victorian home—became all the rage across America. Such houses were built in villages, towns and suburbs while Queen Anne–style town houses were constructed in cities. Heavily ornamented with decorative porches, leaded or art-glass windows, gables and turrets, the Queen Anne style took full advantage of all that modern machinery had to offer. Variations on the eclectic Queen Anne style (such as the smaller Princess Anne) were not unusual and older homes were often "modernized" to incorporate some of the decorative features of the popular style.

*The May 1885* Godey's Lady's Book *included this architectural plan for a modest Queen Anne residence that could be built for approximately $4,000. Note the turret, decorative porches and leaded-glass windows— typical embellishments of the popular Queen Anne style.*

During the second half of the 19th century, especially after the Civil War, middle-class families could refer to popular periodicals as well as architectural pattern books for the latest in home design. For example, in 1878 Palliser, Palliser & Company, the Bridgeport, Connecticut, architectural firm, issued a book of 50 different designs for "cottage" homes and town houses. The preface stated:

> In presenting to the public a new work on Architecture, we have endeavored to meet a demand that has been made on us, for some time past, for practical designs of low and medium priced houses suited to the masses of our country. We have endeavored to combine good design with practical, convenient, plans and sound construction; in fact our aim has been, to get the best effect in design in the simplest, most common sense, and least expensive manner, as it is not expense and ornate decorations, which so many ignorantly believe to be the highest attainment of architecture, but design, which produces true beauty and graceful appearance.[18]

Palliser's book included plans ranging from a "tasty cottage" of six rooms that could be built for $850 to a three-story Queen Anne–row house that was estimated to run $2,400. They also offered plans for a "neat every-day house well adapted for erection in suburbs, villages or country," which could be constructed for $3,000. Whether for young newlyweds or a couple with children, a stylish home could be built with all the latest amenities, including indoor plumbing, a bathroom, spacious parlor and dining room, built-in china closets, a kitchen pantry, laundry area and a front porch or piazza. The surrounding landscape was groomed with flowers, shade trees and sometimes ornamental fences that enhanced the outer beauty and refinement of the dwelling.

Victorian middle-class women were advised to take an active interest in the construction of their homes. This was in fact considered a branch of 19th-century domestic science by such a noted authority as Catharine E. Beecher. For example, in their 1873 *The New Housekeeper's Manual*, Beecher and Stowe told readers:

> The following [chapters] will show, though very imperfectly, how many branches of science and training are included in woman's profession, and thus what needs to be attempted: First, the department of a housekeeper demands some knowledge of all the arts and sciences connected with the proper construction of the family dwelling. A widow, or a woman whose

*husband has not the time or ability to direct, and in communities destitute of intelligent artisans, on building a house would need the guidance of the leading principles of architecture, pneumatics, hydrostatics, calorification, and several other connected sciences, in order to secure architectural beauty, healthful heating and ventilation, and the economical and convenient arrangements for labor and comfort. A housekeeper properly instructed in these principles would know how to secure chimneys that will not smoke, the most economical furnaces and stoves, and those that will be sure to "draw." She would know how dampers and air-boxes should be placed and regulated, how to prevent or remedy gas escapes, leaking water pipes, poisonous recession of sewers, slamming shutters, bells that will not ring, blinds that will not fasten, and doors that will not lock or catch. She will understand about high and low pressure on water-pipes and boilers, and many other mysteries which make a woman the helpless victim of plumbers and other jobbers often as blundering and ignorant as herself. She would know what kind of wood-work saves labor, how to prevent its shrinkage, when to use paint, and what kind is best, and many other details of knowledge needed in circumstances to which any daughter of wealth is liable: knowledge which could be gained with less time and labor than is now given in public schools to geometry and algebra.* [19]

The Queen Anne–style home remained popular until about 1900, but a significant movement was already underway to simplify houses and construct buildings that displayed some measure of craftsmanship rather than factory or machine-made qualities. As a result, the bungalow proved a huge success across the country and could even be ordered precut and ready to assemble from the Sears, Roebuck & Co. catalog. The bungalow's affordability and practicality, combined with interior details such as an open-living floor plan, made it quite popular among the middle class, especially in warm climates where the large veranda and projecting eaves of the bungalow style helped promote interior cooling.

By no means providing a definitive listing of all the 19th-century architectural styles, I have tried to mention several of the more common homes the Victorians were eager to build and reside in. There were of course others, including the short-lived craze for the midcentury-period octagon house; stick-style homes, which made use of "stick" or wooden embellishments on the exterior; Eastlake-style homes, which, like the popular Eastlake furniture made during the 1870s and 1880s, took full advantage of modern machinery to create incised or geometric ornamentation for the facade of the house; shingle-style homes, which, as the name implies, were constructed with shingles rather than clapboard or brick. In addition, vernacular architectural styles native to certain regions of the country no doubt housed many a middle-class Victorian family. Cobblestone houses native to the Great Lakes areas were built during the midcentury in the Greek Revival or Gothic style, while shotgun houses appeared in towns and cities in the South, especially in New Orleans. Constructed so that rooms were aligned one behind the other, the shotgun was ideal for narrow city lots and was often adorned with Greek Revival–trim or Victorian gingerbread. The unusual name was aptly assigned because given the architectural layout, a shotgun could be fired through the front door and exit straight out the back at the rear of the dwelling.

The massive 19th-century housing boom was sparked by the middle-class desire to achieve the American dream. While a newly married couple might begin their life together as boarders in some quaint home on a tree-lined street, during the course of their marriage they undoubtedly purchased or built one or more homes as their financial resources increased and their family grew to include children. As Mark Girouard points out in his introduction to *Victorians at Home* by Susan Lasdun, we must keep in mind that styles often combined or overlapped during the Victorian era and individual households were subject to change as people moved up the social ladder or were influenced by style changes. As a result, architectural styles and home fashions are not so much clearly defined categories as they are pieces of a fascinating puzzle displaying a life story.[20]

Finally, new home construction advanced at a fast and furious pace throughout the 19th century. *Godey's Lady's Book* offered some words of advice in the July 1855 issue when publisher Louis A. Godey wrote: "We have given many plans for building cottages, we now give this one: How To Build A Happy Home—Six things are requisite. Integrity must be the architect, tidiness the upholsterer. It must be warmed by affection, lighted up with cheerfulness; and industry must be the ventilator, renewing the atmosphere, and bringing in fresh salubrity day by day; while over all, as a protecting canopy and glory, nothing will suffice except the blessing of God."[21]

As architectural styles came and went throughout the Victorian era, home spaces or the interior division of rooms were subject to change as well. There were certain priorities important to the typical middle-class family, one of which was that the home must have a parlor for entertaining and conducting the social and ceremonial aspects of daily life. The parlor

*A multigenerational Victorian family gathers around the parlor
table to listen to Father read, perhaps from the Bible. This 1879
chromolithograph entitled "Modern Home" shows a well-appointed
parlor with carpeting, a fashionable window dressing and
modern, simplified furnishings.*

embodied much of the material culture imperative to and associated with respectable middle-class life and served as a showcase for the ornamental needlework and craft projects created by Victorian women.

A descendant of the formal 18th-century drawing room, the Victorian parlor was typically located on the first floor of the home, at the front and off the main hall. In the early 19th century it was not unusual to find a bed in the parlor, as many homes were quite small and space was at a premium. For those eager to participate in true middle-class parlor culture, such homes were either enlarged or the family eventually moved to a more spacious dwelling.

By midcentury the majority of middle-class homes throughout the North and the South had some type of formal parlor and, depending upon the size of the house, may also have had a less formal sitting room or back parlor for everyday family use. For those that did not, the parlor functioned as both the "best room" in the house and the room devoted to family activity.

In an age when most social gatherings were held in the home, the parlor was the setting for formal entertaining, for receiving visitors who paid "calls," for courting and for ceremonial events such as weddings and funerals. Those families that could, often kept the parlor closed when not using it, reserving the sacred space only for special events and entertaining. The wisdom of this was questioned by some household authorities who felt that the family should indeed make full use of their entire house and home. In contrast, others claimed the home should maintain a formal parlor reserved for occasional use. This argument was waged back and forth between advice givers throughout the second half of the 19th century.

Several factors contributed to the eventual decline of the formal parlor after the dawn of the 20th century, including the shift from "parlors" to "living rooms" in open-living architectural plans where one room flowed directly into another. Bungalows especially incorporated this informal arrangement in home spaces. In addition, an increase in the forms of entertainment found outside the home and the invention of the telephone ushered in new ways of socializing and communicating, thereby lessening the importance of having a formal parlor for receiving guests. Lastly, as McDannell points out, the new century's technological promise was reflected in the transition from the house as "sacred hearth" to its new role as a "space in which scientific values and rational planning produced people capable of negotiating modern society."[22]

Even though Victorian sensibilities and a strict code of etiquette lingered until the First World War, household guides and all-purpose compendiums extolled the virtues of the "living room" during the early 1900s. For example, in 1909 *Household Discoveries and Mrs. Curtis's Cook Book* told readers:

> *The old custom of setting apart a "best room" or parlor to be used only on special occasions, as for weddings, funerals, or the entertainment of company, is happily passing away. Only very wealthy people now have drawing-rooms reserved for state occasions. The present tendency is to call all the lower rooms of the house "living rooms," and to have all the members of the family use them freely. A room set apart from ordinary use, and hence shut up much of the time from sun and air, is not good for the physical or moral health of the household. The furnishings themselves, if good care is given them, will be improved rather than injured by ordinary wear, and guests will receive a far pleasanter impression from the easy and graceful atmosphere imparted to a room by daily use, than from the stiff and formal restraints imposed by the old-fashioned parlor. A hostess who takes her friends into a sitting room and tells them frankly that she prefers to "live in her own parlor" will have more friends than critics.*[23]

Despite the fact that advice givers sang the praises of the "living room," the shift away from the parlor did not happen overnight. In her essay "The Decline of the Memory Palace: The Parlor after 1890," Katherine C. Grier notes that the relatively informal modern living room only gradually displaced the "enthusiastically artificial" parlor. Grier observes that "Victorian . . . patterns of room use" persisted even into the 1920s.[24]

While a parlor was vitally important to middle-class culture throughout the Victorian era, a separate room for dining was also a prerequisite for formal entertaining. Dinner parties, usually for 10 or 12 guests, afternoon teas and luncheons were a popular means of entertaining and climbing the social ladder. The dining room was also located on the first floor, often across the hall from the parlor. A butler's pantry often separated the dining room from the kitchen or, if the kitchen was located in the basement, a dumbwaiter transported meals upstairs. Most dining rooms were spacious, allowing for a large table and chairs, a sideboard and a built-in or free-standing china cupboard.

As Kenneth L. Ames notes in *Death in the Dining Room & Other Tales of Victorian Culture*, during the Victorian age dining not only served to satisfy the most basic of human needs but participating in the surrounding formal dining was also a ceremony, a means of conveying gentility.[25] Indeed, if having a proper parlor was evidence of participation in middle-class Victorian culture, knowing how to outfit the dining room (especially the table) and then use myriad pieces of flatware, stemware and china in the proper manner conveyed familiarity with the rules governing proper etiquette and deportment—a knowledge and skill vital to acceptance into genteel society and as evidence of good moral character.

As the 19th century progressed, dining rooms sometimes grew smaller due mainly to changing furniture styles resulting in smaller case pieces and tables that could be extended as needed. After the dawn of the new century, dining rooms were often incorporated into open-living floor plans, but their importance remained steadfast; this ritualistic dining space for family as well as guests never went out of style.

Books, long associated with intellectual endeavors, home study and curiosity about the world had become readily available and affordable by the mid-19th century. It is not at all surprising that a home library—a room devoted to books—became an important space in many middle-class homes. In his 1863 architectural plan book, *Holly's Country Seats*, Henry Hudson Holly wrote: "It is not too much to say that every man owes it to himself, no less than his family, to provide a spot around which he may gather his dear ones for counsel and instruction. Such a home is incomplete without one apartment, too often little regarded, which is a library."[26] Holly's Design No. 4, described as a "cheap cottage" intended for a village lot, included a 15-by-18-foot library on the first floor along with a spacious parlor and dining room. Three chambers or bedrooms and a linen closet were planned for the second floor, and this particular design was estimated to cost $3,000.[27]

Not all middle-class homes had space devoted to a library, and for those that did not, freestanding bookcases full of treasured family books could be found in the sitting room or parlor. With the introduction of more open-living spaces by the end of the 19th century, many living rooms included built-in bookcases or shelves.

The common division of space in the majority of middle-class Victorian homes found the public rooms for entertaining located at the front of the dwelling and the work spaces out of sight (thus out of mind) at the rear. The kitchen and laundry areas faced the backyard or were located in the basement. In the South it was not uncommon for the kitchen to be housed in a separate building connected to the main house by a covered walkway.

*This 1891 illustration from the etiquette book* Manners, Culture and Dress of The Best American Society *conveys the importance of books in the middle-class Victorian home. Whether in a library or a sitting room, books are close at hand, studied and appreciated.*

This not only diminished the threat of fire to the home but prevented all trace of cooking odor from permeating the "best rooms."

Private rooms such as bedrooms, or "chambers" as the Victorians referred to them, were upstairs, tucked away from the scrutiny of public eyes, and the casual family sitting room was generally found behind the formal parlor or toward the back of the house.

As the Victorian era progressed and homes grew larger, it was popular practice to assign specific rooms a special purpose. Since "home culture" was a primary dynamic in Victorian family life, rooms centered around books, music, nature, socializing, ritualistic dining and other designated activities. However, this specialization allowed for a certain ambiguity, as noted by David P. Handlin in *The American Home: Architecture and Society 1815–1915:* "The library, a place for the husband's solitude sometimes served as a room for entertainment or for children's play. The identity of bedrooms was similarly ambiguous. Primarily for sleeping and dressing, a bedroom could also serve as a study and playroom for the children or a sewing room for the wife."[28] Handlin further notes that a second level of ambiguity revolves around the fact that Victorian homes typically incorporated a network of hallways, stairways, doorways and so on to separate and define spaces while at the same time architectural additions such as pocket doors or decorative touches such as fabric portieres hanging in doorways could be opened or pulled back to create access to adjoining areas.[29]

Once the Victorian mistress was settled in her house she set about decorating the public spaces and making the more private areas comfortable and conducive to family interaction, creating a home suitable for the family and acceptable in terms of middle-class Victorian culture.

# HOME DECORATION

For the Victorian women who played an active role in the middle-class cult of domesticity, decorating the home had far greater meaning than simply furnishing home spaces; average women were creating a setting in which domesticity would thrive, social interaction would be a success and self-improvement (intellectual and cultural pursuits) would be promoted. The Beecher sisters noted this in their 1869 domestic treatise *The American Woman's Home:*

*For while the aesthetic element must be subordinate to the requirements of physical existence, and, as a matter of expense, should be held of inferior consequence to means of higher moral growth; it [beauty in home decoration] yet holds a place of great significance among the influences which make home happy and attractive, which give it constant and wholesome power over the young, and contributes much to the education of the entire household in refinement, intellectual development, and moral sensibility.*[30]

In decorating the 19th-century home, furniture as well as floor, window and wall treatments were subject to change as new styles were constantly introduced. Although the middle-class family could not afford to replace their furnishings as each new style made its debut, they often incorporated a piece or two (perhaps a chair, an ottoman or a lamp) into an already furnished room to show they had good taste and the wherewithal to display the latest fashions. Older furniture pieces were often relegated to the bedrooms or possibly the informal sitting room.

In regard to home furnishings, when the Victorian era officially began in the late 1830s American Empire was the predominant furniture style. However, it wasn't long before the romanticism associated with the 19th century spawned a series of flamboyant revival styles having roots in old European culture. Coinciding with the introduction of Gothic architecture, Gothic Revival–style furnishings became popular during the 1840s. Usually crafted of oak or rosewood, elaborate and eye-catching arches, carvings and spool turnings were incorporated into these delicate furnishings that recalled the Middle Ages.

By the 1850s Rococo Revival furnishings, reminiscent of 18th-century France, were in vogue. Flowing serpentine backs were a hallmark of this style on parlor settees and chairs; black walnut and rosewood were often used to produce such upholstered furnishings and case pieces. Sideboards, dressers and tables were ornamented with carved fruits, birds, floral motifs and elegant marble tops.

While cabinetmakers hand-crafted furniture for the well to do, by the mid-19th century the growing middle class could purchase stylish factory-made furnishings available in matching suites. A parlor suite was likely to include a settee, a side chair or two, a gentleman's chair and a lady's chair. Just as certain rooms in the Victorian home were gender specific, so too were furnishings. A lady's chair featured a low back and an obvious lack of arms in order to accommodate the yards and yards of fabric in Victorian

*The informal sitting room, as illustrated in this 1867 lithograph from* Godey's Lady's Book, *was a relaxed setting in which comfortable furnishings, favorite objects and handiwork predominated. Genteel touches such as fresh flowers or a fringed tablecloth add a subtle spirit of refinement to this predominantly female space.*

dresses. A gentleman's chair on the other hand sported a high back and arms, symbolizing the elevated status of the "man of the house."

Renaissance Revival–style furnishings were introduced during the 1860s and in sharp contrast to the demure Rococo Revival–style pieces were quite large and bold in appearance. Mainly crafted of walnut, Renaissance Revival–style furniture featured carved or applied medallions, scroll work, pediments and carved fruit drawer pulls.

During the early Victorian period and until the mid-1870s, advice givers recommended that all the furnishings in any given room should match or be the same style. For example, in his 1873 *The Household Cyclopaedia of Practical Receipts and Daily Wants*, Alexander V. Hamilton advised women: "In furnishing a house let your guiding rules be that the same style, with modifications, be apparent all over your house, that in employment of color you avoid bad contrasts, that walls be well covered with mirrors, pictures, etc., and that the rooms be not overcrowded."[31]

For middle-class Victorian women furniture was one of many symbolic objects found throughout the home. Especially during the period 1830 to 1870 when the revival styles were fashionable, furnishings not only paid tribute to history via their styling but they were also indicative of gentility. Explaining this trend, Katherine C. Grier notes that "while few middle-class families could afford the kind of architecture that made spaces truly gala, some mass-produced furnishings played an important role in commercializing gentility." As an example, Grier cites the popularity of 18th-century-style furniture in the parlors of the 1860s and 1870s: "Their design was meant to encourage formality rather than relaxation; seated comfort, as the concept is understood today, was of little concern."[32]

Historians today look back on the early Victorian parlor as being quite formal in contrast to the last quarter of the 19th century, when this all-important room took on more romantic overtones. This was brought about by several reform movements that introduced not only new furniture styles, but new ways of dressing the walls, floors and windows of the Victorian home. Even seating arrangements were subject to change.

The first of several reform movements in America was inspired by the book *Hints on Household Taste*, written by Charles Eastlake and published in England in 1868. Eastlake's work, which proposed: "The best and most picturesque furniture of all ages has been simple in general form," was being sold in America by the early 1870s.[33] The Eastlake-style furnishings adopted by American manufacturers were primarily constructed of oak, ash, chestnut, cherry or walnut and their rectangular forms were embellished with incised geometric patterns—not exactly what the noted reformer had in mind given his distaste for mass-produced furniture displaying excessive ornamentation. Nevertheless, Eastlake furnishings outfitted many a middle-class home from the early 1870s through the 1890s.

Eastlake's book proved a huge success in the United States, but he was by no means the only notable author on the subject of 19th-century interior design. *The House Beautiful,* 1878, by Clarence Cook was extremely popular, as was *The Decoration of House,* 1897, by Edith Wharton and Ogden Codman, Jr. Wharton, in fact, went on to become a celebrated novelist, writing such works as *The House of Mirth, Ethan Frome* and the Pulitzer Prize–winning *The Age of Innocence.*

As more and more middle-class Americans were exposed to foreign cultures through travel, literature and special exhibitions, interior design began to reflect their expanding world. Tributes to exotica appeared in home spaces in the form of oriental fabrics, Japanese screens and fans, wicker and bamboo furnishings, tufted pillows and ottomans and decorative peacock feathers. The Aesthetic Movement, as this was known, was all the rage during the 1880s and like the penchant that followed for anything Art Nouveau during the 1890s, echoed a love of beauty, nature and various art forms.

The Arts and Crafts Reform Movement was well underway in America in the 1890s, and by blending quality craftsmanship with the beauty of basic, functional design, furniture (mainly oak) was crafted with decidedly simple geometric lines. Gustav Stickley and Elbert Hubbard are two men identified with this furniture style. Stickley began a firm producing handcrafted Arts and Crafts (*aka* Mission style) furniture and Hubbard established the Roycroft Community in East Aurora, New York, where furnishings as well as decorative metalwork for the home were painstakingly created. Although the main objective of this reform movement was craftsmanship, factories began to turn out large quantities of mass-produced Arts and Crafts furniture that proved popular in outfitting bungalows.

Other furniture styles or substyles appealing to the middle class throughout the 19th century included "cottage" furniture, which was highly recommended by Andrew Jackson Downing in his midcentury architectural plan books. Not only was cottage furniture extremely affordable but quite attractive as well. Used mainly to furnish bedrooms and perhaps a sitting room, factory-made cottage pieces were constructed of pine or poplar, painted in soft pastel shades of color and adorned with hand-painted floral motifs or stenciled designs.

Wicker furnishings became popular during the 1880s and 1890s and turned up in almost any room of the Victorian home. Like the factory-made golden oak furniture that appealed to the middle class before the turn of the century, wicker pieces from chairs and rockers to tables and settees were available through home furnishing stores and mail-order catalogs.

With the arrival of the reform movements in the 1870s came a shift in ideology concerning home decoration. Furniture pieces no longer had to match—in fact, a harmonious blend of various styles was recommended, resulting in less formal but more romantic room settings. Regarding furnishing the home, Richard A. Wells, directed women in *Manners, Culture and Dress of The Best American Society*, 1891:

> *Color, form and proportion are the chief features to be observed in house furnishing. It is not necessary to have costly furniture, expensive pictures, fine paintings, elegant draperies, or Haviland and Wedgewood wares to produce pleasant effects; but have the colors harmonize and have nothing too good to use. All stiffness of design in furniture should be avoided. Do not attempt to match articles, but rather carry out the same ideas as to color and form in the whole. Do not have decorations in sets or pairs; the arrangements should all be done with odd pieces.*[34]

Not only was the middle-class Victorian woman concerned about the style, quality and affordability of the furniture she chose for her home, but "decorating" also entailed what she did with her walls, how she treated her floors and how she dressed her windows. In addition, there were the all-important accessories to be considered. During the early Victorian period light colors on the walls were thought advantageous since lighting was limited. Wood floors were painted or covered with matting or floorcloths and window treatments were fairly simple, making use of blinds, curtains and valances. Oil paintings, books (especially the family Bible) and brass candlesticks helped dress the formal parlor, in which furniture was symmetrically placed around the room.

By the 1850s and 1860s factory-made furnishings were designed to be arranged in semiformal intimate groupings; machine-made wallpapers, affordable carpets, elaborate window dressings and changing attitudes toward color harmony altered the interior of the typical middle-class home. A carpet especially was an item women often fretted over, since it was now considered an integral part of home decor. The August 1855 issue of *Godey's Lady's Book* told readers that a carpet should serve as a subtle background

*Home decorating usually included articles created by the
Victorian middle-class mistress, such as the fern screen,
illuminated windowpane and imitation painted glass that
appeared in the 1879 book* The Complete Home.

for furnishings and "give value to all objects coming in contact with it. Composed of sombre shades and tones, and treated essentially as a flat surface, it exerts a most valuable, though subordinate influence upon all other decorations of the day."[35]

In regard to purchasing a carpet women were reminded both in advice books and popular periodicals that great sums of money could be spent on them and frugality was indeed called for. Catharine Beecher addressed the danger of overspending on a parlor carpet in *The American Woman's Home* and Lydia Maria Child wrote along the same lines in her book *The American Frugal Housewife*. Child told readers:

> *A few weeks since, I called upon a farmer's daughter, who had lately married a young physician. Her father had given her, at her marriage, two thousand dollars. Yet the lower part of her house was furnished with as much splendor as we usually find among the wealthiest. The whole two thousand dollars had been expended upon Brussels carpets [Brussels carpets refers to a machine-made, looped-pile carpet], alabaster vases, mahogany chairs and marble tables. I afterwards learned that the more useful household utensils had been forgotten; and that a few weeks after her wedding, she was actually obliged to apply to her husband for money to purchase baskets, iron spoons, clotheslines, etc., and her husband, made irritable by the want of money, pettishly demanded why she had bought so many things they did not want. Had the young lady been content with kidderminster carpets [a long-wearing ingrain carpet] and tasteful vases of her own making, she might have put one thousand dollars at interest.*[36]

Throughout the 19th century the advice manuals attempted to show how the Victorian mistress could have a comfortable yet beautiful home at moderate cost. Unpretentious gentility was the prescribed role for middle-class people.[37] In any case, by the 1870s room-size carpets had become passé. The new reform styles called for exposed wood floors dressed with area rugs featuring oriental designs.

In regard to interior design, perhaps the most significant change during the 1870s and 1880s was the introduction of the tripartite wall treatment. While during the previous decades walls were painted or papered in a singular color or pattern, Charles Eastlake proposed a new horizontal division of wall space that included a dado or wooden wainscoting on the bottom part of the wall, a papered or painted "field" in the midsection and a papered frieze at the top. In many Victorian homes the tripartite wall was created in the parlor and/or dining room by using three distinct but color- or pattern-related wallpapers. Employing a chair rail or wainscoting to create a division of wall space was also common in the dining room.

Interior colors changed dramatically during the 19th century. Pale colors were no longer fashionable for the public rooms in the house and parlors, dining rooms and libraries were painted or papered in shades of olive, plum, claret, peacock blue or terra cotta during the 1870s and 1880s. The elaborate, multilayer window treatments so popular during the midcentury remained in many homes but others chose to simplify, doing away with ornate lambrequins (stationary fabric bedecked with cords, fringe, etc., that hung at the very top of the window). The latest fashion called for a lace undercurtain topped with a simple drapery.

With the Arts and Crafts Reform Movement of the 1890s came a scaled-down look in home interiors. The tripartite wall fell out of favor, subtle rod-pocket lace panels were used at windows and light earth tones replaced the deep colors used on walls during the previous decade.

During the late 1800s, when home decorating reached a feverish pitch, the decorative accessories that filled Victorian rooms to overflow were intended to be a carefully orchestrated blend of material objects that fulfilled cultural, social and domestic needs.[38] Beginning with the front hall, which offered that important first impression, women were advised during the late 19th century to dress their walls in dark, rich colors such as maroon. Wainscoting was also favored in the hallway.

Ideally the hall floor was tile or wooden parquet, but a painted wood floor covered with ornamental area rugs was also acceptable.

Depending upon the size of the hall, it was furnished with one or two high-back chairs, an umbrella stand, a hall mirror, table and hat rack. In tight spaces an all-purpose hall stand was used, combining a seat, mirror, hat rack and umbrella stand in one. Upon a small table could be found the card receiver—an absolute necessity in an age when paying "calls" was a paramount social activity.

In the Victorian parlor, walls were painted and/or papered according to the prevailing fashion. By the 1890s advice givers recommended light tints of olive, gray, pearl or cream and if a wallpaper was used, a delicate scroll or vine pattern was especially nice. Carpets of course were to be cheerful but subtle in relation to the parlor decor.

Regarding parlor furniture, in the 1890s Richard A. Wells recommended:

*The latest design in parlor furniture is in the Turkish style. Rich Oriental colors in woolen and silk brocades are mostly used, and the trimmings are cord and tassels, or heavy fringe. The most tastefully arranged parlor has now no two pieces of furniture alike; but two easy chairs placed opposite each other are never out of place. Here may stand an embroidered ottoman, there a quaint little chair, a divan can take some central position, a cottage piano, covered with some embroidered drapery, may stand at one end of the room, while an ebony or mahogany cabinet, with its panel mirrors and quaint brasses, may be placed at the other end, its racks and shelves affording an elegant display for pretty pieces of bric-a-brac. Tables in inlaid woods, or hand-painted, are used for placing books and albums on. There should be a few good pictures hung on the wall, and a portrait may be placed on a common easel draped with a scarf. An embroidered or India silk scarf with fringed ends may be placed on the back of a chair or sofa in place of the old-fashioned lace tidy. A sash of bright colored plush or silk may be flung across the table, the ends drooping very low. The mantel-piece may be covered with a corresponding sash, over which place a small clock as center piece and arrange ornaments on each side—statuettes, flowerholders, pieces of old china, painted candles in small sconces, may all find a place on the mantel. Those who wish to dispense with heavy curtain draperies in favor of light and sunshine may use the lace curtain alone. Portieres (curtain doors) have superseded folding doors. The fabric mostly used are India goods, but they may be made of any material.*[39]

It is interesting to note that Wells's advice on decorating the parlor includes all the symbolic accessories considered important in a genteel middle-class home. Atop the mantel he recommends the fashionable clock as a center-piece; statuettes, which conveyed cultured good taste; flower holders for the floral displays that expressed a love of nature; pieces of old china reflecting a kinship with generations past; and candlelight, which cast the desired romantic glow on the family hearth.

During the second half of the 19th century the center table was considered a necessity in the typical middle-class parlor. Not only did the center table serve to display the family Bible and other carefully chosen accessories, but it was also a center of family activity during the evening hours. Just as the colonial hearth was frequently depicted as the center of family gatherings, the Victorian counterpart—the center table—became a symbol of family bonds and unity during the 19th century. In this room, lit by a kerosene table lamp or an overhead gas fixture, the family might gather to play a game, listen to Father read aloud, or say evening prayers.

Another item no proper parlor could do without was the étagère, which, in the words of Allison Kyle Leopold, "was the primary means of displaying the family's burgeoning collection of treasures . . . In simpler homes, the humbler whatnot, a triangular corner piece served the same purpose in contributing to a more cultured atmosphere."[40] No matter whether the étagère was laden with heirloom china, cherished figurines, pottery, glassware or a vignette of family mementos, it was a significant furnishing in an era when the parlor reflected the beauty, culture and material objects of the world in miniature. In addition to the numerous collections and items on display in the Victorian parlor (women were becoming full-fledged consumers), handicrafts and ornamental needlework—products of the Victorian woman herself—hung on walls, filled tabletops and accessorized furniture. Such handmade goods showed the world the mistress of the house could not only be frugal in decorating her home, but she was industrious and accomplished as well. (Handicrafts are explored in greater detail in chapter 5.)

How did the middle-class Victorian parlor evolve from the formal and rather reserved room of the 1830s and 1840s into the romantic, excessively ornamented and overdecorated parlor of the 1880s and 1890s? Elan and Susan Zingman-Leith answer this question by observing that the "change in the parlor reflected the change in women's roles." Tracing the development of the parlor from its formal spaciousness in the Greek Revival period through its cluttered intimacy in the late Victorian period, the authors note a corresponding transformation in attitudes toward gender, "in which the workplace has become the man's sphere and the home the woman's." In other words, the relegation of women to an increasingly limited and home-bound status is mirrored in the "obsessive and self-conscious decorating and collecting frenzy [that] resulted when women were cut off from participation in the world and made the guardian of the family's aesthetic and moral well-being."[41]

Regarding the other components of the late 19th-century home, great attention to detail was also common in the dining room, where warm colors on walls, rich carpets, deep-toned draperies and substantial furnishings set the stage for many an elegant meal. Undoubtedly the most noteworthy piece of furniture here was the sideboard. During the midcentury period these were lavishly adorned with detailed carvings of fruits, meats and hunting scenes and were decidedly masculine in appearance and form. They

*Flowers, trailing vines and potted ferns were used as decorative elements in the typical middle-class Victorian home. This 1879 chromolithograph illustrates the popular window garden, with vines being trained to frame the window setting.*

WOMEN AT HOME IN VICTORIAN AMERICA

were also symbolic of the relationship between mankind and the natural world.[42] During the late 1800s sideboards, while still quite large, became somewhat simpler. They did, however, retain myriad shelves for displaying choice items in the dining room and could often be the most costly furnishing in the house.

The sitting room (if indeed the home had a second parlor) was to be comfortable and cozy. It often mirrored the proper parlor on a scale less grand but more intimate. Domestic authorities recommended furnishings to include a large table to serve as a catchall, a low divan with pillows, a rocker and a small sewing table and chair. Hand-me-down furniture from the parlor might be reupholstered with a cheerful chintz fabric and used in this setting. A bookcase was often included, especially if the home had no library, and along with books, ornaments such as family photos, odd pieces of china, mineral specimens, shells, vases and so on were displayed there. Family portraits, pastel landscape scenes and chromolithographs adorned the walls. Many sitting rooms also included a card or game table for cribbage, chess or board games. Window gardens showing an appreciation and love of nature were also common in the sitting room, and climbing and trailing vines became another form of decoration. The bright and cheerful sitting room was decidedly feminine—essentially a woman's space even though other members of the family gathered here on a regular basis.

In contrast, the library was a manly domain, a room where the master of the house could escape to conduct business, read, smoke or pursue other interests or hobbies. The decor typically reflected his masculinity, with hunting or nature scenes decorating the walls and strong, deep colors contributing to the air of quiet repose. Furnishings in the library included built-in or freestanding bookcases, easy chairs, low tables for books and magazines, footstools and often a handsome desk.

Bedrooms or chambers, private spaces that also included an area for one's toilette before indoor plumbing made a separate bathroom a possibility, were furnished with the bare necessities to avoid harboring dust and germs. Especially during the late 19th century, light colors on walls were preferred and only small area rugs were recommended. The bed, dressers and dressing table were often a matching set, and a washstand was included to hold necessary items such as a pitcher and bowl, chamber pot and slop jar. A decorative screen was used in the absence of a dressing room.

Last but not least, kitchens were rarely considered a space to be decorated in antebellum America. This utilitarian room or work center was often the domain of domestic servants in the North or slaves in the South. However, once middle-class women began to spend more time there in the late 1800s (due to a shortage of domestics and the rising cost of employing same), advice givers recommended that the room could be made cheerful—but kept sanitary.

Regarding home decoration, especially during the late 19th century, Harvey Green notes in *The Light of the Home: An Intimate View of the Lives of Women in Victorian America*, 1983, that the use of multiple patterns and fabrics in interior design and the collection and abundant display of bric-a-brac in the late 1800s home was more than a symbol of wealth or social standing. It was also woman's response to the industrializing world —a world that created separate lives for men and home responsibilities for women.[43]

The Victorian home and the middle-class woman who resided there were touched throughout the 19th century by changes great and small. As the largely agrarian society of the early 1800s was replaced by industry, the woman's role shifted from hands-on labor for the good (and often the very existence) of the family, to one defined by intangible qualities. Her self-worth was frequently expressed throughout her home and even extended to the appearance of the house itself and the surrounding grounds. The Victorian home was material proof of her earthly existence in an era marked by analogies comparing her to angelic or celestial beings.

# 3

# MOTHERHOOD AND FAMILY LIFE

First and foremost, you are a wife and mother.

—*A Doll's House* (1879) by Henrick Ibsen

The Victorians celebrated and revered motherhood throughout the 19th century. The Victorian family—a patriarchy in which the father was paid tribute as the head of the house—was based on stringently defined relationships intended to provide stability in the face of technological and social changes. Family dynamics evolved around emotions, sentiment, reserve and gender ranking. Culturally, the cult of motherhood was entwined with this cult of domesticity, and procreation not only empowered the family unit but was thought the height of achievement for the stereotypical middle-class woman.

Physically, the realities of pregnancy and childbirth during the 19th century were filled with dangers, and the high rate of infant mortality was a horrific reality. At the same time, women were told pregnancy and childbirth would make them stronger and prevent physical problems later in life.

Young children, and the care they received, were the subject of numerous books and magazine articles. Their rudimentary education, religious training, introduction to the social graces and health and well-being were solely the mother's responsibility. Sheltering young children from the harmful influences of the outside world was imperative.

# MOTHERHOOD

For the middle-class Victorian woman, motherhood was the answer to her higher calling. Once she had given birth, she had arrived at her final destination; the journey through her own childhood, young womanhood, courtship and marriage having laid the groundwork for this daunting event. Joys and sorrows relating to her children would dominate the rest of her life and her success as a mother would be determined by the character of these children. Ideally, her virtuous nature would help instruct and mold good little citizens that could make the family proud.

Motherhood was portrayed as the most noble work on earth in popular song, poetry and fiction, and behavior manuals and advice books underscored the importance of child rearing at every turn. For example, in 1848, George W. Burnap wrote:

> *We come in the next place to speak of woman in the most important and responsible relation which she sustains, as the mother. In this relation Providence fully makes up to her the inferiority of her physical powers, the narrowness of her sphere of action and the alleged inferiority of her intellectual endowments. She governs the world in the capacity of mother, because in the forming period of life, the cords of love and gentleness are stronger and more prevailing than all the chains which mere force has ever forged. She sways the world, because her influence is on the whole paramount in the primary element of all society, the domestic circle.*[1]

Mothers and a mother's love were also immortalized in various writings during the 19th century, as the bonds of love between a mother and child were recognized as the most potent in the world. The January 1867 issue of *Godey's Lady's Book* sentimentalized mother love in an anonymous essay appropriately titled "A Mother's Love":

**THE MOTHER'S PRAYER.**

BY ROSE HARTWICK THORPE

Twilight spreads her dusky mantle
  O'er the blossoms sweet and fair,
Blooming near a low-roofed cottage,
  And a hush is in the air,
Only broken by the murmur
  Of a mother's evening prayer.

Kneeling low beside the cradle,
  Where her precious darling lies,
With the golden lashes drooping
  O'er his wondering baby eyes,
All her heart goes out in pleading
  For the soul that never dies.

Far beyond earth's gloomy shadows,
  Past all doubt, all pain and care,
Rises her heart's fond petition;
  And the angels bending there,
Hush their rapturous songs to listen
  To the mother's evening prayer.

*This 1883 engraving from the book* The Heart of the World
*portrays motherhood and the Victorian mother's love and
concern for the well-being of her infant child.*

MOTHERHOOD AND FAMILY LIFE

*Happily, a mother's love is something upon which the great majority of mankind can look back—reverently and fondly look back—for an objective representation of its main characteristics. Oh, the unselfishness of it! And then the patience and long-suffering of it. There is nothing quite like it in this world of ours—nothing so morally beautiful: a self-fed, self-sustaining love, yet, under any circumstances, chiefly a sorrow-bearing love, of which the joys are cares, the duties are inflictions of pain upon itself, the pride is nourished to be bestowed elsewhere, and the fondest gain is the sorest loss. About every true mother there is a sanctity of martyrdom—and when she is no more in the body, her children see her with the ring of light around her head.[2]*

It is interesting to note this author draws a parallel between motherhood and martyrdom that once again points to women—especially mothers—as celestial or angelic beings.

Many 19th-century writers paid tribute to their mothers in the printed page and credited them with raising children of moral character and worldly success. One such writer, William Graham, told readers that although he'd traveled around the world during his adult years, no memory was as beautiful as the old log cabin and rolling hills of Pennsylvania where he'd spent his childhood: "That humble cabin was the home of my mother! Her name and character and influence are associated with all that is endearing in that picture of memory."

Recalling that his mother bore and raised 11 children, Graham continued:

*So wise were her counsels, so pious her life, so consistent her example, and so great her influence that at the time of her death, her ten living children were all church members, and four of them ministers of the Gospel. Who will say that she lived and toiled in vain? She never moved in fashionable circles, never visited a watering-place, and never traveled beyond her own native state; yet in fruitful labors she surpassed many who in worldly advantages were more highly favored.[3]*

Graham's testimonial is but one of many such writings that appeared in popular magazines throughout the 19th century illustrating the widespread veneration of a mother's influence and a mother's love throughout Victorian culture.

Even under the best of circumstances motherhood was a conflicting state of affairs. On the one hand, the Victorian mother was responsible for a child's upbringing and well-being. At the same time, a patriarchal society, especially in the antebellum South, allowed her little if any real power to make decisions. In the words of historian Anne C. Rose: "Not only did fathers feel free to ask families to serve their needs, but all household members acted on the tacit assumption that families, no less than society at large, were based on the preeminence of men."[4]

In regard to the physical aspects of motherhood, pregnancy and childbirth were often feared not only because of the pain involved but the very possibility of death. During the late 1800s physicians argued that a woman was not fully developed physically (i.e. the pelvic bones) until she reached her early twenties and that childbirth before this age would undoubtedly be difficult and risky. Ideally, marrying and bearing children were to be done between the ages of 21 and 30.

Young wives often wore tight stays and dressed in an attempt to hide their pregnancy during the early to mid-Victorian period, but by the late 19th century advice givers warned this was a dangerous practice. Loose clothing and undergarments such as stays with bones removed were recommended for comfort and the safety of the unborn child. Likewise, loose garters and elastic stockings would make legs more comfortable.

Exercise during pregnancy was to be limited to short, frequent walks and plenty of fresh air. Such activity would relieve the unpleasant side effects of pregnancy and help maintain a cheerful disposition. Dancing and horseback riding, on the other hand, were prohibited because of the threat of miscarriage. The soon-to-be mother was to strike a proper balance between rest and activity. Lolling about all day on a sofa or divan and ignoring household duties and exercise would prolong labor and make for a difficult birth.

Concerning the Victorian woman's diet during pregnancy, she was to eat light, healthy meals. Rich soups and pastries, highly seasoned stews and spirits of any sort were to be avoided. Meats, poultry, game, fish, milk, rice, suet pudding, batter-puddings and fruits such as roasted apples, grapes, pears, stewed prunes and orange juice were highly recommended.

Proper rest was vitally important during pregnancy, as Monfort B. Allen, M.D., and Amelia C. McGregor, M.D., advised in their 1896 book *The Glory of Woman or Love, Marriage and Maternity*:

> *A pregnant lady must retire early to rest. She ought to be in bed every night by ten o'clock, and should make a point of being up in good time in the morning, that she may have a thorough ablution, a stroll in the garden,*

*and an early breakfast; and that she may afterwards take a short walk either in the country or in the grounds while the air is pure and invigorating. The importance of bringing a healthy child into the world, if not for her own and her husband's sake, should induce a wife to attend to the above remarks.*[5]

Throughout the Victorian period, and regardless of whether a woman lived in the North or the South, as delivery was drawing near she would retire to her "lying-in" room and prepare for her "confinement." Her chamber or bedroom usually served this purpose and great attention to detail made sure the room was prepared for the "sitting-up" visits people would pay after the child was born. Since the typical confinement after childbirth lasted at least a month, the "lying-in" room became a temporary "public" space in which to receive guests and well-wishers.

At the time of birth a midwife or doctor was present to help with the delivery, and a woman, usually a beloved relative (such as a mother or sister) or a close friend, was there to lend moral support and encouragement. *The Glory of Woman* advised readers:

> *In making the selection of a friend, care should be taken that she is the mother of a family, that she be kind-hearted and self-possessed, and of a cheerful turn of mind. All "chatterers," "croakers" and "potterers" ought, at these times, to be carefully excluded from the lying-in room. No conversation of a depressing character should for one moment be allowed. Nurses and friends who are in the habit of telling bad cases that have occurred in their experience, must be avoided as the plague.*[6]

There were indeed bad cases and women's fears of childbirth were not unfounded, as they likely knew—or knew of—women who had died during delivery or shortly thereafter from the dreaded "childbed fever." The modern social historian Elizabeth Donaghy Garrett notes that this was the cause of untold apprehension that followed women throughout pregnancy. The fear of dying as a result of childbirth "far outweighed their dread of dying in any other manner."[7]

During the early Victorian period there were undoubtedly many long and painful births, but if the middle-class wife was able to secure the services of a physician her pain might be relieved with opium or laudanum. By the late 1840s chloroform was available to ease the pain of hard, lingering labor. Chloroform was also considered quite useful when the expectant mother was crazed with fear or extremely nervous. Inhaling the anesthetic for a prescribed amount of time would produce semiconsciousness or unconsciousness and freedom from pain.

Once the baby was safely delivered the new mother was to rest without moving for at least an hour. A cup of cool black tea was offered for refreshment and if she was hungry warm gruel was thought safe for her delicate condition.

By the late 1800s medical experts were advising that the new mother should have no visitors (except immediate family) for at least 10 days so she had ample opportunity to rest and recoup her strength. Most likely this advice was seldom followed and, as was typical of the early and mid-Victorian years, a constant stream of visitors was the norm. This of course applied to women in urban areas only, for those isolated on small plantations and farms had few daily visitors to contend with. Not only were constant "sitting-up" visits hard on the new mother; they were disruptive to the household in general. The entire lying-in period could in fact turn a household upside down, with chores being neglected by servants and other children in the family going unsupervised.[8]

While the majority of middle-class women gave birth at home throughout the 19th century, by the early 1900s increasing numbers of babies were born in hospitals with a physician in attendance. Not only were the hospitals considered safer and more sanitary, but new drugs for pain relief had become available; the state of being pregnant and childbirth itself were increasingly looked at from a scientific viewpoint as opposed to natural processes and components of the cult of domesticity.[9]

Even after a baby was safely delivered and both mother and child seemed to be doing well, parents feared for their newborn's well-being as infant mortality was a constant threat. Statistics for the early Victorian period are scarce, but during the last quarter of the 19th century it is estimated disease and illness caused the death of one in ten children before they reached the age of one.[10] Infant death was such a common occurrence that most extended families—if not the immediate family—were affected by the passing of a little one. The sadness, sorrow and grief associated with the death of a young child were the subject of countless stories and poems throughout the Victorian era. Many such works reflected the religious convictions and faith in God that helped parents through the hours, days, weeks and years of loss. For example, an 1897 book *The Great Hereafter, or Glimpses of The Coming World,* included a chapter entitled "Our Children in Heaven" that offered several poems about infant death. While many of

*Entitled "The Vacant Chair," this circa 1880s lithograph conveys
the reality of a child's death during an era when many families
were struck by such tragedy due to epidemics and diseases.*

the poems in this anthology were written by women, it is interesting to note this particular poem was the work of a man:

## A MOTHER'S LAMENT

I loved thee, daughter of my heart;
　My child, I loved thee dearly;
And though we only meet to part,—
　How sweetly! How severely!
　Nor life nor death can sever
　My soul from thine forever.

Thy days, my little one, were few;
　An angel's mourning visit,
That came and vanished with the dew.
　'Twas here,—'tis gone—where is it?
　Yet didst thou leave behind thee
　A clue for love to find thee.

Sarah! my last, my youngest love,
　The crown of every other!
Though thou art born in heaven above,
　I am thine only Mother!
　Nor will affection let me
　Believe thou canst forget me.

Then—thou in heaven and I on earth—
　May this one hope delight us,
That thou wilt hail my second birth,
　When death shall reunite us,
　Where worlds no more can sever
　Parent and child forever.

—James Montgomery

Infant mortality impacted on family size throughout the 19th century but there was also a deliberate decrease in the birthrate toward the late 1800s. Harvey Green points out that statistically, among white, Anglo-Saxons, the average family size decreased from 5 children in 1800 to an average of 3.42 children per family by the year 1910.[11] Given the fact that women in both the North and the South seemed to be in a constant state of pregnancy during the early Victorian years, this does not seem surprising. Giving birth to large numbers of children in rapid succession, and then caring for same, was not only physically draining but emotionally demanding as well. In writing about Southern women during the pre–Civil War years, Anne Firor Scott points out the prevailing custom of having a large family, religious influences and men were the controlling factors in regard to a woman's fertility. As a result, motherhood was often "the most widespread source of discontent" for Southern women.[12]

While effective contraception was unavailable during the early Victorian era, by the late 19th century periodic abstinence, special douches, protective sheaths and primitive diaphragms were helping to lower the birthrate. In addition, to end unwanted pregnancies, home remedies, patent medicines and abortions were not all that uncommon. The advice givers, members of the clergy and physicians strongly objected to such practices, continually reminding women that sexual intimacy did indeed have a higher purpose. For example, Dr. Allen and Dr. McGregor wrote:

*And it is also to be observed that the natural period for sexual union is when it is demanded for the purpose of procreation, and that the use of marriage or the sexual act for mere pleasure, and using any means to avoid impregnation, are unnatural.*[13]

In contrast to the above, radical social reformers did advocate limiting family size during the late 19th century, but middle-class Victorians undoubtedly had their own reasons for doing so. Not only was it an attempt by women to gain control over their lives, but smaller families allowed parents (especially mothers) the luxury of tending to their children's needs in a comfortable fashion. The expense of food, clothing, toys, education, vacations and so on were more affordable in a smaller family. Appearances after all, were important in maintaining middle-class status and acceptance in one's social circle. Also, a smaller family gave the mother additional time to devote to the development of each child.

For those Victorian children that survived the crucial first years of life, their childhood would ideally blossom within the sanctity of the Victorian home and the safe arms of mother's love.

# CHILDREN AND CHILD CARE

Children were viewed quite differently at the start of the Victorian era than they had been during the 1700s and early 1800s. Rather than considering infants innately sinful, and childhood (until around the age of seven) a bothersome period of no particular value to the family, the Victorians believed their newborns were innocent little beings and their early years a delight. Not only had stern religious views been altered to bring about such change, but the family unit itself, decreasingly dependent upon child labor for economical survival, saw motherhood and childhood in a whole new light. Karin Calvert notes that this concept of children as innocent little beings meant that any undesirable characteristics they might develop were the result of unsavory contact with the world outside the home.[14] This line of thinking naturally reinforced the responsibility of mothers as moral guardians and protectors.

Because such innocence denied any relation to gender at such a young and tender age, mothers tended to dress little boys and girls alike during the 1830s and 1840s, with common attire being a frock and pantaloons. It was also not unusual for little boys to have long, curly hair or girls, short cuts. As a result, it was sometimes difficult to tell if the little person was male or female. Interestingly, this was the subject of a major 1995 exhibition entitled "Is She or Isn't He? Identifying Gender in Folk Art Portraits of Children" at the Art Museum at Heritage Plantation in Sandwich, Massachusetts. With over 75 children's portraits on display (painted circa 1800–1865), visitors were offered clues in looking at the paintings to help determine the sex of the subject since dress, hairstyles and jewelry were often alike on boys and girls. Over 1,400 such portraits were examined in preparation for this exhibit; its curator, Jennifer Yunginger, noted that significant differences in telling boys from girls could be found in the subject's hair part—girls usually sported a center part and boys, a side part or no part at all. In addition, boys were often depicted with dogs or gender-specific toys such as a buggy whip while girls were frequently posed with a cat, a doll or a basket containing flowers or fruit.[15]

*This circa 1855 fashion plate from* Godey's Lady's Book *illustrates popular clothing styles for children. Note that the small boy sitting on the left is dressed in a frock or dress and pantaloons similar to the little girl on the right. In examining such fashion plates, paintings etc., boys can usually be identified by the side part in their hair, while girls usually sported a center part.*

Along with new costumes, babies and young children were allotted their own space within the Victorian home and limited furnishings and accessories to fill it. Material culture surrounding childhood was indeed a product of the Victorian age. Nurseries, typically located on the upper floor of the house, were a safe, protected environment for the little ones in the family, equipped with a crib, a miniature chair or two and a small number of educational toys that helped prepare children for adult life. All the younger children in the family typically slept, ate and played in this same space, sheltered from the outside world, and at the same time restricted so that they were unable to inflict harm on the "public" rooms generally reserved for guests.

The home training and care of children was the subject of numerous books targeting mothers beginning in the 1830s. For example, in 1833 Dr. John Abbott wrote *The Mother at Home* and around the same time Lydia Maria Child authored *The Mother's Book*—a work that proved so popular it went through several printings and was still in wide use a decade later. Catharine Beecher addressed motherhood and child rearing in her 1847 *Treatise On Domestic Economy* and her best known book, *The American Woman's Home*, explored these same subjects 20 years later. Given the enormous responsibility and social implications of child rearing, such instructional guides became popular for the "expert" advice they offered in a changing world. Also, with large segments of the population leaving family ties (and helpful advice) behind to move to urban areas, such books helped fill the void when questions arose or general guidance was needed.

In addition to the above, popular periodicals offered women advice and pearls of wisdom regarding children, such as this passage from an essay entitled "Little Children" that appeared in the June 1867 issue of *Godey's Lady's Book*:

> *We think them the poetry of the world—the fresh flowers of our hearts and homes—little conjurors, with their "natural magic," evoking by their spells what delights and enriches all ranks, and equalizes the different classes of society. Every infant comes into the world like a delegated prophet, the harbinger and herald of good tidings. A child softens and purifies the heart, warming and melting it by its gentle presence; it enriches the soul by new feelings, and awakens within it what is favorable to virtue. It is a beam of light, a fountain of love, a teacher whose lessons few can resist.*[16]

Women's magazines also offered the latest in fashions so children could be made beautiful, and they routinely included practical advice for mothers

*For the middle-class Victorian mother, providing children with religious training was an important duty. This illustration from the January 1856* Godey's Lady's Book *portrays a loving mother instructing her young daughter in prayer.*

such as remedies for childhood illness, food recipes for sick children and instructions on proper etiquette and deportment for the little people.

By the 1860s there was growing acceptance of the theory that pointed to specific periods of development in a child's life: infancy, childhood and youth. Horace Mann, a noted educator and politician, and Horace Bushnell, author in the 1860s of the popular *Christian Nurture*, are credited with bringing these stages of development to light.[17] Adolescence, however, was not recognized as a stage of development until the 1904 publication of *Adolescence: Its Psychology and Its Relations to Physiology, Anthropology, Sociology, Sex, Crime, Religion and Education* by G. Stanley Hall.[18]

Middle-class Victorians adopted specific dress and codes of expected behavior for each stage of a child's development, and to help children advance successfully from one stage to the next, periodicals and weekly publications for them became an important learning tool. Some of the better-known examples included *The Children's Hour: A Magazine for the Little Ones, Harper's Round Table, The Girls' Own Paper, Harper's Young People, The Young Ladies' Journal* and *St. Nicholas*. Such papers and monthly publications included games, stories (with morals, of course), fashions, deportment and poetry. Magazines for young children were enjoyed by both boys and girls, but many publications were gender specific for youths.

In the last quarter of the 19th century a new ideology concerning the nature of children altered the manner in which they were perceived and raised. Karin Calvert has pointed out that child-rearing authorities of the time "began to doubt the absolute innocence of all children." If children were no longer seen as morally perfect, their minor transgressions and acts of disobedience were no longer viewed as falls from grace. Rather, misbehavior was seen as natural, relatively harmless, and open to correction.[19]

With this shift in ideology regarding infants and children came a change in the language used to describe them. "Angelic," "angel from heaven" and so on gave way to pet names such as "Princess" or the "Little King." The September 1896 issue of *Ladies' Home Journal* offered a perfect example of this in select lines from a poem entitled "The King of Lapland":

I know a tiny monarch who has taken his command
Within a quiet region, where a faithful little band

Of people do his bidding, or yield him homage true,
And watch his faintest gesture, as old vassals used to do.
If you would find his royal seat you need not sail the sea,
For—strange enough—his throne is set in this home of the free.
Just find the nearest nursery, and bow to the command
Of the loving little monarch, who is king of all Lapland.

—By Alice Cary

Thus childhood as we are familiar with it today began to emerge, no doubt to the relief of many a Victorian mother. One can imagine the frustration, confusion and feelings of failure the early Victorian mother must have felt when a supposedly good and innocent child did act up—she no doubt blamed herself for inadequacies in home training or overexposing her child to the bad influences of the world outside the home.

For the children too, it must have been difficult to keep their physical exuberance and merrymaking in check in order to be angelic and well behaved. The December 1855 *Godey's Lady's Book* included a story, "Ellen Goodwin; or, A Sense of Duty," that addresses this issue. Author Virginia DeForrest wrote about a young girl named Ellen, who loved the outdoors. Her aunt was constantly fearful she would come to harm if allowed to run in the fields, climb trees and so forth, and encouraged Ellen to spend her time reading and to be more "gentle and quiet." Ellen was also encouraged to give more thought to "how can I be most useful in the world? How can I best do my duty?" Her aunt told her, "If you are quiet, gentle and ladylike, you will win more love." Ellen made an attempt to spend her time reading, but upon the arrival of two male cousins she went out to the lane on horseback to greet them. She raced them back to the house—most dreadful behavior—and her horse threw her in an attempt to jump a fence. Poor Ellen was in bed several weeks after the fall and would be lame for life. She tells her aunt, "I know, I know that I needed discipline—I know that it is right or God would not have permitted it to be, and I do try hard to bear it patiently. But oh! to be a useless burden all my life!" After some time Ellen decided she must come to terms with her condition, telling her cousins, "I will be happy. Not gay yet perhaps, but cheerful. I feel a new meaning to a sense of duty."[20]

*To be "quiet, gentle and ladylike" and spend time reading
were admirable qualities for a young girl. From the story
"Ellen Goodwin; or, A Sense of Duty" in the December 1855
Godey's Lady's Book, young Ellen attempts to do as told,
and as expected of her—keeping her childlike exuberance in check.*

With changing views regarding childhood during the late 1800s came new advice on child rearing and an explosion in material goods catering to children. In the 1879 edition of *The Complete Home: An Encyclopaedia of Domestic Life and Affairs*, Mrs. Julia McNair Wright devoted a chapter to "Children in the Family." Readers were advised that children are not perfect and that "childhood has errors which we may reprove or correct very gently, or even ignore altogether, rather than to be always condemning." Wright continued, pointing out that one childhood error, falsehood, was often the result of a "very vivid imagination that causes them to state things as they appear to them, which look like very false statements to grown people. We must consider how new the world is to him [the child] before we call his misstatements lying."[21]

Mrs. Wright's book was published in 1879, at a time when, as the above passage indicates, infants were being thought of as imperfect. Even more important, however, is the mention of childhood imagination. As the period of childhood became more specialized, middle-class parents (especially mothers) were targeted as consumers, ready, willing and able to provide for their child's development. Since children needed stimulation to develop both physically and intellectually, myriad toys, books, games and furniture became available and proved a huge success. Such items were no longer strictly educational; they also relied on the child's imagination to create enjoyment. For example, the 1895 Montgomery Ward & Company catalog for Spring & Summer offered a variety of illustrated books, including the Brownie Books, Aunt Louisa's Big Picture Books, Little ABC Books, The Knockabout Club Series, Elephant Series, Cock Robin Series and the Round the World Series. Toys too were available in ever-increasing numbers; popular examples included baby rattles, marbles, tops, iron train sets, pull toys, mechanical novelties, stuffed animals, jumping ropes, Jack-in-the-Boxes, Noah's Arks, wooden ships, wooden soldiers, toy guns and pistols, toy musical instruments, building blocks, dolls and doll furniture, toy kitchen sets, wash or laundry sets, stoves, paper dolls and a large number of folding board games. Child-size table and chair sets, rockers, settees and blackboards were available for the Victorian nursery or playroom. While toys for little boys often encouraged imaginative adventures in the outside world (train travel, cowboys and Indians), the toys created for girls mirrored the practical aspects of domestic life—dolls to dress and care for, toy stoves to cook on, etc. That is not to say little girls spent all their playtime in the house while brothers were allowed—and expected—to explore the great outdoors. As the contemporary historian Anne Scott MacLeod points out,

*As the 19th century progressed, views regarding childhood evolved considerably. By the 1880s it was understood that a child's imagination could lead to learning and harmless fun, as seen here in this circa 1860s illustration of a simple childhood game.*

autobiographies written by women who grew up in middle-class families during the Victorian era detail their participation in many happy hours of outdoor play. Gender-specific distinctions in regard to behavior did not become so stringent until a girl reached the age of 12 or 13, at which point she was expected to start preparing for womanhood in earnest.[22] (See chapter 1.)

Clothing for children was less restrictive during the late 19th century. With new theories regarding childhood the emphasis shifted away from prim and proper to comfortable clothing allowing children freedom of movement. Clothing designed specifically for play was quite common during the early 20th century.

During the late Victorian era childhood was no longer a stage passed for the most part in the home, with mother in attendance. Schools now played an important role in educating and training young children; a variety of experts—doctors, scientists, domestic science authorities—advised on their upbringing, and middle-class children were allowed greater freedom than their predecessors to explore the world at large.

Just as the ideology surrounding childhood changed during the 19th century, so too did child-care practices. For example, until the 1880s infants were usually breast-fed by their mothers unless there was just cause, such as a mother's illness, to seek the services of a wet nurse. Maternal duty demanded that the Victorian middle-class mother tend her infant in this manner until he or she was nine months to one year old, and any frivolous excuse for shirking this duty reflected poorly on her. There were, however, exceptions to this in the antebellum South. It was not uncommon (or frowned upon) for Southern women to secure the services of a wet nurse, or to turn the responsibility of suckling a newborn over to a slave, so they could tend to the burdensome responsibilities of the slave community as well as their immediate family on smaller plantations.[23]

In weaning babies, concoctions made of flour and water or tapioca, rice, bread or arrowroot were often bottle-fed to the child on a part-time basis, but by the late 1800s cow's milk had become widely accepted. As the whole process of child rearing became more scientific, prepared baby foods were advertised and widely promoted as a safer way to feed small children. Made to be mixed with cow's milk, prepared foods were reportedly a healthy alternative to the starch-laden mixtures prepared at home. For example, the March 1897 *Ladies' Home Journal* included an advertisement for "Mellin's Food" by the Doliber-Goodale Company of Boston, Massachusetts. Their ad, depicting an adorable young child, ran a testimonial from a satisfied mother that read: "It is a pleasure for me to write you how much good your Mellin's Food has done for my little family. My two girls were brought up entirely on Mellin's Food and cow's milk, and two healthier children never existed. The physician's bill for the two has amounted to much less than five dollars. I have now begun to use the same food for my baby boy, and it agrees with him perfectly." Once the year-old child was started on table foods, animal meats were to be avoided (or given in small amounts) in favor of pureed fruits and vegetables and bland puddings.

Mothers, of course, were receptive to any product or information that would safeguard the health of their small children. The very real and frightening possibility that a little one would become ill was always imminent. During the 1870s one household guide listed the common childhood illnesses as convulsions, jaundice, thrush, croup, nettle rash, summer rash, mumps, scald head, worms, measles, scarlet fever, whooping cough and chicken pox.[24] Because certain illnesses could become epidemics, and often proved fatal, protecting a child's health was no small matter. For that reason many Southern families, especially during the pre–Civil War years, left the heat and humidity of the summer months in favor of a more moderate climate where illness wouldn't thrive.

Throughout the 19th century, mothers kept on hand an arsenal of ingredients to concoct poultices, brews and home remedies when a child became ill. The carefully measured use of opium and its derivative, laudanum, was common during the Victorian period in treating a wide range of illnesses. While many such "recipes" for cures and treatments were handed down from one generation to the next, by the second half of the 19th century patent medicines had become available, and household guides routinely included sections on home nursing and medical care. For example, *The Household Cyclopaedia of Practical Receipts* recommended the following in treating croup: ". . . [T]he doctor should be sent for, the child placed in a bath, as hot as it can bear it, right up to the neck, and an emetic administered. When the patient has been sick, put a mustard plaster round its neck, and keep it on as long as the child can bear it. If the doctor has not arrived, you must give it a powder made thus: Mix six grains of calomel, one grain of tartar emetic, and fifteen grains of powdered loaf sugar together, and give one every twenty or thirty minutes until there is relief."[25] Mothers, of course, had to keep a well-stocked medicine chest so they could prepare home remedies and poultices.

As for intellectual development, children received the bulk of their learning at home during the early Victorian period. Training began as soon as a child was born. In her hugely popular *The Mother's Book* (1831), Lydia Maria Child advised mothers to nurture even newborn babies with an eye to their future development, emphasizing that such children should be treated with a gentleness and tenderness commensurate with their extremely delicate moral and physical condition. Waxing lyrical, Child rhapsodized that "gentleness . . . enters into a child's soul, like the sunshine into the rose-bud, slowly but surely expanding it into beauty and vigor."[26] This floral image is more than just simile, however; Child seriously believes that a nurturing environment is the first medium of education, and she goes on to enumerate specific ways of fostering such an environment:

> *All loud noises and violent motions should be avoided. Attention should be easily aroused by presenting attractive objects—things of bright and beautiful colors, but not glaring—and sound pleasant and soft to the ear. It is important that children, even when babes, should never be spectators of anger, or any evil passion. They come to us from heaven, with their little souls full of innocence and peace; and, as far as possible, a mother's influence should not interfere with the influence of angels. Therefore the first rule, and the most important of all, in education, is, that a mother govern her own feelings, and keep her heart and conscience pure. The next most important thing appears to me to be, that a mother, as far as other duties will permit, take entire care of her own child. I am aware that people of moderate fortune cannot attend exclusively to an infant. Other cares claim a share of attention, and sisters, or domestics, must be intrusted; but where this necessarily must be the case, the infant should feel its mother's guardianship."[27]*

As the baby grew older, child care included instructing the little one in religion, proper etiquette and deportment and useful knowledge. Teaching children prayers to be recited daily, reading to them from the family Bible and attending Sunday service were imperative to religious upbringing. Equally important, instructions regarding deportment were begun early, when a child, usually by the age of four, could be seated in a high chair to join the family in the dining room for dinner or at least dessert. Learning the intricacies of Victorian middle-class culture, and especially the customs surrounding the elaborate ritual of dining, began at a young and tender age. One popular 1880s deportment manual advised: "At the table a child should be taught to sit up and behave in a becoming manner, not to tease when denied, nor to leave his chair without asking. A parent's wish at such time should be a law from which no appeal should be made."[28] After all, a child's deportment at the table was a direct reflection on mother and how well she was doing her job.

Growing children were, of course, instructed in other areas of Victorian middle-class culture, including courtesy, cheerfulness, politeness and the advantages of an industrious nature. One expert told parents, "There should never be two sets of manners, the one for home and the other for company, but a gentle behavior should always be required."[29] Toward this end, the 1880 book *The Manners That Win* included "A Chapter for Children," in order that they become a "manly man" or a "womanly woman." Addressing young boys, the authors largely discussed the dos and don'ts of their physical behavior; "Never stamp, jump or run in the house." Also, the rules of etiquette were addressed, such as "Be prompt at every meal."[30]

In contrast, girls were offered very different instructions in this same book. The development of their virtuous nature was of the utmost importance and advice to them had more to do with molding the proper character. To girls, the authors wrote:

> *Boys are expected to have more or less of the bear in their natures but girls are born and bred to modest and lady-like behavior, and a saucy, pert and selfish girl is simply beyond endurance. A girl who is disrespectful to her mother or to her superiors, can never acquire the charm of manner which throws all beauty, style, fine dressing, and diamonds into shadow. That charm comes of a kind and unselfish heart. Clothes should always be neat and pretty. It is within the reach of everyone to be graceful and genteel in manner. Above all, let girls remember that to be safe they must guard against all appearance of evil in their conduct. To be pure and to seem pure at all times and in all places, is to establish a character which is an armor proof against envy, malice and slander.*"[31]

A child's intellectual training also came under the heading of nurturing. Once common schools were established during the second half of the 19th century, young children spent more structured (rather than sporadic) time in the classroom and away from mother each day. Catharine Beecher thought this was a good thing. In *The American Woman's Home* she and Harriet Beecher Stowe recommended:

> *In regard to the intellectual training of young children . . . [I]t is very important to most mothers that their young children should be removed from their care during certain school hours; and it is very useful for quite young*

*children, to be subjected to the discipline of a school, and to intercourse with other children of their own age. And, with a suitable teacher, it is no matter how early children are sent to school, provided their health is not endangered by impure air, too much confinement, and too great mental stimulus, which is the chief danger of the present age.*[32]

In contrast to the Beecher sisters' opinion that "it is no matter how early children are sent to school," doctors and social reformers such as Lydia Maria Child proposed children under the age of six or seven should not be sent from the home to participate in formal education. Rather, by the 1860s, kindergartens with a protective and nurturing environment were being established to offer the very young a setting in which to participate in structured playtime instead of the rigors of hard learning.[33]

In regard to the formal education of children, during the early and mid-1800s, schoolhouses were established in rural areas while city children were usually tutored at home. Such a haphazard approach to educating the young moved social reformers and educators to develop more structured settings for learning, especially given the influx of immigrants needing assimilation into American culture. As noted by Barbara Finkelstein and Kathy Vandell, these foreign children needed to learn "Anglo Saxon civic virtues."[34] The result then was the common school, as these early versions of public schooling were called, and boys and girls were taught reading, writing, spelling, geography, arithmetic, civics and Bible study. Coed classes were the norm in rural areas while classes were sometimes divided by gender in the cities.

The curriculum of the common school was altered during the late 1800s as science and "scientific methods" gained a stronghold on various aspects of Victorian daily life. By the year 1900, along with academics, school programs also included manual courses in woodworking for boys and home economics for girls and vocational training such as typing and bookkeeping. Extra activities such as social clubs, bands, theater productions etc., also expanded the social aspects of the turn of the century public school.[35]

Throughout the Victorian era *McGuffey's Eclectic Readers* by William Holmes McGuffey were the most popular schoolbooks for teaching children how to read and spell. McGuffey's books included stories and poetry that reinforced the concept of a loving God, good citizenship and the benefits of hard work. Good behavior was a common theme in many of his instructional and entertaining stories. By the late 1800s, McGuffey's series of schoolbooks had been adopted as the standard school texts in over 35

*This late Victorian-era photograph depicts a typical middle-class family.
With the advent of affordable photography, many such family portraits
were taken and became cherished mementos displayed on parlor mantels
or saved in special albums. Such a sitting was cause to dress in finery.
Though these family members wear their typical Victorian reserve,
the mother has just a hint of a smile captured by the camera.*

states and were especially popular in the South. They were revised several times and used in schools across the country through the early 1920s.

Dependent upon proper child care and a nurturing, devoted mother, Victorian middle-class childhood could be a wondrous and widely celebrated stage of life. While the bond between mother and child was viewed as sacred, the family unit as a whole was a primary component of middle-class Victorian culture.

# THE VICTORIAN FAMILY

Throughout the early 19th century family life was idealized in popular songs, romantic fiction and poetry. The power of the family unit as a social institution was driven home again and again in the Sunday sermon and in the pages of behavior manuals and advice books. The Victorian middle-class family was also immortalized in numerous folk art paintings and later, lithographs, and many such works were included in the pages of the leading periodicals.

The Victorian family of the late 1830s–1850s was evolving from an economy-based unit in which everyone labored for the economic survival of the family, to one in which relationships were based on love, feelings and sentimentality. This new concept of family was repeatedly compared to the heavenly family above, as the Beecher sisters noted in *The American Woman's Home*: "The family state then, is the aptest earthly illustration of the heavenly kingdom, and in it woman is its chief minister."[36]

The early Victorian family was a patriarchal unit in which the father held a dominant position—not only within the family but society as well—since women and children had virtually no legal rights. Patriarchy was especially important in the antebellum South, where male dominance within the family was vital to the slave culture, politics and economic power.[37]

During this pre–Civil War period family relationships both North and South were based largely on emotional bonds, and historians have noted that fathers and daughters often became close just as mothers and sons did. Anne C. Rose notes that in father-daughter relationships the daughter served as a companion and as such, father was able to exert some measure of power over her in a loving fashion.[38] Victorian mothers, by contrast, developed close relationships with their sons, not only because fathers and sons frequently experienced conflict with each other but also because family

Mother and child seated in the library watch for Father to
arrive home in this 1890 illustration entitled "Looking for Papa."
While the early Victorian-period family was typically a
patriarchal unit, as the century progressed feelings of love
and affection dominated family relationships.

MOTHERHOOD AND FAMILY LIFE
95

ties could best be experienced through mothers. In addition, in a society governed by men, close ties with a son brought the middle-class Victorian mother that much closer to freedoms she herself could not experience first hand.[39]

Such close bonds between a parent and child were more common in the North, where the cult of domesticity was largely sentimentalized. After the Civil War, however, Southern families also turned to mutual affection as a basis for relationships, in light of the massive changes that forever altered their way of life.

Behavior books and periodicals published throughout the 19th century offered a wealth of advice concerning family relationships. For example, the March 1867 *Godey's Lady's Book* included an essay, "Golden Maxims For Families," which emphasized the importance of "feelings" within the family unit. The four points discussed included:

1. The parental character must be highly respected.
2. Domestic order must be maintained.
3. The love of home must be fostered.
4. Sympathy under domestic trials must be expressed.

Regarding this last point, the essay continued: "There must be no cold, no unfeeling heart displayed. Family difficulties will occur; family changes will be experienced; family sorrows will be endured; family bereavements will be undergone; and, in these situations, there must be sympathetic and tender emotion cherished."[40] Women were largely responsible for seeing to it that such "Golden Maxims For Families" were carried out. While the parental character of both the mother and the father was ideally beyond reproach, women had full control over domestic harmony and instilling in the young child a love of home. Also, it was usually the mother who expressed tender emotions during times of trials and tribulations.

Advice books too offered suggestions for family life, many containing chapters devoted to the subject of "Home Government." In the 1882 book *The Voyage of Life: A Journey From the Cradle to the Grave*, readers were told: "The importance of sacredly guarding the family relation cannot be overestimated. It is the foundation-stone of all that is good and pure both in civilization and religion." Dealing mainly with discipline and family relationships, this chapter on "Parental Government" advised: "Always send your little child to bed happy. Always allow them to tell you all that has happened to interest or annoy them while absent from home. Mothers, don't whip them! Treat God's lambs tenderly. Compel obedience, but not with the rod . . . They will not trouble you long. Children grow-up—nothing on earth grows so fast as children."[41]

In sharp contrast to the relative indulgence expressed above, in the 1883 book *The Heart of the World: or Home and Its Wide Work*, G. S. Weaver favored a disciplinarian approach, telling readers: "Parental government should be strong and active. Children love those best who govern them well. There are two extremes in family government; one is tyranny, the other anarchy; and probably anarchy is worst. One great need of our time is a more vigorous family government."[42]

Although women were largely responsible for disciplining children throughout the 19th century, advice targeting middle-class families during the late 1800s made a point of addressing both parents, not just the mother. The late Victorian era saw a subtle shift away from patriarchy to increasing numbers of families in which both mother and father governed (at least in the home) on a more equal footing. This shift in ideology concerning the family structure coincided with the changing role of women—from domestic goddesses (their virtue and the safety of home protecting family members) to one which has been labeled educated motherhood. In studying this change in family dynamics, sociologists have named it the "companionate family."[43]

The 1888 edition of *Hill's Manual* offered the dos and don'ts of home government, and under the heading "What *Parents* Should Never Do" included the following:

1. Never speak harshly to a child.
2. Never use disrespectful names.
3. Never use profane words in the presence of a child.
4. Do not be so cold and austere as to drive your child from you.
5. Never misrepresent.
6. Never withhold praise when the child deserves it.
7. Never waken your child before they have completed their natural slumbers in the morning.
8. Do not reproach a child for a mistake which was made with a good motive at the time.
9. However wealthy you may be, teach the child the value of money.
10. Never demean yourself by getting angry and whipping a child.

*Etiquette manuals published during the late 1800s*
*offered advice on child rearing, family relationships,*
*home, government etc. The Victorian child,*
*such as the one seen here in this vintage photo,*
*was the very heart and soul of the late Victorian-era family.*

*Hill's Manual* also included the following list of "What *Parents* Should Do":

1. Always speak in a pleasant voice.
2. Always teach your child how to work.
3. Explain the reason why.
4. Teach your children the evil of secret vice, and the consequence of using tobacco and spiritous liquors.
5. Encourage your child to be careful of personal appearance; to return every tool to its place; to always pay debts promptly; to never shirk a duty.
6. Teach your children to confide in you by conference together.
7. Give your children your confidence in the affairs of your business.
8. If you are a farmer do not overwork your children, and thus drive them off to the cities.
9. Teach your child the value of the Sabbath.
10. Teach your children those things which they will need when they become men and women. As women they should understand how to cook, how to make a bed, how to preserve cleanliness and order throughout the house, how to ornament their rooms, to renovate and preserve furniture and clothing, how to sing, and play various games, that they may enliven the household. They should be taught how to swim, how to ride, how to drive, how to do business, and how to preserve health.[44]

Although women were largely responsible for raising the children, they undoubtedly realized the importance of spending time together as a family. Interaction between family members or family activities during the early and mid-Victorian period often focused on simple home pleasures or games such as checkers, chess or charades. Sing-alongs were another popular form of family entertainment, and one or more members of the family often played a musical instrument. With much of the middle-class population still living in rural areas during the early 19th century, family celebrations were commonly held at harvest time in the late summer or fall, and there were of course holiday festivities such as those centered around Christmas. Children's birthday parties were annual events in which the entire family took part.

As more and more families took up residence in growing urban areas, family activities and socialization in general became more elaborate. One circa 1880s deportment manual discussed private theatricals such as charades, dramatic readings and the presentation of short dramatic pieces.[45] Also, table games were a common form of entertainment and the Victorian family might amuse themselves with thought-provoking games like "Consequences," "Adjectives" or "Definitions." Dominoes and other games such as "The Whist Game" and "Tiddle-A-Wink" played with dominoes were also a favorite pastime. Such activities no doubt served to strengthen family bonds and reflected positively on women in charge of family life. In addition, the educational or morally uplifting aspects of certain family activities were yet another means of preparing children for adulthood.

By the late 1800s the concept of leisure and relaxation was gaining wider acceptance among the Victorian middle class. As a result, games and activities no longer had to have a higher meaning or be morally, educationally or religiously stimulating. Donna R. Braden has noted the irony in the fact that, as leisure choices increased, family coherence decreased. She points out that traditional "home amusements and family pastimes were looked upon as potential means of reuniting the segmented family."[46] Toward this end games and toys were created and marketed purely for entertainment, as opposed to strictly educational. Parents were encouraged by advice givers to participate in the new games and sports with their children to maintain close family feelings and ties.

Popular board games during the 1890s included a variety of sports, travel and leisure activity themes. For example, "The Yale-Harvard Game" was based on football; "The Limited Mail and Express Game" focused on train travel; "Hopity," a game of skill, offered amusement in the form of a "jumping move" in which game tokens were allowed to jump their opponents; "The Game of Travel" allowed players to journey across the board to Europe and back; and "The Grand Race Game" offered a board representing a horse track and cardboard horses and riders that raced each other around the track.

As for outdoor recreation, sports such as archery, croquet and lawn tennis were enjoyed by all. Parents often joined the youngest members of the family in outdoor games for children such as "Catching the Weasel," "The Flying Feather," "Blind Man's March," or "Little Washer-Women." The increased focus on health and exercise during the late 19th century also encouraged family members to take up boating, horseback riding, fishing, cycling and camping. On the subject of camping, one advice giver wrote in 1890: "Despite our boasted civilization and culture there is enough of the original savage in the majority of men and women to make them thoroughly enjoy a season of camping out with its hundred and one privations, its comical make-shifts, its homey occupations done in the spirit of play, but its blessed freedom from fashionable toilets, inane watering-place gossip, and ordinary, every-day, nineteenth-century routine."[47]

By the late 1800s and early 20th century, motherhood, child care and Victorian family life had altered considerably from what they actually were —and what they were perceived to be—in the early Victorian era. The risk associated with pregnancy and childbirth had lessened due to advances in science and medicine; the smaller family became the norm for many middle-class couples as women struggled for release from outdated precepts of womanhood; and children and child-rearing practices were viewed in a more realistic and healthy light. The typical Victorian family evolved from a dictatorship in which the father ruled in a strict or loving fashion to an institution in which the bonds of mutual respect helped balance the power between husband and wife. Throughout it all, the Victorian mother was the anchor that kept her family, especially her children, safely rooted in the home until such time they were ready to make their own mark on the world.

# 4

# MANNERS, POLITE SOCIETY AND PERSONAL APPEARANCE

There is always a best way of doing everything,
if it be to boil an egg.
Manners are the happy ways of doing things.

—Ralph Waldo Emerson

Throughout the Victorian era a middle-class woman's conduct and appearance allowed—or denied—her entry into desirable social circles. Knowledge of proper etiquette and deportment was essential to the achievement of social rank and reflected positively or negatively on her husband and children.

The intricate codes of 19th-century behavior became more complex with each passing decade, ultimately acquiring the status of social "laws." Moreover, the complex variations of these laws was more pronounced between urban and rural societies of a single geographic area than between the North and the South.

Entertaining and socializing was akin to a part-time job for the Victorian mistress who sought her family's entry into polite society and strove to maintain contact with the best of the best. Afternoon teas, receptions, dinner parties and the late 19th-century custom of paying calls were carefully orchestrated events designed to cultivate social contacts and friendships, return social favors and, yes, socialize in an era when a great deal of entertainment was home based.

Proper conduct also included striving for beauty in appearance and fashionable dress. Styles varied greatly throughout the Victorian era, and women's fashions from the sublime to the ridiculous (such as crinolines) played an important role in how women were perceived by society in general.

# PROPER ETIQUETTE AND DEPORTMENT

As a hallmark of gentility, ideal womanhood and good religious standing, etiquette and deportment—manners—were vital achievements for the middle-class Victorian mistress. More important, good manners were viewed by 19th-century advice givers as a necessity for all in a young, democratic society where people from all walks of life interacted on a regular basis. One high-toned etiquette manual published in the 1880s bluntly drove this point home by telling readers: "We are all forced, in spite of individual objections and protests, to put into practice the national theory of equality. We must mix together, and it therefore behooves us, for our own comfort, to make the mixture as smooth and agreeable as possible."[1] This of course was done by practicing good manners at all times.

During the early Victorian era, etiquette manuals served to "instruct" or "guide" the middle class with specific information on everything from the art of conversation, dress and social engagements to walking in public, riding in a carriage and looking (or rather, not looking) at strangers. Popular books reflecting this effort to "instruct" included *Etiquette for Ladies: With Hints on the Preservation, Improvement, and Display of Female Beauty* (1838); *A Guide to Good Manners: Containing Hints on Etiquette, Business, Morals, Dress, Friendship, Weddings, Balls, Dinner Parties, Compliments, and Letter Writing* (1848); *Guide to Good Behavior: Being A Complete Book of Instructions on the Subjects of Dress, Conversation, Balls, Parties, Dinners, Dancing etc.* (1856); and an 1868 work entitled *Manners: or, Happy Homes and Good*

*Home etiquette illustrated in this 1891 sketch from* Manners,
Culture and Dress of The Best American Society *was an important
part of genteel womanhood, as were the art of conversation,
proper behavior in public, appropriate dress and so on.*

*Society All the Year Round*, written by Sarah Josepha Hale, long-time editor of the popular *Godey's Lady's Book.*

During the later 19th century the natural obsession with etiquette and deportment elevated good manners to a set of "rules" or "laws." Rather than referring to etiquette manuals as social "guide" books (as in previous decades), advice givers hoped the implications of such lofty words as "rules" would inspire a following not only among the growing middle class, but among black Americans and immigrant populations as well.[2] Etiquette books published during the last quarter of the century sported heavy-handed titles such as *The Social Mirror: A Complex Treatise on the Laws, Rules and Usages that Govern Our Most Refined Homes and Social Circles* (1886); *Rules of Etiquette and Home Culture; or, What to Do and How to Do It* (1889); and the 1896 *Social Etiquette or Manners and Customs of Polite Society Containing Rules of Etiquette for All Occasions.*

While etiquette books published early in the 19th century offered basic instructions on such topics as cutlery, personal hygiene and proper public behavior (behavior long since assimilated by society and taken for granted), the concept of good manners became increasingly complex. By the mid-Victorian period urban areas were experiencing rapid growth and industrialization was in full swing. During the postbellum era life took on a different pace, especially for the growing middle-class population experiencing the benefits of increased wealth. New guidelines were called for and intricate codes of acceptable behavior became the norm.

On a more personal level, for middle-class Victorian women these strict laws of etiquette and deportment to a great extent limited their involvement with the world at large and served to reinforce the notion that their place was in the home. Consider for example the "Etiquette of the Street," as several 19th-century authors referred to it. Aside from social outings, women often left home during daylight hours to shop or run errands. According to Mrs. E. B. Duffey in her 1877 book *The Ladies' and Gentlemen's Etiquette: A Complete Manual of the Manners and Dress of American Society:* "That is a true lady who walks the streets wrapped in a mantle of proper reserve so impenetrable that insult and coarse familiarity shrink away from her, yet who carries with her a congenial atmosphere which attracts all and puts all at their ease."[3] In other words, leaving the safe haven of home, the middle-class woman subjected herself to the scrutiny of strangers. She was to do nothing to draw attention to herself and yet to present herself as a true lady at the same time. In order to accomplish this, her attire when venturing into the streets was to be plain and serviceable. Her dress was to be a "quiet" color with a linen collar and cuffs. A matching bonnet was appropriate. Gloves were a necessity and no display of jewelry was called for with the exception of her wedding rings, a watch and perhaps a simple brooch. Correct behavior, as described by one advice giver, was as follows:

> *A lady walks quietly through the streets, seeing and hearing nothing that she ought not to see and hear, recognizing acquaintances with a courteous bow, and friends with words of greetings. She is always unobtrusive, never talks loudly, or laughs boisterously, or does anything to attract attention of the passers-by. She walks along in her own quiet, lady-like way, and by her pre-occupation is secure from annoyance to which a person of less perfect breeding might be subjected. A lady never forms an acquaintance upon the street, or seeks to attract the attention or admiration of persons of the other sex. To do so would render false her claims to ladyhood, if it did not make her liable to far graver charges.*[4]

Thos. Hill, author of the 1888 *Hill's Manual of Social and Business Forms*, concurred and added: "Swinging the arms when walking, eating upon the street, sucking the parasol handles, pushing violently through a crowd, whispering in public conveyances, are all evidence of ill-breeding in ladies."[5]

A detailed code of behavior applied to every and all situations when the Victorian woman ventured forth into society or the outside world. For example, while it was permissible for her to go out alone during daylight hours, she was not to go out in the evening "unattended." She required an escort to see her safely to and from her destination. If a lady recognized an acquaintance when out, she could bow or offer words of greeting but shaking hands was to be avoided.

Women were considered the fair and weaker sex. If a lady went out with a gentleman escort, he was expected to shelter her from possible harm, exertion or strain. The gentleman was to carry all packages for a lady, she was to have the "inside" of the walkway to protect her from being bumped by passersby or splashed with water or mud from the street, and she was to hold the gentleman's right arm for protection, especially during the evening hours. Cultural historian John F. Kasson has noted that "the entire ritual structuring of urban life, although performed in the name of honoring women, assumed and encouraged their subservience to men."[6]

Especially after the Civil War, life for middle-class women in small towns or rural areas differed significantly from the life lead by their urban counterparts. The rules of etiquette were more strictly adhered to in the city and, in many cases, applied only to city life. For example, a 1903 publication, *Correct Social Usage: A Course of Instruction in Good Form, Style and Deportment*, brought the differences between city and country life to light:

> *There is more heart, more good-fellowship, more spontaneity in human intercourse as it is seen in rural sections. There is less of rigid formality. I am willing to assume for the sake of argument that country etiquette is in a measure the adaptation of city etiquette. But that the difference must be greater than the likeness, I think, can be shown in a sketch illustrating the wide divergence of habits of life. Let me call it:*
> *"The Parable of Mildred."*
> *Mildred, who is just seventeen, ambitious and well ahead with her studies, lives in a big farmhouse with her papa and mama and brother Thomas. She has read all that admirably equipped writers have set down about etiquette, and she understands it, but it doesn't seem to fit. Mildred is soft-spoken. She is respectful to old people. She is a busy little person, anxious always to persuade mama to rest, and to get dinner herself for the four hired men who come in from the fields in their shirt sleeves, perspiring and hungry, to eat with the family. They are good men. She doesn't feel above them. But as she passes them the boiled pork and greens, and sweetens their tea, and sees them putting generous slices of butter on the edges of their plates, she wonders whether they would know the difference between a fish fork and an oyster fork, and reflects on the question whether theirs is not a code of etiquette fitted as nothing she has read is fitted to the demands of a farming community. Mama isn't a musician, but she can help Mildred with her geometry and correct her faulty pronunciation and give valuable hints about her use of the nearest village library. Mama is impressive when she puts on her one black silk gown. But mama's hands are hard and her face is a trifle red. She never used a skin lotion in her life. She would not know what to do with a compound of oil soap, and rosewater and spermaceti, and pounded almonds. As for gymnastics, she has all she wants in the making of beds and sweeping of floors and the kneading of bread. Mildred doubts whether it is worth while to read mama the etiquette books. That mama is as true a lady as any in the world all her own reading will never make her doubt at all.*

The author's point, of course, was that readers of *Correct Social Usage* should "adopt and follow strictly the rules that seem to fit the time, place and person."[7] In other words, regardless of whether a woman lived in the city or country, North or South or boom towns of the West, she was to be well

*Knowing how to participate in various parlor amusements and conduct oneself accordingly were popular topics in Victorian etiquette manuals. In this circa 1891 sketch a young woman plays a board game with perhaps a gentleman caller. Note that the young couple are chaperoned.*

versed in good manners so she'd be prepared for—and could adapt to—any situation or location she might find herself in.

Along with "The Etiquette of the Street," popular advice manuals also explored the fine art of making introductions, salutations, conversation, traveling etiquette, shopping etiquette, the etiquette of public places, the etiquette of riding in and driving a carriage, etiquette at Washington and business etiquette. They also routinely discussed appropriate dress, the toilette, the etiquette of making calls, the etiquette of visiting cards, dinner parties, table etiquette and receptions, parties and balls—all of which are explored in greater detail later in this chapter.

The etiquette of conversation was a priority during the 19th century because a woman's ability to converse well could determine social success in life. General knowledge was a must, as well as command of the language and formulation of sentences. Confidence too was required. As a means to an end, being able to converse—and do it well—afforded middle-class Victorian women the opportunity to develop friendships, acquire knowledge on timely topics, climb the social ladder and participate in their limited realm of social activities. They were never to discuss money, and it was inappropriate for them to converse in detail about manly topics such as politics or business. Rather, women were to concern themselves with lighter subjects that wouldn't be so mentally taxing, such as craftwork, literature, entertainments, charity work, fashions and so on.

Just as the vast majority of etiquette books published during the antebellum period were the product of publishing houses located in the larger cities of the Northeast, so too did many of the prerequisite "good manners" originate in these same urban areas. Richard L. Bushman has noted that middle-class women of the Northern states had increased opportunity early on to participate in the material culture (e.g., home decor) associated with gentility and to enter social venues where they could observe and emulate the display of good manners. It took time for both material goods and the latest fashions and customs to make their way South and, later, West.[8] Following the Civil War and the Reconstruction period, improved transportation, widespread industry and celebrations surrounding the nation's centennial helped foster a national unity. There was a marked decrease in differences between the middle class of the North and the South as the 20th century approached.

Gentility and increased consumerism went hand in hand during the Victorian era and, as a proliferation of machine-made goods gave rise to numerous small shops and then department stores, etiquette or conduct in such establishments became yet another area of instruction for women. For example, deportment manuals published during the last quarter of the 19th century told readers that when shopping they should speak softly, handle goods carefully, be courteous to other patrons, and never lean upon a store counter. To do otherwise would clearly convey "ill-breeding." Women especially were never to haggle over a price; they were to treat clerks respectfully and avoid making any unfavorable comments about the quality of goods offered. According to one advice giver, "Ladies should not monopolize the time and attention of salesmen in small talk, while other customers are in the store to be waited upon."9 Paying cash  was favorable to purchasing on credit, but if a line of credit were established "promptitude" in paying debts was vital to maintaining a good reputation.

Just as domestic-science authorities wrote about the importance of striking a proper balance between industry (in other words, household labor) and leisurely pursuits during the mid-19th century, writers used sentimental fiction to temper the excesses of polite society during the late Victorian era. Many perceived fashions and entertainments as taking on more importance than the concepts of "home" and "virtue." Stories with a common theme—one that would point women in the right direction—began to fill the pages of popular periodicals.

For example, during the year 1889 *Harper's New Monthly Magazine* ran a serial story, "A Little Journey in the World," by Charles Dudley Warner. The heroine, Margaret, is a young woman from the country visiting friends in New York City. Margaret seems at times overwhelmed by the fast pace of city life but she is well versed in proper etiquette and therefore able to participate in all the gay festivities and social engagements. After an evening at the opera and an elegant dinner, Margaret tells her handsome escort, "It is so different from the pleasure one has in an evening by the fire." The author then notes: "It was a deeper matter than she thought, this about worldliness, which had been raised in Margaret's mind. Have we all double natures, and do we simply conform to whatever surrounds us? Is there any difference in kind between the country worldliness and city worldliness?" As the story continues, Margaret does indeed reflect on the vast differences between the two worlds. We are told: "She felt that in the whirl of only a few days of it [city life]—operas, receptions, teas, readings, dances, dinners where everybody sparkled with a bewildering brilliancy, and yet from which one brought away nothing but a sense of strain; such gallantry, such compliments, such an easy tossing about of every topic under heaven; such an air of knowing everything, and not caring about anything very much; so much mutual admiration and personal satisfaction!" Margaret's escort grows very fond of her, finding her true heart and simple charms a refreshing change from the city women concerned only with the latest fashions or gossip. At yet another social engagement he asks Margaret if she finds New York agreeable.

*Yes. Yes and no. One has no time to one's self. I have a feeling of having lost myself. Do you know, the world seems much smaller here than at home. The interests of life don't seem so large—the questions, I mean, what is going on in Europe, in literature, in politics. I get a wider view when I stand off—at home. I suppose it is more concentrated here. And, oh dear, I'm so stupid! Everybody is so alert in little things, so quick to turn a compliment, and say a bright thing.*[10]

Margaret's words—her impressions of city life—clearly convey the superficial hustle and bustle at the expense of quieter moments, intellectual endeavors and home comforts. Margaret is a true lady and not surprisingly, wins the heart of the kind gentleman who falls in love with her simple elegance, industrious nature and good mind.

Balance was all important; home and family were never to be upstaged by worldly entertainment and modesty never replaced by vanity. How did the middle-class Victorian woman acquire the skills to mingle with her peers? In chapter 1 we explored the advice manuals that served as primers on the road to ladylike behavior; along with studying to improve one's self-culture, advice givers also recommended that one carefully observe and emulate the etiquette of others. Practice could indeed make perfect, or close to it.

By the First World War the social order as the Victorians had known it was becoming a thing of the past. New forms of entertainment, communication and transportation made many social "laws" obsolete. John F. Kasson has noted the virtues of "character" were replaced by the expression of "personality" in a modernizing world.[11] Women, no longer content to walk through the streets with their heads bowed, were fighting for the right to vote, improved working conditions and a place in the male-dominated world outside the home.

# ENTERTAINING AND SOCIALIZING

Throughout the 19th century, as entertaining and socializing became increasingly elaborate, the middle-class Victorian woman continued to play a pivotal role in the planning, execution and success of any given social undertaking.

Entertaining, most often in the home, frequently included formal dinners, private balls or more casual afternoon teas. To assist the growing middle class in the fine art of entertaining, etiquette books as well as household manuals provided detailed instructions on everything from how to send invitations and set the table to what foods should be prepared and in what order they be served. In *Miss Beecher's Domestic Receipt-Book*, published in 1846, Catharine Beecher noted among her objectives the wish to "furnish such directions in regard to small dinner-parties and evening company as will enable any young housekeeper to perform her part, on such occasions, with ease, comfort, and success."[12]

Social "seasons" were the norm throughout the Victorian era and New Year's Day usually marked the start of a whirlwind period that lasted until the beginning of the religious period known as Lent. In the South, families whose lives were centered on the plantation would often travel to cities or towns for a brief stay in order to participate in myriad social functions. In many cases this was the only opportunity a woman might have to enjoy a lavish party or ball, given the isolation associated with plantation life. On the other hand, for Northerners (especially those living in large cities) it was the busiest time of year. Summer, of course, was a time for vacationing and entertaining, and socializing during the warmer months was done on a more relaxed and casual basis than during the winter.

During the early Victorian period stylish dinner parties became labor-intensive affairs requiring a multitude of table accessories and meals that stretched through several courses. For example, in *Miss Beecher's Domestic Receipt-Book* Catharine Beecher described preparations for a "substantial" dinner for 10 or 12 guests. The mistress would

> make a list of all the articles to be used, either for table furniture or cook-
> ing, and then examines her cupboard, store-closet, and cellar, to see if every-
> thing is at hand and in order. All the glass and silver to be used is put in
> readiness, the castors, salts, and everything of the kind arranged properly. In
> order to be more definite, the exact dishes to be provided will be supposed to
> be these: Soup. Fish. A boiled ham. A boiled turkey, with oyster sauce.

*Three roasted ducks, and a dish of scalloped oysters. Potatoes, Parsnips, Turnips, and Celery. For dessert, Pudding, Pastry, Fruit and Coffee.*[13]

Miss Beecher went on to offer the house servants and cooks specific instructions for preparing the meal and making the table ready. Regarding the table setting, attention to detail was all important. For example, the woman of the house was to supervise the servant responsible for this task to assure proper placement of everything from the table rugs and tablecloths to castors (glass condiment jars), dishware, cutlery, napkins, salt stands, tumblers and carving knives and forks. Also, Miss Beecher explained how to set up the side table with the dessert offerings and dishes. She also explained in minute detail the manner in which food dishes were to be passed about the table and the responsibility of the host to do the carving. Servants stood by to replenish bread, water and wine and remove dishware from the table as each course was finished. A servant also cleared the table and removed one of the tablecloths to make way for dessert dishes.[14]

This type of formal dinner, in which the host did the carving and dishes were passed at the table, had become somewhat old-fashioned by the 1870s when dinner à la Russe (in the Russian style) was introduced. This fashionable new mode of serving dinner called for all the food to be placed on the sideboard and for domestics to do the carving and serving. This allowed women to display elaborate centerpieces on the table (usually floral arrangements) at dinner and left the host and hostess free to concentrate on their guests. Dinner à la Russe, however, required a staff of several servants, so in households where only one or two domestics were employed older methods prevailed. *Godey's Lady's Book* discussed both styles of serving dinner in an 1885 "Practical Hints for the Household" column. In regard to the "old" way, readers were instructed:

*The host and hostess should sit at the ends of the table, the hostess should serve the soup, salad, dessert and coffee at dinner; the host the fish and meat; and the servants, the vegetables and the entrées. At a dinner served à la Russe, the fruit and flowers only are placed upon the table, the several courses being served from the side. Many volumes have been written upon table etiquette; but it is hard to follow all suggestions, as what is considered proper at one place or time is not always approved under other circumstances; it is sadly perplexing to always keep pace with the variations of fashion. Utter deference should be paid to the evident arrangement of the house at which you are.*[15]

As the century progressed advice givers looked unfavorably upon multicourse meals and ostentatious table settings and dining room decor. Rather, they recommended simple but elegant meals and surroundings. Accordingly, the 1898 *Smiley's Cook Book and New and Complete Guide for Housekeepers* told readers: "This is not the age of heavy dinners nor heavy decorations. The dinner tables of fashionable people are things of lightness and delicacy, and the menus to correspond."[16] Even simplified dinners, however, required careful attention to detail. The Victorian era gave rise to so many and varied accessories for the table that when preparing for guests, even considering which cutlery, flatware and service pieces to use remained a daunting task. Depending upon the menu, there were place settings or serving spoons for berries, bouillon, coffee, crackers, eggs, gravy, ice cream, jelly, mustard, nuts, olives, peas, salads, salt, sorbet, soup, sugar, tea and vegetables. Likewise, forks were designed for asparagus, cheese, meats, fish, lettuce, oysters, pastry, pickles, pie, sardines, toast and vegetables. Different knives, also in assorted sizes, were required for butter, cake, cheese, fish, ice cream, jelly, macaroni and waffles, and special servers were used to dish up everything from fried oysters and cucumber to Saratoga Chips and tomatoes. Miscellaneous items included tongs for serving asparagus, sugar, ice and sandwiches, and butter picks, cheese scoops and sifters for sugar. The handsome, well-dressed Victorian dinner table was a sight to behold, and an embodiment of Victorian material culture second only to the parlor.

If the table setting was upstaged at all, it may have been by the centerpiece or floral arrangement the Victorian woman prepared for the formal dinner party. One late 1800s household guide reported:

> *The tasteful decoration of the table is no small item. In some circles the hostesses vie with each other as to whose table shall be the most elegant, and in some cases as much is spent on the flowers as on the dinner itself. It is a mistake to think that it is necessary to go to large expense in order to decorate a table prettily. Many flowers which are perfectly adapted for the table decoration can be bought for a mere trifle, or grown at home. Ladies with taste will find this a very pleasant task, while young people should be allowed to assist in decorating the table, and have their taste for arranging flowers encouraged.*[17]

There were of course rules women were to follow in creating a floral display for the dinner table. Important guidelines called for light floral scents and

# POLITENESS AT THE TABLE.

ROPERLY conducted, the dinner-party should be a pleasant affair; and if rightly managed, from the beginning to the end, it may prove a very enjoyable occasion to all in attendance, the dinner being from 5 to 8 P. M., the guests continuing at the table from one to two hours.

For a very pleasant social affair the rule is not to have the company when seated exceed twelve in number. With a party of that size the conversation can be general, and all are likely to feel more at ease than if the number be larger, provided a selection of guests is made that are congenial to each other. None of them should be conspicuously superior to the others, and all should be from the same circle of society.

Having determined upon the number of guests to be invited, the next thing in order will be the issuing of notes of invitation, by special messenger, which should be sent out ten or twelve days before the dinner is given. Their form will be—

*Mr. and Mrs. L——request the pleasure of the company of Mr. and Mrs. T—— at dinner on Wednesday, the 10th of March, at six o'clock P. M.*
*R. S. V. P.*

The answer accepting the invitation may read—

*Mr. and Mrs. T—— accept with much pleasure Mr. and Mrs. L——'s invitation for dinner on the 10th of March.*

If declined, the form may be as follows:

*Mr. and Mrs. T—— regret that a previous engagement* (or for other reasons which may be given) *will prevent their accepting Mr. and Mrs. L——'s kind invitation for dinner on the 10th of March.*

Should the invitation be declined, the declination, which should state the reason for non-acceptance of the invitation, should be sent immediately by a messenger, that the hostess may have an opportunity for inviting other guests in the place of those who decline.

Should the invitation be accepted, nothing but serious difficulty should prevent the appointment being fulfilled. Should anything happen to prevent attendance, notification should be given the hostess immediately.

It is of the utmost importance that all of the company be punctual, arriving from ten to fifteen minutes before the appointed time. To be ten minutes late, keeping the dinner waiting, is a serious offense which no one should be guilty of.

The host, hostess and other members of the family should be early in the drawing-room to receive guests as they arrive, each of whom should be welcomed with a warm greeting.

The hostess having determined who shall accompany each other to the table, each gentleman should be informed what lady he is expected to escort. The hour having arrived, the host offers his right arm to the most honored or possibly the eldest lady guest, and the gentleman most distinguished will escort the lady of the house.

Proceeding to the dining-room when all is in readiness, the host will take his seat at the foot of the table, and the hostess at the head, the lady escorted by the host taking her seat at his right, and the escort of the hostess sitting also at *her* right. The next most honored seat is at the *left* of the hostess. The illustration (Fig. 12) upon this page shows a company thus seated.

It is fashionable to have cards laid upon the table, bearing the name, sometimes printed very beautifully upon silk, indicating where each guest shall sit, which saves confusion in being seated. The ladies having taken their places, the gentlemen will be seated, and all is in readiness for the dinner to be served, unless grace be said by a clergyman present or by the host.

Let us hope if there is any carving, it will be done before the meat is brought to the table, and the time of the company saved from this sometimes slow and tedious work. Should soup be passed, it is well for each one to take it, and also the various courses as they are served, making no special comment on the food.

The gentleman will, when a dish is brought, having seen the lady he escorted provided for, help himself and pass it on; he will pay no attention to the other lady near him, but will leave that to her escort. In all cases he will be careful and attentive to the wants of the lady in his charge, ascertaining her wishes and issuing her orders to the waiters.

No polite guest will ever fastidiously smell or examine any article of food before tasting it. Such conduct would be an insult to those who have invited him; neither will the host or hostess apologize for each other, the cook or the waiters; all having done the best they could, there is nothing left to do but to make the best of everything that is provided.

Especial pains should be taken by the host and hostess, as well as all the company, to introduce topics of conversation that shall be agreeable and pleasing, that the dinner hour may be in the highest degree entertaining. When all the

FIG. 12. GENTILITY IN THE DINING-ROOM.

The evidences of good breeding with a party of ladies and gentlemen seated about a table, who are accustomed to the usages of polite society, are many. Among these will be the fact that the table is very beautifully and artistically spread. This need not require much wealth, but good taste is necessary to set it handsomely.

Again, the company evince gentility by each assuming a genteel position while eating. It is not necessary that an elaborate toilet be worn at the table, but careful attention should always be given to neatness of personal appearance, however plain may be the dress which is worn.

Another evidence of good manners is the self-possession with which the company deport themselves throughout the meal.

guests have finished their eating, the hostess, with a slight nod to one of the leading members of the party, will rise, as will all the company, and repair to the drawing-room, where, in social converse, the time should be spent for the next two or three hours. Etiquette demands that each member of the company remain at least an hour after the dinner is finished, it being impolite to hurry away immediately after rising from the table. Should he do so, however, he will ask to be excused.

---

*Familiarity with the etiquette of the dining table was equally important for the hostess and guests, knowledge that their social standing might well depend upon. The page illustrated here with hints for "Politeness at the Table" appeared in the 1888* Hill's Manual of Social and Business Forms.

a low dish of flowers was preferred to avoid blocking the view across the table.

The ultimate goal of any Victorian dinner party was assuring that a pleasant time be had by all. The middle-class home could be well-appointed and the dining room the ideal refined setting, but if small talk and conversation did not flow smoothly the evening was a social failure. According to one popular 19th-century etiquette book: "A host and hostess generally judge the success of a dinner by the manner in which conversation has been sustained. If it has flagged often, it is considered proof that the guests have not been congenial; but if a steady stream of talk has been kept up, it shows that they have smoothly amalgamated, as a whole. No one should monopolize the conversation, unless he wishes to win for himself the appellation of a bore, and be avoided as such."[18]

Another advice book laid responsibility for the outcome of a dinner party squarely on the hostess. *Collier's Cyclopedia of Social and Commercial Information* reported:

> *The duties of hostess at a dinner-party are not onerous; but they demand tact and good breeding, grace of bearing, and self-possession of no ordinary degree. She does not often carve. She has no active duties to perform; but she must neglect nothing, forget nothing, put all her guests at their ease, encourage the timid, draw out the silent, and pay every possible attention to the requirements of each and all around her. No accident must ruffle her temper. No disappointment must embarrass her. She must see her old china broken without a sigh, and her best glass shattered with a smile.[19]*

Familiarity with proper etiquette was imperative when entertaining. Once guests, dressed in their finest evening wear, were led from the parlor to the dining room, place cards indicated where they should be seated. Topics of conversation at the table were to be light and lively. Discussing money, the stock market, religion and social gossip were taboo but conversations related to the literary world, art and music were appropriate. Also, while discussing politics was considered bad taste, talk about the city of Washington was acceptable. During the late 1800s, Washington gossip was a popular topic of conversation, for middle-class Victorians were curious about the social aspects of the nation's capital as well as the doings of the first family and other prominent political figures.

While playing the role of hostess could be a daunting task for women, being a guest at a dinner party also had clearly defined responsibilities.

*Collier's Cyclopedia* did not mince words in emphasizing the importance of good manners when telling readers: "To be acquainted with every detail of the etiquette pertaining to this subject [the dinner party] is of highest importance to every lady. Ease, savoir-faire, and good-breeding are nowhere more indispensable than at the dinner-table, and the absence of them is nowhere more apparent. How to eat soup and what to do with a cherry-stone are weighty considerations when taken as the index of social status and it is not too much to say, that a young woman who elected to take claret with her fish, or ate peas with her knife, would justly risk the punishment of being banished from good society."[20]

Another form of entertainment and socializing popular among middle-class Victorian women was the morning tea or reception. Although they were commonly referred to as "morning" receptions, such social events typically took place between four o'clock in the afternoon and seven o'clock in the evening. Informal invitations were sent and on the appointed day the hostess would oversee arranging the refreshments. An 1897 issue of *The Ladies' Home Journal* offered timely advice in regard to preparations for a morning tea or reception, telling women:

> *In serving tea the table, especially if it is in the parlor, should be arranged before any visitors arrive. Its cover may be a linen teacloth embroidered or trimmed with lace, while the cups and saucers, with the spoon resting in each saucer, the thin slices of lemon, the small wafers, or cakes, or sandwiches, or thinly-cut, buttered bread, on plates, on pretty doilies, should be artistically arranged upon it. The tea kettle should be in its place . . . [t]he teapot just in front of it, the teacaddy at one side, while the cream pitcher and sugar bowl should be within convenient reach. If the hostess pours the tea she allows the guests to put in the sugar and cream for themselves. If she expects many visitors, then there will be wisdom in asking a friend to pour tea for her.*[21]

Similar to a morning reception but less formal, the "kettledrum" became popular during the late 19th century. The kettledrum can be compared to the modern-day "open house" because guests usually visited only for a short time (30 minutes or so) and light refreshments were served. Conversation with friends was the main objective but entertainment in the form of music was often supplied. A lady's dress for a morning reception, or kettledrum, called for a demitoilet with or without a hat. Her dress might be of velvet, silk, muslin or grenadine, but simple jewelry was to be worn.

In the hierarchy of Victorian social functions, the private ball ranked second to the formal dinner party. In the larger homes of the middle class a dining room or parlor (ideally a room more square than rectangular) was cleared of most furniture to accommodate musicians and dancing couples. Invitations were sent at least ten days before the event but more likely three to four weeks notice was extended. The hostess always tried to assure an equal number of dancers of both sexes so young women would not be left without partners.

In addition to the room set aside for dancing at a ball, the hostess also had to see to it that a bedroom was available for ladies to freshen up, leave their wraps and trade confidences. Another room, close to the ballroom, was used for refreshments and the midnight supper that was usually served.

Knowledge of the etiquette of the ballroom was imperative for hosts and guests alike. The manner in which introductions were made, invitations to dance were extended, and the dance itself were performed, all required a familiarity with what was considered proper and socially acceptable. Of the dances themselves, quadrilles and round dances were the most popular forms; the quadrille basically required the ability to walk gracefully but a round dance called for skill and practice. Dancing was subject to some controversy during the Victorian age, and a brief article published in the September 1867 issue of *Godey's Lady's Book* warned of the dangers of overexertion. In regard to dancing as a form of exercise for girls, readers were told:

> *But while it is true that amusements are, or ought to be, favorable to the health of the body, it is as true that they are often abused, and perhaps on the whole are productive of more evil than good, produce more sickness than health. This results from the fact that they are sought, not always because they are naturally favorable to health, but for the sake of hilarity, frivolity, and fun which they afford. The dance, for example, which in our own parlors, with no injurious appendages, if it could remain subject to proper parental restraint, might be safely encouraged, probably under the present circumstances is among the most fruitful causes of pulmonary consumption and some other forms of disease among the victims of the ballroom. It is unfortunate for those who resort to the dance "for exercise" as many claim that it is practiced at a time when rest, not exercise, is needed, at the close of the labors of the day, and continued until a late hour, often varying from midnight till the dawn of day. Instead of healthful exercise it often becomes violent exertion, crushing effort, sufficient to impair, if not destroy the strongest constitutions.*[22]

Even as late as 1905, experts were still cautioning women regarding the "dance." In *What a Young Woman Ought To Know*, Dr. Mary Wood-Allen commented: "Dancing is a most fascinating amusement, and if only it could be conducted under proper circumstances it would be very delightful. If dancing could be conducted out of doors, in the daylight, with intimate friends, without the round dances, only those forms of dancing which may be likened to gymnastics, as the contra-dance, the cotillion, the objections to dancing would be largely removed, but I am of the opinion that a large share of the fascination of dancing would go at the same time."[23]

Dancing was indeed fascinating. At the ball, dance programs were distributed to young ladies so they could plan their evening by allowing gentlemen to pencil themselves in as dance partners for assorted waltzes, quadrilles, polkas, the galop, the cotillion and the Virginia Reel. Propriety dictated that no young lady allow her behavior to be subject to speculation by dancing with the same man more than twice. In addition, husbands and wives did not usually dance together in public, although by the 1880s some advice givers were offering their consent for married people to do so. One expert offered the following explanation:

*It is not decorous for husband and wife to seek each other's company in society, nor should they be partners at cardtables, or, as a rule, in the dance. The reason of this rule is apparent—it is only necessary to consider what would be the state of things, if each family made a selfish circle of its own. Members of a family accept an invitation out to meet other people, not to enjoy each other's society, for they could do that better at home.*[24]

While fashions changed constantly throughout the Victorian era, the attire for the ball was to be the finest evening wear. Generally, young women and ladies with brunette coloring were to wear rich colors, while blondes with a fair complexion were well suited to delicate shades. Gloves were a prerequisite, and, just as the parasol was an integral part of the dress when venturing out during daylight hours, the fan was a necessary part of the ballroom attire. One circa-1880 etiquette book instructed: "An indispensable article of toilette for a lady is a fan. This may be carried even in dancing, by suspending it from the waist by a chatelaine chain."[25]

Fans were an important accessory item throughout much of the 19th and early 20th century. Middle-class Victorian women carried demure fans for daytime outings during the 1850s and 1860s (they were especially useful during the warm weather months), but by the last quarter of the century they were usually reserved for evening functions. Fans heightened the aura of gentility and served as a romantic prop of sorts since they could be used to convey messages, thoughts or feelings to eligible young men. Just as the "language of flowers" added a certain romance to the courtship process, so too did the handheld fan. For example, by drawing the fan across her cheek, a young woman could send the message "I love you." Fanning fast told gentlemen nearby "I am engaged," and by holding a fan with the handle to the lips a young woman invited a kiss.[26]

Among the most beautiful decorative objects of the Victorian era, fans were often created of silk, lace, ivory or tortoise shell and embellished with bead-work, braiding, artistic hand-painted designs, feathers or embroidery. Japanese fans were quite fashionable during the 1880s, when anything exotic was in vogue. As both an adornment and practical accessory, the fan held its place among women until the end of the Edwardian era (the outbreak of the First World War) and was de rigueur for evening entertainments.

Along with the various forms of entertaining and socializing already discussed, paying "calls" became a very structured way for women to socialize during the late 19th century. The etiquette and deportment surrounding "calls" was quite elaborate and one had to be intimately acquainted with the dos and don'ts of visiting to assure it was done properly. Paying calls was practically a daily ritual for urban middle-class women and became an important means of establishing and maintaining social position. The importance of social calls was even a topic of discussion between sisters Jo and Amy in Louisa May Alcott's hugely popular *Little Women*. Jo was reluctant to accompany her sister on a round of visits because "she hated calls of the formal sort and never made any till Amy compelled her with a bargain, bribe or promise." Amy's retort, "I'm sure it's no pleasure to me to go today, but it's a debt we owe society . . ." typifies the duty-bound mentality of many middle-class Victorian women.[27]

That paying social calls was women's work was clearly conveyed in one 19th-century deportment book, which stated:

*The bent of nature, and early training, combine to teach ladies attention to details and develop a quick perception of the nice shades of conduct that constitute the polish of good society. For these reasons, society is more exacting in its demands upon woman, and a neglect of formalities, which would be pardoned in a man, is not readily overlooked if the fault of a careless or ill-bred sister. Ladies are expected to be observant of the apparently trivial points of etiquette.[28]*

*Calling cards with a special message or honoring a certain occasion such as New Year's were popular during the late 19th century.*

*While simple, engraved calling cards were recommended by etiquette manuals, many women chose beautiful chromolithographed cards during the late 1800s and often collected and saved examples such as this one in scrap albums.*

For paying calls, between three o'clock and five o'clock in the afternoon were acceptable hours, insofar as they eliminated the risk of intruding upon the luncheon hour or interrupting household chores. When a woman set out from home to attend to her social duty she was often dressed in special garb known as a "visiting toilette" that included a fine dress for daytime wear, hat, gloves and parasol. At each home she visited she was to stay no longer than 15 to 30 minutes, and the time was spent in polite, general conversation. Either upon entering or departing, she made sure to leave one of her calling cards in the card receiver strategically placed near the front door. Several calls could be made during a single afternoon in an effort to maintain acquaintances, climb the social ladder, and offer condolences or congratulations. According to the 1873 *Household Cyclopaedia of Practical Receipts and Daily Wants*, by Alexander V. Hamilton, "A visit of ceremony should not last more than a quarter of an hour, and you should not remove either bonnet or shawl. You should retire easily and quietly, as soon as possible after the arrival of other visitors, but do not let it appear that their arrival is the cause. When they are seated, take leave of your hostess, and bow to the guests."[29]

During the mid-Victorian period, as calls evolved into an elaborate social responsibility, calling cards became increasingly important. First introduced during the 1850s, calling cards eventually became intricately entwined with the ritual surrounding ceremonial visits. If a lady found the subject of her visit not at home or "otherwise engaged" and unavailable, leaving her calling card was proof positive that she had attempted to pay a visit. While generally engraved, handwritten or, later, machine-printed with a lady's name and address, the calling card could also state, in the lower left-hand corner, the day of the week a lady would be "at home" to receive callers.

It was common for calling cards to be placed in an ornate calling-card receiver (a platelike or footed receptacle often made of sterling silver or silverplate) placed on a tabletop in the front hall. Cards were often saved and put in scrapbooks as keepsakes or mementos. Although the advice givers recommended simple but elegant engraved cards as most suitable, the penchant for ornamentation throughout the Victorian era left no stone unturned. By the 1880s chromolithographed cards, sporting beautiful floral, foliage and nature-inspired designs, or novelty cards were the most popular. Lovely calling-card cases kept the small cards crisp, clean and handy.

In the 1870s and 1880s women used calling cards as an especially handy form of communication when someone was not at home or was unavailable to receive callers. By simply turning down the upper right-hand corner of her card a woman left the message that she had called in person. By folding the lower right-hand corner she extended a good-bye (often done before embarking on a journey); folding the upper left-hand corner sent congratulations, and by folding the lower left-hand corner condolences were conveyed. If a woman left a calling card with the entire left side folded it was understood she had come to visit all the women of the family. This "language of the calling card" had become obsolete in many social circles by 1890. Mrs. John Logan made note of this in her book, *The Home Manual*, telling readers that "cards should not be turned down at the corners, nor bent over at one end—the fashion is now out of date."[30]

Throughout the 19th century the various forms of entertaining and socializing were done on a lesser scale in rural areas or small towns and villages than in the large cities where social "seasons" were the norm. In small communities, tea parties and receptions were more informal and balls were generally reserved for special occasions. Also, paying calls or visits was less structured for country women. Rather, women in rural locations might gather together for tea and conversation while completing a needlework project or planning a town festivity. In the South, holidays were a popular time to open the house to visitors, and agricultural communities enjoyed celebrations in conjunction with harvesttime. While entertaining and socializing may have been less frequent for them, such middle-class women were still familiar with the necessary accoutrements of dress and their parasols, fans and calling cards were available when needed.

# FASHION AND BEAUTY

For middle-class Victorian women, fashion and beauty were closely linked to the concept of gentility. A demure and virtuous nature along with a firm grasp of the laws of etiquette were vital to success in life, but so too were appearance and manner of dress. The prevailing styles of fashion during the Victorian era prompted numerous magazine articles, lectures and books on female health—or lack of it. The constricting restraints and bodily harm resulting from the often discussed "unmentionable," the corset, was of special concern.

During the early 1800s popular fashions found women dressed in flowing, high-waisted Empire-style gowns that emphasized the bust. By the dawn of the Victorian age the focus had shifted to the waist—the smaller

*During the mid-19th century women wore crinolines to achieve the then popular full, hooped-skirt look. This 1864 fashion plate from* Peterson's Magazine *shows a ball gown on the left and an evening dress on the right with crinolines and tightly corseted waists. Note that the woman on the left has that all-important accessory, a handheld fan.*

the better—and corsets made with iron or whalebone stays shaped and molded female figures draped in full-skirted dresses with enormous puff sleeves and masses of ribbons, ruffles and bows. The concept of beauty during the 1830s was epitomized in then-popular magazine illustrations depicting angeliclike creatures with expressions of childlike innocence and tiny features.

By the next decade the much-discussed concepts of Republican Motherhood and domesticity influenced fashion trends somewhat, and the ideal Victorian woman began to dress more in keeping with her role as a "domestic goddess." Calf lengths gave way to floor-length hems and dresses were simpler, sans bows and ribbons. Close-fitting modest bonnets were worn over spaniel-style ringlets that hugged the face.

Fashions in America changed in accordance with what was being worn in France. During the 1850s women found the crinoline a necessity in achieving the full, hoopskirt look, and in subsequent decades corsets were laced tighter and tighter. Historian of fashion Lynn Schnurnberger, in discussing the destructive persistence of this trend, notes that by midcentury "corsets are so tightly laced . . . that they restrict breathing, cause ribs to overlap, and are a general pain in whatever they happen to be constricting. Doctors, philosophers, and reformers rail against the confounded contraptions. But fashion is fashion, and no matter how uncomfortable, women aren't willing to throw them out until styles change. That happens around the turn-of-the-century when designer Paul Poiret creates the corsetless chemise."[31]

George Burnap warned about the danger of corsets in 1848, noting that young women were subjected to the "tyranny of fashion in dress" and the desire to achieve the smallest figure possible through tight lacing; the result of this practice was to put all vital organs in jeopardy.[32] Similarly Mrs. Sigourney cited the ills associated with tight corsets in her 1854 book, *Letters To Young Ladies*: "Few circumstances are more injurious to beauty, than the constrained movement, suffused complexion, and laboured respiration, that betray tight-lacing. That pulmonary disease, affections of the heart, and insanity, are in its train, and that it leads some of our fairest and dearest to fashion's shrine to die, is placed beyond a doubt, by strong medical testimony."[33]

Women were warned throughout the century regarding tight lacing. Why then did they continue the practice? In part they were influenced (as women are today) by the "ideal beauty" portrayed in leading magazines, with her perfect figure, lovely features and fashionable dress. Also, on a

ELIZABETHAN beauties simply cramped themselves in their corsets, which added nothing to beauty of form.

## Women's Beautiful Figures

are more often the result of the corset they wear than is generally supposed. The matchless *Flexibone* fabric, in its form‑making and shape‑preserving quality, yields to every curve, intensifying graceful carriage and adding charm to every movement of the body: distinctive features obtained only in the famous

## Flexibone
## Moulded Corset

Think this out now and remember this truth when dress fitting begins.

### From $1.50 to $3.00

Extra long, long and short waist, in the most beautiful selections of fabric.

For sale by leading dealer in your town. If not, address card for name of nearest dealer, and booklet, *"How to Select."*

**CORONET CORSET COMPANY, Jackson, Michigan**

*This advertisement for the Flexibone Moulded Corset appeared in the September 1896 issue of The Ladies' Home Journal. While the corset was long targeted by physicians as a threat to a woman's health, women nevertheless continued to wear them until fashions changed with the dawn of the 20th century.*

*This circa 1870s illustration shows the demise of the crinoline for the latest new fashion: the bustle. This wire or bone cagelike undergarment gave dresses a notable "lift" in the back and remained popular through the late 1800s.*

subliminal level, the tight corset implied a refined lifestyle. As Harvey Green points out in *The Light of the Home*, corsets were the equivalent of a status symbol for women. Since wearing a corset made routine physical movements associated with household chores virtually impossible, women were sending the message their family had the wherewithal to employ domestic servants.[34]

Along with the tight corsets and steel-hooped crinolines worn during the 1850s, evening wear became more sensual with off-the-shoulder gowns. Simple but elegant hairstyles called for a carefully arranged chignon or a center part with drooping ringlets covering the ears. Curls were highly favored according to an 1855 issue of *Godey's Lady's Book*, which told readers: "In or out of fashion, we contend that curls are pre-eminently beautiful and becoming. As weapons aimed at men's hearts, no other revolvers are half so deadly. They look youthful; they look modest; they look caressing."[35]

Clothing became more colorful, elaborate and readily available during the late 1850s and the 1860s with the introduction of chemically produced dyes for cloth, paper dress patterns and widespread use of the sewing machine. Not only was it easier and less time consuming to make clothing at home with the sewing machine (rather than by hand) and paper patterns (rather than cutting out muslin forms), but before long women would be able to buy off the rack at department stores and via mail-order catalogs.

Dresses during the 1860s often had multilayers of fabric and were created in a combination of colors. Fashion plates in magazines of the late 1860s show the crinoline loosing favor to the bustle, a wire, padded or bone cagelike garment worn under dresses to give fullness to the back of the outfit. These same fashion plates also depict a change in thought regarding hair coloring. While color fashion plates in magazines of the 1850s generally featured blondes (symbolic of purity and an angelic nature), by the 1860s brunettes were given their due. Dark hair was increasingly viewed as having a sensual quality, especially appealing on the worldly middle-class Victorian woman. In short, the ideal mid-Victorian woman was as adorned, ornately dressed and accessorized as the finest high-style parlor rooms. This seems hardly a coincidence, given the material display in the parlor and its provenance as the center of her domestic sphere.

Fashion did however take a brief hiatus during the Civil War years. Many women in the North went to work in office jobs vacated by men off to fight the war. Women of the South were occupied with caring for the wounded, running farms or plantations and, in many cases, simply trying to survive and meet basic needs. Personal beauty and adornment were insignificant compared to the important work at hand for women on both sides of the cause. Plain and practical clothing was needed and became a fashion statement in and of itself, reflecting hard times as well as the very real contributions made by women to the war effort. In the South a ballad, *The Homespun Dress*, reflected these sentiments:

*My homespun dress is plain, I know.*
*My hat's palmetto, too.*
*But then it shows what Southern girls*
*For Southern rights will do.*
*We have sent the bravest of our land*
*To battle with the foe*
*And we will lend a helping hand—*
*We love the South you know.*[36]

During the last quarter of the 19th century fashions kept pace with changing lifestyles rather than lifestyles conforming to fashionable modes of dress. The pale, almost sickly look that women aspired to during the early Victorian era (considered a show of delicacy) was traded for a healthy glow and a full figure. Corsets were still worn but fashions were no longer high waisted. Large bustles gave women a distinct "lift" in the back, and height along with a strong constitution was no doubt needed to carry the 10 to 30 pounds of clothing worn by a fully outfitted woman.

A complete wardrobe called for a variety of dresses, gowns and outfits. The middle-class Victorian woman required a simple morning dress for home, a morning dress with a fitted waist to be worn when visitors were expected, a plain morning dress for the street (short enough that it would not drag on the ground), an elegant dress for the promenade and for making calls (such as a walking suit), a rich dress (silk or velvet trimmed with lace) for a carriage ride and assorted dresses and gowns for evening wear. Special outfits were also required for horseback riding and other outdoor or leisure activities. Women increasingly participated in sports such as bicycling, golf and tennis, and this influenced fashions. By the mid-1890s smaller bustles were being used for formal wear and the ornamented, often heavy dress and multiple undergarments for daytime use were traded for blouses—shirt-waists, as they were known—and crisp tailored skirts. Women were no longer unquestioning slaves of fashions. Unyielding wardrobes were slowly cast aside in favor of fashions more comfortable and conducive to simplified lifestyles. As evidence of this an article appearing in an 1890 issue of *The House Wife* magazine reported:

> *Fashionable women, those who buy without regard to cost, are in a very small minority. Statistics show that of all the families in the United States, a comparatively small number are able to keep even one servant; the very large majority of women do the work of their own homes; and three hundred thousand of these are engaged in paid avocations, as well. This shows that dress for the great mass of them, means a rigid observance of the law of* must—*a law which fashion is not supposed to take into account except in accordance with its own behests. But fashion, as fashion, is today much less a power than formerly. In fact, it hardly exists for intelligent women. They dress as they please. Undoubtedly they are influenced in this direction, or that, but it is more by movements antagonistic to fashion, than by fashion itself. Indeed it is a little surprising to find that even women who are supposed to stand as representatives in the world of society, and its conventions, sometimes lead in the adoption of an idea that recommends itself to their common sense.*[37]

The healthy, voluptuous female of the 1890s was portrayed in the "Gibson Girl" illustrations created by Charles Dana Gibson. Beginning in 1890 his works were featured in numerous national magazines and the "Gibson Girl" with upswept hair, full figure (still corseted), aristocratic features and stunning beauty became the ideal late Victorian-era woman. She did, in fact, hold this place of honor for about 20 years.

After the turn of the century, clothing continued to have a simple, tailored look. Skirts and shirtwaists with high collars were worn with a jacket, gloves, boots and perhaps a straw hat during the warmer months. Around 1910 high collars lost favor to low-cut bodices and a softer look began to take center stage in the fashion world.

Beauty and fashion were goals to be achieved and, while physical beauty was aspired to, women were continually cautioned by advice givers that inner beauty was more valuable and important. For example, the January

6914

*This fashion illustration from the June 1912 issue
of* The Ladies' Home Journal *depicts the trend
toward a more natural but soft and
elegant look in dress.*

1856 issue of *Godey's Lady's Book* included the following directions for "The Young Lady's Toilet":

*Self-Knowledge—The Enchanting Mirror.*
*This curious glass will bring your faults to light,*
*And make your virtues shine both strong and bright.*
*Contentment—Wash to Smooth Wrinkles.*
*A daily portion of this essence use,*
*'Twill smooth the brow, and tranquillity infuse.*
*Truth—Fine Lip-salves.*
*Use daily for your lips this precious dye,*
*They'll redden, and breathe sweet melody.*
*Prayer—Mixture, giving Sweetness to the Voice.*
*At morning, noon, and night, this mixture take,*
*Your tones improved, will richer music make.*
*Compassion—Best Eye-water.*
*These drops will add great lustre to the eye;*
*When more you need, the poor will you supply.*
*Wisdom—Solutions to prevent Eruptions.*
*It calms the temper, beautifies the face,*
*And gives to woman dignity and grace.*[38]

Regardless of this type of advice, cultivating a beautiful physical appearance was viewed as a powerful tool in the socializing, courtship and marriage rituals of the Victorian age. Luxurious long hair, a milky white complexion and delicate facial features were revered, and women employed an arsenal of homemade concoctions during the early and mid-19th century to achieve or maintain such desirable attributes. Makeup was frowned upon, as one article in *Godey's Lady's Book* told women:

*. . . the great principle in dress is to develop beauties by appropriate treat-*
*ment of costume and decoration, not to conceal any defects which may un-*
*fortunately be found on our persons. Whatever is false or artificial is as*
*reprehensible in dress as in morals. Pearl powder, and rouge, false and dyed*
*hair, are falsehoods addressed to the eye instead of the ear; and, like other*
*untruths, seldom escape detection and contempt. In spite of the skill with*
*which they are employed, their artificiality is betrayed by their utter want*
*of harmony with the surrounding parts.*[39]

Nevertheless, cheeks were pinched to add a spot of color and lips were bitten to produce a rosy glow. For longer lasting color, rouge could be made at home by combining two quarts of distilled water with two ounces of grain cochineal (red dye made from dried cochineal insect bodies) and then boiling the concoction for six minutes. Sixty grains of Roman alumin powder were then added and the entire mixture allowed to boil an additional three minutes before cooling. It was then strained through white silk and the red residue put out to dry in the shade. Along with rouge, cold cream for the face and tinted lip salves could also be made at home.[40]

Ever so slowly, makeup was assimilated into a lady's daily toilette. As early as the 1840s, apothecaries in large urban centers were employing cosmeticians and just a few decades later booming department stores included cosmetics counters. Advertising played a key role in promoting the widespread, acceptable use of cosmetics from the 1880s on, as magazine ads and whimsical trade cards (given free and distributed by companies, merchants or through the mail) hailed the healing properties and healthful benefits of assorted beauty products. In 1905 an advertising booklet entitled *Beauty, a Woman's Birthright* was put out by the Pond's Extract Company. The author, Harriet Hubbard Ayer, wrote: "The time has gone by, fortunately, when it was regarded as sinful for a woman to take the same tender care of herself and her appearance as she previously bestowed on the parlor furniture and the dining-room silverware." By this time makeup was well on its way to becoming a commercial success.

A prerequisite of feminine beauty throughout the Victorian era, beautiful long hair was treated to a number of home recipes for shampooing and maintaining a healthy shine. One popular cleansing solution was a rosemary wash in which one gallon of rosemary water was combined with one-half pint of rectified spirits of wine and one ounce of pearlash.[41] Many household manuals including such "domestic chemistry" recipes also offered women instructions for making various hair oils and "pomatums" (perfumed ointments for hair grooming). Magazines too aided women in preparing home beauty products. *Godey's Lady's Book* frequently included recipes for "The Toilette" and in one 1855 issue advised that to restore hair "when removed by illness or old age rub the bald places frequently with an onion."[42] If one was a brunette, color could be improved upon by washing the hair with a recipe calling for walnut husks, but vigorous and frequent brushing was considered the best way to achieve beautiful hair.

Advertisements for commercial hair-care products also turned up in magazines by the late 1800s, and before long homemade recipes fell by the

# LABLACHE FACE POWDER

## The Queen of Toilet Powders

IS PURE and PERFECT
It makes the skin soft and beautiful, and is delightful and refreshing.

LABLACHE
FACE POWDER
is endorsed by society and professional ladies in Europe and America, and the sale of over one million boxes annually is a marked testimonial to its worth. This powder imparts to the face, neck and arms, a delicate softness, with the tint and fragrance of the lily and rose.

Take no other.

Flesh, White, Pink and Cream Tints
Price, 50c. per box
Of all druggists or by mail
BEN. LEVY & CO., French Perfumers
34 West St., Boston, Mass., U. S. A.

*This 1896 advertisement for face powder assured middle-class women that the use of this makeup was endorsed by socialites. Ever so slowly, commercially prepared cosmetics were accepted. After all, beauty was viewed as a means to having some measure of power over men.*

Halls Vegetable Sicilian Hair Renewer Beautifies the HAIR and restores its youthful Color

While homemade recipes for hair care were the norm
throughout much of the Victorian age, commercial products
were being successfully marketed and sold by the late 1800s.
This appealing trade card for Hall's Vegetable Sicilian Hair Renewer
told potential customers, "Never fails to restore gray or faded hair
to its original color and beauty. It cures humors, removes dandruff,
and all impurities from the scalp. It prevents the hair from falling,
and renders it soft and silken . . . Its quality
is zealously maintained."

wayside. For example, the 1900 Sears, Roebuck and Company catalog offered numerous beauty enhancing products including "Princess Hair Restorer," advertised as "A wonderful new hair tonic and producer" that would "Restore the Natural Color, Preserves and Strengthens the Hair for Years, Promotes the Growth, Arrests Falling Hair, Feeds and Nourishes the Roots, Cures Dandruff and Scurf, and Allays all Scalp Irritations." At 65 cents a bottle, women were told to "use it always if you want a head of fine, silky, glossy hair, the PRIDE OF EVERY WOMAN."

Just as beautiful hair was symbolic of Victorian womanhood, so too was a milky white complexion. The middle-class woman could not be caught with a sun-tanned face, freckles or rough, red hands, associated with outdoor labor or strenuous work in the home. Toward this end, long sleeves were worn during daylight hours and bonnets or hats, along with a parasol, protected her face while gloves covered her hands. If by chance she did expose herself to the effects of the sun, freckles could be removed by combining horseradish and a cup of cold, sour milk, then allowing it to stand 12 hours before applying it three times a day.[43] Milk of almond, which could be obtained from a chemist at a drug store, was thought a good remedy for sunburn, and rough, chapped hands could be treated with a mixture of lemon juice, white wine vinegar and white brandy.

With more active lifestyles during the 1890s and on through the early years of the new century, a lily-white complexion fell off as a measure of middle-class social standing. According to Drs. Allen and McGregor, authors of *The Glory of Woman*, 1896, "Constant exposure to diffused daylight and to sunlight, when not too vivid, for some little time daily, is favorable to the health and beauty of the skin, and improves the hue of the complexion. An insufficient exposure to light, on the contrary, causes the skin to assume a pale and sickly hue, and to become lax and unhealthy."[44]

Popular opinion and changes regarding beauty did not happen over-night, however. In a question and answer page appearing in a 1912 issue of *Ladies' Home Journal*, a reader submitted the following to the "Pretty Girl Questions" column: "The present tint of my hands and arms does not encourage me to wear elbow sleeves. Please tell me something to whiten the skin." Emma E. Waker, M.D., responded with "the application of lemon-juice solution will whiten and soften the skin."[45]

The model Victorian woman was transformed in illustrations through-out the 19th century from a tiny, angelic creature to a more maternal-look-ing figure and then finally, by the late 1800s, into a more sophisticated and sensual being. Notably, she was always depicted with an innocent, childlike

*Throughout much of the Victorian era a milky white complexion
was a hallmark of a woman's middle-class social standing and an
indication of genteel womanhood. Toward this end, an advertising
trade card for Laird's Bloom of Youth and White Lilac Soap
proclaimed "Every lady desires to be considered handsome. The most
important adjunct to beauty is clear, smooth, soft and beautiful skin . . .
Ladies afflicted with tan, freckles, rough or discolored skin, should lose
no time in procuring and applying Laird's Bloom of Youth. It will
immediately obliterate all such imperfections . . ."*

face and according to Allison Kyle Leopold, author and lecturer on the Victorian age, "This interesting contradiction reveals a lot about what was considered desirable in those days—i.e., the body of a woman, the mind of a child."[46] Not until the Gibson Girl ideal of the turn of the century was woman depicted with a more mature attitude and self-assured air—a belated but fitting tribute given the changes women were forging.

# 5

# HOME WORK, HANDIWORK AND LEISURE

I slept and dreamed that life was beauty.
I woke—and found that life was duty.

—Ellen Sturgis Hooper

For the middle-class Victorian woman, domestic work was a never-ending series of tedious, often mundane tasks. Even with the assistance of domestic servants, or slaves in the antebellum South, the wife as home manager faced a daunting workload. Cooking, cleaning, laundry work, tending the kitchen garden, sewing and the production of numerous household supplies involved so much time and intensive labor that individual days of the week were given over to specific chores to maintain orderly routine or "economy of time," as it was called.

Throughout the 19th century, advice givers set high standards in regard to all manner of home work, cementing the bond between women and the home and placing yet more pressure on wives and mothers to achieve perfection.

141

If she wasn't tending to housework, the domestic goddess could likely be found sewing, doing needlework or completing an ornamental craft project to embellish her home. Sewing skills were of course a necessity and the ability to turn out decorative items for the home was symbolic of a well-bred and industrious nature. What leisure time the Victorian woman did have was best spent gardening (indoors and out) or reading for self-improvement or pleasure.

# DOMESTIC CHORES

As the middle class acquired increased wealth during the early Victorian period, women ideally made a shift from laborer to manager in many households. In reality, this was often difficult to achieve and even more difficult to maintain as the century progressed.

Whereas a family may have had a young girl known as the "help" to assist the wife and mother with domestic chores during the early 1800s, by the 1830s differences in social standing found the "help" commonly being referred to as "domestic servants." Social historian Faye Dudden observes that this change in the title of the servant also signaled a change in the status of the mistress. Noting that in the 1820s and 1830s the number of servants working "in an explicitly domestic sphere" had increased, Dudden sees evidence of the newly managerial status of middle-class women, who had "found the means to make domesticity more flexible, accommodating roles of authority and activity, rather than passivity and isolation."[1]

Early on, domestic servant roles were filled by young women making the transition from country life to city life and in search of employment. By the 1840s, however, immigrants were hired in the majority of house-holds, as young American women sought other options for work.

As the middle class became more affluent, their homes increased in size. With domestic servants in residence, the Victorian woman devoted additional time to entertaining and decorating the home. As household manager, she would instruct and oversee her staff, but she still remained a "hands-on" policy in regard to certain tasks. For example, many middle-class women prided themselves on their ability to bake excellent breads or turn out exquisite cakes and would balk at turning such jobs over to domestics. These were better suited to laundry work, house cleaning and preparing the everyday meals.

For women in the antebellum North, having two or three servants—usually a cook and chambermaid—may have decreased their physical labor, but it created new problems. Often the mistress had to spend a great deal of time educating poorly trained young girls, many of whom presented linguistic barriers, in routine tasks, cooking methods and the ways of the household. According to the advice manuals the wife was to consider it a blessing and a social obligation to train others in the art of housekeeping.

In contrast, for women in the South, slave plantations and farms actually increased the physical workload of the stereotypical Southern belle. She was responsible for the basic necessities of the slaves (food and clothing) and had to tend to their health needs. She saw to a large garden that produced fruits and vegetables and the dairy, which provided milk and eggs. At a time when many Northern women could increasingly rely on store-bought goods, the Southern mistress was constantly working to provide and replenish the food supply. Catherine Clinton notes that "although women in commercial society were able to become conspicuous consumers, plantation mistresses were far likelier to be inconspicuous producers."[2]

For young women who had been schooled in foreign languages, music and needlecrafts, the early Victorian period had its share of advice and cookery books that guided them in the art of housekeeping. Favorites included *The Virginia Housewife or Methodical Cook* by Mary Randolph, *The American Frugal Housewife* by Lydia Maria Child, *The Lady's Receipt Book* by Eliza Leslie and the *The House Book; or a Manual of Domestic Economy for Town and Country*, also by Eliza Leslie. In *The House Book*, 1840, Leslie discussed the importance of housekeeping, telling readers:

*A neat and well-conducted house, with fires and lights always as they should be; and a table where the food is inviting, from being good both in material and cooking; also clothes well washed and ironed, are comforts that are not lightly prized by any married man; and it is but just that he who perhaps labours hard in his business or profession to procure the means of obtaining them, should not be disappointed in their application, particularly when the deficiencies are caused by the inertness or the mis-management of the woman who should consider it her especial care to render his home agreeable to him.*[3]

During the 1860s drastic changes took place in middle-class households both North and South. The Civil War and the 13th Amendment, freeing slaves, forever altered the way of life in the South, and unstable economic conditions forced many Northeners to cut costs and simplify their lifestyles.

An 1869 book entitled *The Philosophy of Housekeeping* commented on these changes:

> *One of the effects of the war which has just closed has been to bring our American society into much closer resemblance to the European civilization. It has exaggerated the differences between the upper and lower classes. By this means, the large middle class has been greatly diminished. A fraction of it has been raised above modest independence, which they formerly enjoyed, to the possession of wealth and the indulgence in luxury; while by far the larger portion, with incomes but little increased, and prices often more than doubled, have a far harder struggle to make ends meet than they had ten years ago.*[4]

Even those middle-class families that could afford to keep or hire domestic servants often found such help was difficult to obtain after the war. With the industrial revolution came a variety of factory and service-related jobs, and many newly arriving immigrants chose the questionable working conditions and meager pay of such positions over domestic work with its implied class distinctions and isolation from family and friends. As a result, by the late 1860s and early 1870s many Victorian women had little choice but to manage their homes with limited help (or no help at all) and began to assume responsibility for a greater number of tasks within their own kitchens and laundry rooms.[5]

To help women complete the mind-boggling array of chores carried out in the typical middle-class household, domestic science authorities recommended they follow habits of "system" and "order." The Beecher sisters offered a model schedule for housework in *The American Woman's Home:*

> *Some persons endeavor to systematize their pursuits by apportioning them to particular hours of each day. For example, a certain period before breakfast, is given to devotional duties; after breakfast, certain hours are devoted to exercise and domestic employments; other hours to sewing, or reading, or visiting; and others, to benevolent duties. But in most cases, it is more difficult to systematize the hours of each day, than it is to secure some regular division of the week . . . Monday, with some of the best housekeepers, is devoted to preparing for the labors of the week. Any extra cooking, the purchasing of articles to be used during the week, the assorting of clothes for the wash, and mending . . . these, and similar items, belong to this day. Tuesday is devoted to washing, and Wednesday to ironing. On Thursday,*

*A typical middle-class kitchen of the 1870s included a worktable,*
*coal and/or wood-burning cast-iron range, a pantry for storing staples*
*and dishware and a wooden "dry sink" with water faucets.*
*Small attempts at decoration can be seen in the*
*framed print on the wall above the table*
*and the potted plant.*

*the ironing is finished off, the clothes are folded and put away, and all articles which need mending are put in the mending-basket, and attended to. Friday is devoted to sweeping and house-cleaning. On Saturday, and especially the last Saturday of every month, every department is put in order; the casters and table furniture are regulated, the pantry and cellar inspected, the trunks, drawers, and closets arranged, and everything about the house put in order for Sunday. By this regular recurrence of a particular time for inspecting every thing, nothing is forgotten till ruined by neglect.*[6]

The kitchen was the primary factorylike work center in the Victorian home. During the early 19th century, plantation kitchens in the South were frequently located in a separate building at the rear of the main house, while in urban centers both North and South, the kitchen was often located in the basement. In other homes the kitchen was typically found in the back of the house, as far away as possible from the "public" rooms used for entertaining.

Since it was a work center, little thought was given to making the kitchen attractive and comfortable. It was serviceable but lacking in any sort of planned convenience. The main furnishings consisted of a worktable and assorted free-standing cupboards for storage. A pantry was included for keeping staples and extra kitchenware. The industrial revolution provided a wide assortment of machine-made gadgets and utensils designed to ease workloads and speed up production in the kitchen. Not all improved gadgetry lived up to its expectations but cast-iron apple parers, egg beaters and cherry stoners were among the new items that were put to use during the 1850s and 1860s.

Hearth cooking had become obsolete by the mid-19th century as cast-iron cookstoves and ranges took center stage in the kitchen. The introduction of the cookstove advanced cooking methods, redefined meal planning and also eliminated the strenuous work of lifting heavy iron cookware to and from the hearth. However, many of the new stoves were difficult to operate and required constant attention.

To help women master their cookstoves, prepare a variety of meals and tend to all the other duties associated with housekeeping, a plethora of cookbooks and home manuals were published during the second half of the 19th century. Among other things, the all-purpose household cyclopaedias (as they were called) usually included chapters on household management, cooking recipes, cooking for the sick, domestic medicine, tables of weights and measures, nursing the sick and destroying domestic pests. A select

The frontispiece of the cookbook section found in Catharine
Beecher's 1873 book The New Housekeeper's Manual.
This work was published as an expanded and
updated version of her hugely popular
The American Woman's Home.

listing of the more popular cookbooks and home manuals of the day includes the *Common Sense in the Household* series by Marion Harland, *The Successful Housekeeper* by M. W. Ellsworth and F. B. Dickerson, *The White House CookBook* by Mrs. F. L. Gillette and Hugo Ziemann, *Cooking Manual* by Miss Juliet Corson, *Appledore Cook Book* and *Miss Parloa's New Cookbook and Marketing Guide* by Maria Parloa, *Boston School Kitchen Text-Book* by Mrs. Mary Lincoln, *The Boston Cooking-School Cook Book* by Fannie Farmer and of course, the hugely popular *The American Woman's Home* by Catharine Beecher and Harriet Beecher Stowe.

Like the authors of etiquette books, those who wrote cookbooks and home manuals used their publications to convey strong opinions on popular concerns of the Victorian era. Marion Harland routinely included a "Familiar Talk with the Reader" in her works to emphasize the value and importance of housekeeping during a time (the last quarter of the century) when many women were questioning their roles and the sacrifices they made in the name of keeping house.

Marion Harland and others were also adamant that daughters learn to cook and keep house. For example in *The Everyday Cook-Book and Family Compendium* by Miss E. Neil (circa 1880s), the author wrote:

*Yes, yes learn how to cook, girls; and learn how to cook well. Let all girls have a share in housekeeping at home before they marry; let each superintend some department by turns. It need not occupy half the time to see that the house has been properly swept, dusted, and put in order, to prepare puddings and make dishes, that many young ladies spend in reading novels which enervate both mind and body and unfit them for everyday life. Women do not, as a general rule, get pale faces doing housework. Their sedentary habits, in overheated rooms, combined with ill-chosen food, are to blame for ill health. Our mothers used to pride themselves on their housekeeping and fine needlework. Let the present generation add to its list of real accomplishments the art of properly preparing food for the human body.*[7]

Magazines, too, played an important role in educating women in cookery methods and household work and routines. Publications such as *Godey's Lady's Book* and *Peterson's Magazine* included recipes, home-related advice and needlework projects. Others, such as *The House Wife* magazine, focused specifically on cooking, domestic chores, child rearing and sewing skills.

VOL. 5.—No. 11.      NEW YORK, MARCH, 1890.      50 CENTS A YEAR.

Advice pertaining to household matters, cooking, cleaning and so on
could be found in several popular magazines including The House Wife.
From the title page of the March 1890 issue, the slogan
"The housewife makes the home and the home makes the
nation" echoed increasingly old-fashioned sentiment.

Housework involving cleaning also benefited from new inventions and improved 19th-century technology. For example, by the 1860s, carpet sweepers had been invented and the old-fashioned method of "dusting" rugs with a broom was happily left by the wayside. Also, laundry work was supposedly made easier with one of the new washers introduced during the 1860s; nevertheless, in many households older methods (using a washboard and copper boiler) prevailed, for some of the new machines had a tendency to rip or stain clothing and precious linens.

Having a well-stocked pantry or storeroom was a priority during the Victorian age and the mistress of the house was responsible for making sure necessary supplies were on hand. In addition, as increasing numbers of women were forced to return to the kitchen during the late 19th century, they welcomed new and innovative kitchen tools, household gadgets and packaged or canned foods as time savers. With this in mind, *The White House Cook Book* included the following list of items every housekeeper should have on hand in the kitchen:

2 Sweeping Brooms and 1 Dust Pan
1 Wisk Broom
1 Bread Box
2 Cake Boxes
1 large Flour Box
1 Dredging Box
1 large-sized tin Pepper Box
1 Spice Box containing smaller Spice Boxes
2 Cake Pans (two sizes)
4 Bread Pans
2 square Biscuit Pans
1 Apple Corer
1 Lemon Squeezer
1 Meat Cleaver
3 Kitchen Knives and Forks
1 large Kitchen Fork
4 Kitchen Spoons (two sizes)
1 Wooden Spoon for Cake Making
1 large Breadknife
1 Griddle
1 Griddle Cake Turner
1 Potato Masher
1 Meat Board

1 dozen Patty Pans and the same number of Tartlet Pans
1 Large Tin Pail and 1 Wooden Pail
2 small Tin Pails
1 set of Tin Basins
1 set of Tin Measures
1 Wooden Butter Ladle
1 Tin Skimmer
1 Tin Steamer
Dippers (two sizes)
2 Funnels (two sizes)
1 set of Jelly Cake Tins
4 Milk Pans
1 Strainer
1 dozen iron Gem Pans or Muffin Rings
1 coarse Gravy Strainer, one fine
1 Colander
1 Flour Sifter
2 Scoops (one for flour, one for sugar)
2 Jelly Molds (two sizes)
1 Can Opener
1 Eggbeater
1 Corkscrew
1 Chopping Knife
2 Wooden Chopping Bowls (two sizes)
1 Meat Saw
2 large Earthen Bowls
4 Stone Jars
1 Coffee Mill
1 Candlestick
2 Market Baskets (two sizes)
1 Clock
1 Ash Bucket
1 Gridiron
2 Frying Pans (two sizes)
4 Flat-irons (two #8 and two #6 pounds)
2 Dripping Pans (two sizes)
3 Iron Kettles (Porcelain-lined if possible)
1 Corn Beef or Fish Pan
1 Tea Kettle
2 Granite-ware Stewpans (two sizes)

1 Wire Toaster
1 Double Kettle for cooking custards, grains, etc.
2 Sugar Boxes (one for coarse, one for fine)
1 Waffle Iron
1 Step Ladder
1 Stove (and one coal Shovel)
1 Pair Scales
4 Pie Pans
3 Pudding Molds (one for boiling, two for baking, two sizes)
2 Dish Pans (two sizes)
2 Cake or Biscuit Cutters (two sizes)
2 Graters (one large, one small)
1 Coffee Canister
1 Tea Canister
1 Tin or Granite-ware Teapot
1 Tin or Granite-ware Coffeepot
2 Coal Hods or Buckets
1 Kitchen Table, two Kitchen Chairs
1 large Clothes Basket
1 Wash Boiler, one Washboard
8 dozen Clothes Pins
1 large Nail Hammer and one small Tack Hammer
1 Bean Pot
1 Clothes Wringer

Regarding the above list the authors remarked, "An ingenious housewife will manage to do with less conveniences, but these articles, if they can be purchased in the commencement of housekeeping, will save time and labor, making the preparation of food more easy—and it is always economy in the end to get the best material in all wares."[8]

During the late 19th and early 20th centuries the growing houseware industry employed savvy marketing techniques to attract the middle-class consumer. In an era when employing domestic servants was on the decline, many household and kitchen items were promoted as the new "servants." According to a 1904 article, in 1870 one out of every eight families had a domestic servant while by the year 1900 it was only one in fifteen families.[9]

Regardless of how many labor-saving devices a middle-class Victorian mistress acquired for her home, there was still an overwhelming amount of work to be done—much more than one servant could possibly tend to. While reluctant to give up her role as household manager, the majority of women nevertheless assumed responsibility for an increasing number of tasks to maintain appearances and a socially acceptable standard of living. Toward this end, the advice literature published during the 1890s and early 1900s offered work schedules for the one-servant household. For example, in her book *Home Comfort*, Mrs. Logan proposed the following arrangement in regard to a weekly work schedule: Beginning with Monday, she wrote:

*The one maid must rise early enough to accomplish part of the washing before breakfast. By rising at five, there will be two hours before it is time to lay the table and prepare the first meal. After having cooked the breakfast and waited the table, the girl sets before her mistress a neat dish-pan, a mop, and two clean towels; then takes the heavy dishes, knives and forks into the kitchen, while the lady shakes and folds the table-cloth, sweeps the dining room with a light broom and dusts it carefully, opening the windows to air the apartment, and then proceeds to set the parlor in order. Meanwhile, the servant should go to the chambers, turn the mattresses, make the beds, and then go back to the kitchen, clean the pots and kettles used in preparing breakfast, and then devote her undivided attention to the heavy work of washing. Care should be taken to choose a plain dinner—steaks or chops, potatoes, and some ready-made dessert. The afternoon is occupied by finishing the washing, hanging out the clothes, and getting the tea, which must be a meal easily cooked; for the tidying up of the kitchen is yet to be done before the girl can rest. It will be of great assistance, in places where the visiting is sufficiently informal to permit it, if some member of the family opens the door on busy days. Tuesday by general consent, is assigned to the work of ironing; and here it will usually be necessary for the mistress to lend a hand, and aid in clear-starching and ironing the fine clothing. Wednesday is devoted to baking part of the cake, bread and pies that will be needed during the week. In this work the mistress helps by washing the currants, stoning the raisins, beating the eggs, and making light pastry. Often a lady who has a taste for cooking makes all the desserts, cakes and pies. She should never consider it extravagant to supply herself with the best cooking utensils—egg-beaters, sugar-sifters, double-boilers, etc., and, if a good housekeeper, she will find both pride and pleasure in her jars of home-made pickles and preserves. Thursday the maid must sweep the house thoroughly, for this work, if the carpets are heavy, requires strength. The mistress then dusts room after room, and, last of all, the servant follows with a step-ladder to wipe off mirrors and windows. Friday is commonly occupied in general house-cleaning: scrubbing the floors, cleaning the brasses and silver, scouring the knives, and putting linen-*

*closets and drawers in order. Saturday is filled with baking bread and cake, preparing the Sunday dinner so that the servant may have her Sunday afternoon out, and the toil of the week closes with a thoroughly swept and orderly house, a clean kitchen, and all the cooking done except the meat and vegetables for the Sunday dinner.*[10]

Women who could not afford a live-in domestic servant or could not find someone suitable to fill the position often hired part-time workers to do the laundry (if the laundry was not sent out), assist with preparations for formal dinners and help with seasonal house cleaning.

Another area of Victorian home management centered on spring and/or fall house cleaning. Oil-burning lamps, gas lamps and coal/woodburning stoves left soot and residue on furnishings, draperies and bric-a-brac, requiring seasonal cleanings. The Victorian house was literally torn apart from garret (the attic) to cellar and walls, windows and floors were dusted, washed, disinfected and often painted. Furniture was polished, repaired or reupholstered, and rugs and curtains cleaned. Every room was tended to in this ritualistic cleaning that usually took a week or more to complete. Also, if the major cleaning was done in the spring, the house was often made ready for the warm summer months by packing away heavy draperies and rugs to make way for lighter lace window dressings, sisal floor coverings and furniture slipcovers.

The work involved in maintaining a household was increasingly viewed from a "scientific" standpoint as the century progressed. By the late 1800s concern over the spread of disease, availability of packaged foods and new technologies related to the home transformed the factory-like kitchen of the period between the 1830s and 1880s into a down-sized, sanitary work center. By the turn of the century middle-class kitchens were commonly found on the first floor of the home and indoor plumbing made hot and cold running taps a reality. This laboratory-like kitchen sported crisp painted or tiled walls, linoleum floors and sinks with exposed undersides to prevent the harboring of germs. Wooden iceboxes kept perishables cool and close at hand and the baker's cupboard (a free-standing cupboard with a built-in flour bin, storage areas and a wooden or zinc work top) gave women a centralized work station for preparing meals. Gas stoves were slowly replacing coal/woodburning models. This "planned" kitchen with more organized space eliminated the need for servants.

Even the work itself was now referred to by experts as the "Science of Housewifery" and the American Home Economics Association had been formed to help instruct women across the country in housekeeping "techniques" and more nutritional meal planning. During the early 1900s the Science of Housewifery focused on the four branches of housework: cooking, cleaning, laundry and chamber work.

Cooking increasingly involved prepared foods as women continued the shift from producer in the kitchen to full-fledged consumer of everything from boxed cereals and canned meats to store-bought breads and ready-to-heat soups. In addition, electric appliances were making their debut during the early 1900s and many women found they had traded physical labors for the mind-numbing drudgery associated with opening boxes and cans and turning dials on the stove.

Cleaning still revolved around daily, weekly, monthly and seasonal schedules during the early 1900s, and the Victorian housewife continued to prepare most of her own cleaning solutions, although soaps and polishes were available at stores.

Laundry work, usually begun on Monday or Tuesday, continued to take two days to complete with all the ironing involved. Sadirons made of cast iron were heated atop the stove and most women had several on hand, along with a smaller iron for pressing collars and delicate trim.

Chamberwork referred to the daily routine of washing bedside commodes and slop jars in homes without indoor bathrooms. Also, the washstand and accessory items were cleaned, beds were aired and then made and the entire room put in order.

Throughout the Victorian era popular mantras in regard to domestic undertakings included "A place for everything, and everything in its place," "The way to a man's heart is through his stomach" and "Cleanliness is next to godliness." Most women zealously complied, but at what cost? Perhaps one young housekeeper said it best when she wrote the following letter to author Marion Harland during the 1870s:

*I wish you could set me right on one point that often perplexes me. Is housekeeping worth while? I do not despise the necessary work. On the contrary, I hold that anything well done is worth doing. Is it worth while for a woman to neglect the talents she has in order to have a perfectly appointed house? To wear herself out chasing around after servants and children that things may always be done well, and at the started time? I have seen so many women of brains wear out and die in harness, trying to do their self-imposed duty. And these women could have been so happy and enjoyed the life they threw away, if they'd only known how **not** to keep house. I should not mind if one*

*could ever say "it is a well-finished thing!" But you only finish one thing to
begin over again, and so on, until you die and have nothing to show for
your life's work. It looks hopeless to me, I confess. I wish you would show me
the wisdom—or the folly of it all.*[11]

## HANDIWORK AND ORNAMENTAL NEEDLEWORK

Throughout the Victorian era, sewing skills were considered a necessity, both for the utilitarian purpose of making clothes and linens and as a banner of womanly virtue.

As soon as a young girl could hold a needle (often by the age of five or six), she was instructed by her mother or female members of the family in needlecraft arts. Samplers, a popular learning tool in the 17th and 18th centuries, continued to be an important means for young girls to develop reading skills and practice sewing stitches during the early Victorian period. According to C. Kurt Dewhurst, Betty MacDowell and Marsha MacDowell, authors of *Artists In Aprons,* "Essentially a piece of cloth containing examples of embroidered letters, design motifs, verses, pictures, and the maker's name, the sampler was an almost universal creative medium."[12] In addition to proving a young girl had indeed mastered a vitally important skill, samplers were also viewed by many "as badges of readiness for womanhood."[13]

The importance of mastering the sewing needle was driven home again and again in the advice literature of the day. In *Letters To Young Ladies,* Mrs. Sigourney wrote:

> *Needle-work in all its forms of use, elegance and ornament, has ever been
> the appropriate occupation of woman. From the shades of Eden, when its
> humble process was but to unite the fig-leaf down to modern times, when
> nature's pencil is rivaled by the most exquisite tissues of embroidery, it has
> been both their duty and their resource. While the more delicate efforts of
> the needle rank high among accomplishments, its necessary departments are
> not beneath the notice of the most refined young lady.*[14]

While samplers were a common means of practicing sewing skills during the early decades of the 19th century, by the mid-Victorian period "amusing" ways of instructing daughters in needlework were recommended. The Beecher sisters advised readers:

*When a little girl begins to sew, her mother can promise her a small bed*
*and pillow, as soon as she has sewed a patch quilt for them; and then a*
*bedstead, as soon as she has sewed the sheets and cases for pillows; and then*
*a large doll to dress, as soon as she has made the undergarments; and thus*
*go on till the whole contents of the baby-house are earned by the needle*
*and skill of its little owner. Thus the task of learning to sew will become*
*a pleasure.*[15]

The Beecher sisters also believed young girls should master a variety of
sewing stitches, including the overstitch, hemming, the running stitch,
backstitching, the buttonhole stitch, chain stitching, darning, gathering
and the cross-stitch.[16]

Prior to the invention of the sewing machine in the 1840s, women spent
a major portion of their time making clothing for all the members of the
family. Daughters were trained early to the task, and sometimes a seamstress
was hired by the family to assist with the bulk of the work, which was done
during the cooler months. For special articles of clothing, such as fancy
evening wear, a dressmaker might be commissioned to complete the
garment.

Popular periodicals such as *Godey's Lady's Book* early on included color
and black-and-white fashion plates of the latest styles from Paris. Such plates
depicted evening dresses, carriage dresses, walking dresses, bridal gowns,
riding habits and morning dresses. Children's clothing was included as well
as bonnets, caps and cloaks. Women could send to the magazine for tissue
paper patterns to make assorted items of wear featured in the magazine, and
they could even purchase hats or shawls illustrated and advertised by
big-city specialty shops.

Publications such as *Godey's Lady's Book* welcomed the sewing machine
as a "celebrated family aid." In the August 1855 issue, publisher Louis
Godey told readers that

*every family in the United States ought to have one, and would if they only*
*knew the saving and quality of work that can be done in a day. Once hav-*
*ing mastered the little difficulties incident to a proper understanding of the*
*machine, the housekeeper feels that with its help she can easily compass the*
*important part of her duties—the clothing of her family. The spring sewing*
*or the fall sewing for half a dozen children, loses its formidable aspect,*
*when a yard of handsome and substantial stitching can be run off in two*
*minutes. That never-ending, still-beginning drudgery of the needle need not*

*much longer be counted among the grievances of humanity; for no woman
of the least enterprise or spirit will long submit to sit stitching from dawn to
dark, at a garment which could be better done in forty minutes. As to the
cost of the machine, where there is an objection, several families in a neighborhood may contribute to the purchase.*[17]

With the average sewing machine costing around $70 during the
mid-1850s, it was indeed a sizable investment in terms of money. The
popularity of the machine, however, was indicative of its time-saving
benefits, and by the 1860s few middle-class households could make do
without a sewing machine. Sarah J. Hale, highly respected long-time editor
of *Godey's Lady's Book*, elaborated on the advantages of the sewing machine
when she reported that hand stitching a man's shirt required "more than
twenty thousand stitches."[18]

As women became accustomed to using their machines, they became
more elaborate in decorating and accessorizing their garments. The September 1855 *Godey's Lady's Book* made note of this:

*The autumn ribbons are, as usual, very rich in color and variety of shad-
ing. Plaids and stripes of moire and velvet, with taffeta, either in the same
or contrasting colors, are the favorites. Never was there a season when
ribbons were more in use for dresses, mantles, even chemisettes and un-
dersleeves. In all our large cities ribbon stores have become a feature. They
sometimes have embroideries also; but other establishments deal in nothing
else. Every hue of the rainbow—every shade of heaviness or delicacy in
material is represented.*[19]

This penchant for ornamentation continued, and 12 years later the February 1867 *Godey's Lady's Book* was reporting that decorative beads were in
vogue for dresses as well as bonnets, and silk fringe, crystal fringes and
buttons were turning up in beautiful designs.[20]

Given the amount of work that must have been required to ornament
women's clothing, even in middle-class households where a sewing machine
was in use the wife often employed a seamstress to assist with the sewing.
In those homes without benefit of this new technology, a seamstress would
bring her own machine and stay for two or three weeks to complete the
family wardrobe.

Some domestic science experts were concerned the sewing machine
would be the demise of women's needlecraft skills. In an advice tome

published in 1879, a wise and experienced woman known as Aunt Sophronia dispenses advice on all manner of household concerns. In regard to sewing, she questions her audience:

> *Can you sew? Can you cut out garments? Can you make, mend and re-make? Rich or poor, every woman should know how to do this; if she is rich, she may be poor some day and need the knowledge, or she can now do this work for the objects of her charity, and so increase her means of usefulness. Every woman should be a good seamstress as well as a good housekeeper, whether she be obliged to use her needle herself or not. There is a growing neglect of nice hand-sewing.*[21]

Along with the actual work of making clothing (as well as towels, bedding and linens), there was also constant mending and altering to be done. One advice giver of the early 1870s commented that "things neatly mended last four times as long as those carelessly repaired. All things should be periodically examined. Sew up torn linings, rebind frayed edges, and replace broken strings, buttons, and hooks, directly seen, or the trouble will be greatly increased. Never forget the well-known aphorism, 'A stitch in time saves nine.'"[22]

Ready-made clothing was increasingly available during the second half of the 19th century, but many middle-class women, especially those living in small towns and rural areas, continued to produce the family clothes. Store-bought clothing was the exception rather than the rule until department stores and mail-order catalogs became commonplace during the last quarter of the century. For example, the Spring and Summer 1886 Bloomingdale's catalog touted the success of the store's Dressmaking Department, boasting that "neither pains or expense are spared in securing the services of the most skillful artists, who are able to reproduce the original European designs, and competent to design modes to suit the demands of this fashionable country. No pains are spared in the execution of orders entrusted to us."[23] Nancy Villa Bryk, a modern curator of domestic artifacts who wrote the introduction to a recent reprint of this catalog, notes the extraordinary degree to which the store was willing to follow its female customers' specifications. Not only were clothes custom fitted, but fabrics, colors and trims were all carefully chosen to suit the purchaser's particular needs and tastes. Even her complexion was recorded so that the dressmakers and milliners could recommend appropriately flattering colors.[24]

*Entitled "A Stitch in Time Saves Nine," this illustration from an 1866 issue of* Peterson's Magazine *conveys the importance of learning sewing skills at an early age and reminds women of the economy of time and labor saved by prompt attention to mending work.*

A wide variety of clothing and accessory items could be ordered from Bloomingdale's and other mail-order catalogs, including dresses or suits for women, children's suits and dresses, cloaks, shawls, underwear for the entire family, night gowns, infants' wear, hosiery, gloves, hats, shoes and clothing for men. By 1910 women's clothing was available in standard sizes, eliminating the need to send precise measurements when ordering.

Although middle-class women were increasingly active consumers of ready-made garments during the late Victorian era, home sewing remained a popular practice. Magazines continued to depict the latest fashions with patterns available for home use, and advice columns, such as "The Home Dressmaker," which ran in *Ladies' Home Journal* during the 1890s, were widely read.

Where did Victorian women perform the bulk of their handiwork? If the middle-class home was large enough, a bedroom was often designated a "sewing room." If not, the sitting room would include a sewing stand or workbox and a tabletop or free-standing treadle sewing machine. The tools of this particular area of her domestic trade included sundry items such as scissors, pincushions, needles, threads, bolts of fabric, buttons, buttonhole scissors, a darner, embroidery hoops, a tape measure, thimbles, etc.

Making clothing (whether by hand or machine) resulted in large amounts of scrap material that was put to good use as hand-stitched blankets or coverlets. Victorian women were avid quilt makers and young girls were trained early on in the production of these utilitarian bedcovers. Patchwork quilts were created by stitching scraps together in often beautiful designs that where then "quilted" to a filling and a backing. While many such quilts were individually crafted the enormity of such a project often made it a communal effort, resulting in groups that were united by shared labor and camaraderie and were known as "quilting bees." Especially popular in small towns and rural areas, the quilting bee was a "uniquely American institution" that gave middle-class women the opportunity to socialize with others as they completed a quilt project.[25]

Quilting not only provided serviceable goods for the home and gave women an opportunity to share advice, common concerns and conversation; it also served in many cases as an outlet for creativity. The Victorian woman with an eye for color or a talent for design could express herself in the beauty of her quilt. Pattie Chase notes that "a woman made utility quilts as fast as she could so her family wouldn't freeze, and she made them as beautiful as she could so her heart wouldn't break."[26] Toward that end, one 19th-century advice giver suggested scraps of silk, satin, velvet, calico and cambric ideal for patchwork quilts, while rich fabrics were especially nice in creating mosaic, star or diamond-pattern quilts.[27] The more traditional quilt patterns remained popular throughout the Victorian era, especially in rural areas. In contrast, the "crazy quilt," inspired by the late 19th-century penchant for anything of an exotic nature, was typically produced by urban middle-class women during the late 1800s. A crazy quilt was made of silk patches (of various shapes and bold colors) stitched together and embellished with gold thread.

In regard to ornamental needlework, the early Victorian period found women knitting and practicing crochet. Berlin wool work (similar to needlepoint) was also quite popular. Tatting, point-lace work, silk embroidery and macramé became favorite pastimes during the late 19th century. Women created a variety of decorative objects for the home, including knitted baskets, needlework that was framed, wall pockets, bookmarks, pillows, hooked rugs, crocheted antimacassars (a protective doily for chair or sofa backs), assorted tea cloths, table scarves, and linens embellished with silk embroidery. Decorative needle arts were so widely practiced that if the Victorian woman had callers while she was occupied with a needlecraft project, it was perfectly acceptable for her to continue her work while conversing with guests. This, in fact, reflected very positively on her, proving her both accomplished and industrious.

As the century progressed and industry made great strides, all sorts of kits became available for needlecraft enthusiasts. Especially popular during the last quarter of the 19th century, perforated cardboard with stamped or printed words or mottoes were embroidered and framed for home use. As moral guardians of the home and all who dwelled within, many such needlework projects had a religious theme. The concept of the "Christian Home" as described by the Beecher sisters in *The American Woman's Home*, along with the Romantic Evangelicalism and Protestantism of the age, gave rise to the popularity of such works. Typical mottoes included "God Bless Our Home," "Give Us This Day Our Daily Bread," "Bless This House," "Faith, Hope and Charity," "Rock of Ages," "God is Love" and "In God We Trust." A modern scholar might take a somewhat critical view of such mottoes, noting, as Kenneth L. Ames does, that they were an accessible, inexpensive, relatively simplistic way to dramatically state one's "commitment to the community of the faithful." Ames adds that "these mottoes made it easy to be a moral mother . . . It was easy to create and enshrine words to live by."[28] Such modern distaste notwithstanding, mottoes were ubiquitous in Victorian America. Placed above the mantel, over a doorway

*Along with sewing to provide the necessary clothing and linens*
*for the Victorian family and household, middle-class women*
*also became skilled in other types of needlework to decorate*
*their homes. Patterns such as this circa 1867 basket,*
*which could be used in making curtains or antimacassars,*
*were regularly featured in leading women's magazines.*

HOME WORK, HANDIWORK AND LEISURE

or in a high place of honor upon the wall, various mottoes (the majority of which did convey religious sentiments) embellished the homes of the middle class until the 1890s, when home was no longer viewed in idealistic terms.

Along with the needlework kits made available to women during the late 1800s, women's magazines contained sections, such as the "Work Department" in *Godey's Lady's Book*, offering instructions, patterns, stencils and whatever else was needed for decorative needlework projects; thread companies produced small advertising booklets with assorted projects as well. Specialty publications such as *The Home Needlework Magazine*, were quite popular during the early years of the 20th century. Also, in addition to needlework projects for decorating the home, magazines and all-purpose home manuals included instructions for smaller items that could be quickly made as gifts or to raise funds at fancy fairs and charitable bazaars. For example, the August 1885 *Godey's Lady's Book* contained the following: "Pretty sachets for wedding presents are made of white or pale-blue satin, in the form of large envelope turned down at one corner and fastened with a silver button. This is trimmed all around with a silver lace. On the back can be embroidered a wreath of orange-blossoms or other flowers, with the monogram of the bride embroidered in silver in the centre. The same makes a lovely quilt for a sofa."[29]

Domestic needlework, whether for utilitarian or decorative purposes, was directly influenced by assorted machinery arising from the industrial revolution. By the last quarter of the 19th century technological advances in the sewing machine had, for the most part, turned the home-based production of clothing into a factory-based commercial industry. In addition, domestic needlework often became "a solitary pastime where it had once been the handmaiden of many a social event."[30] In other words, progress in the form of the sewing machine had reduced women's burden significantly but at the same time eliminated the need for communal gatherings such as the quilting bee.

# HOME CRAFTS AND LEISURELY PURSUITS

For middle-class Victorian women, advice givers recommended that whatever leisure time they had was best spent pursuing specific, acceptable craft works (such as those already discussed), instructional or light reading, and gardening.

Although many 19th- century women were zealous needleworkers, they also spent a considerable amount of time on other parlor crafts that contributed to the home's decor. Natural materials were highly favored for creating decorations on assorted objects, such as baskets embellished with moss or pine cones and picture frames bedecked with seashells.

Shell craft in fact had been a popular pastime throughout the Victorian period but reached its peak during the late 1800s. In the early decades of the Victorian era, shellwork resulted in small-scale projects such as figurines crafted from shells, or elaborate shell flowers that were protected under glass domes.[31] By the 1860s shellwork had become such a fad that Victorian women could purchase shells at seaside souvenir shops or order them from magazines such as *Godey's Lady's Book* if they were so inclined, rather than collect them on their own.

In *The American Woman's Home*, the Beecher sisters elaborated on the use of such natural materials in their chapter devoted to "Home Decorations." They were of the opinion that decorative items handcrafted for the home were not only economical, but a "means to educating the ingenuity and the taste."[32] They described in detail a picture frame that could be made for inexpensive "chromos" (chromolithographs):

> . . . you can make for yourselves pretty rustic frames in various modes. Take a very thin board, of the right size and shape, for the foundations or "mat;" saw out the inner oval or rectangular form to suit the picture. Nail on the edge a rustic frame made of branches of hard, seasoned wood, and garnish the corners with some pretty device; such, for instance, as a cluster of acorns; or, in place of the branches of trees, fasten on with glue small pine cones, with larger ones for corner ornaments. Or use the mosses of the wood or ocean shells for this purpose.[33]

Victorian women adorned innumerable objects, including plaques, frames, baskets, boxes, novelty items, flowerpots and small tables with shellwork and other natural materials. Craft books published during the last quarter of the 19th century offered countless ideas as well as instructions, and even the all-purpose household manuals included directions for working with shells. For example, by the late 1890s, when shellwork items could be bought ready-made at tourist destinations, one household guide instructed women "to fasten shells on wood or pasteboard—melt common resin and stir in about twice as much brick dust; use it like sealing wax. Or, use very thick gum water, in which finely-powdered whiting is stirred until it is thick."[34]

The romantic Victorian age had close ties to nature in all her forms, especially flowers. Throughout the 19th century, many craft projects revolved around floral or foliage motifs. Flowers were crafted from a variety of mediums and adorned numerous objects. For example, in the parlor craft known as potichomania (from the French word *potiche*, which means porcelain vase), women decorated the insides of glass vases with pasted paper cutouts and paints in floral motifs that resembled the beautiful artwork found on Chinese and Japanese porcelain. Découpage on the other hand, involved gluing paper cutouts on a surface in a pleasing design, and then covering it with several coats of varnish or lacquer. This also involved floral designs and was especially popular in decorating trays, privacy screens or vases.

Other parlor pastimes revolved around actually crafting flowers of fabric, wax, feathers or tissue paper. In regard to paper flowers, the June 1867 *Godey's Lady's Book* offered instructions for making tissue-paper hyacinths:

> *The paper may be pink, blue, violet, or yellow and white, according to taste. In the winter months, when flowers are scarce, a few of these hyacinths put into pots or glasses in a conservatory have a very good effect.*[35]

Likewise, an 1870s household guide told women:

> *Paper flowers may be easily made. They serve admirably to ornament a ball-room, to add to evergreens for Christmas decorations etc. Roses are simple in construction; a few sheets of pink, yellow, and crimson paper, a little green moss, iron wire, and green cotton being all the materials necessary. Hyacinths are also pretty and easily made. Dahlias require more careful cutting, and a paper pattern. The real flower should be carefully imitated.*[36]

The European custom of making hairwork jewelry and decorative items was another popular home craft introduced in America at midcentury. Victorian women were smitten with the concept of creating jewelry, wall art and trinkets from a loved one's hair as a token of remembrance and mourning as well as a sentimental gesture of love. This was noted in May 1855 *Godey's Lady's Book*: "Hair is at once the most delicate and lasting of our materials, and survives us, like love. It is so light, so gentle, so escaping from the idea of death, that with a lock of hair belonging to a child or friend, we may almost look up to heaven and compare notes with the angelic nature—may almost say 'I have a piece of thee here, not unworthy of thy being now.'"[37]

During the 1850s and 1860s, at the height of its popularity, making hairwork jewelry involved sorting hair by lengths and boiling it in soda water for several minutes before the actual work of braiding could be done. The finish work of applying clasps, etc., was done by a local jeweler.[38] *Godey's Lady's Book* gave the parlor craft its stamp of approval in December 1850:

> *Of the various employments for the fingers lately introduced among our country women, none is, perhaps more interesting than that we are about to describe, via. hairwork; a recent importation from Germany, where it is very fashionable. Hitherto almost exclusively confined to professioned manufacturers of hair trinkets, this work has now become a drawing-room occupation, as elegant and as free from all annoyances and objections of litter, dirt, or unpleasant smells as the much practiced knitting, netting or crochet can be. By acquiring a knowledge of this art, ladies will be themselves enabled to manufacture the hair of beloved friends, and relatives into the bracelets, chains, rings, and ear-rings.[39]*

Other attempts at handcrafting and home decoration during the late 19th and early 20th centuries included the art of pyrography, also called burned wood or poker decoration. Store-bought kits came complete with everything needed to burn a design into soft wood in order to make a variety of objects for home decoration. Boxes embellished with a burned-wood design were used for everything from sewing supplies and candy to collars and cuffs and hankies. Novelty items, picture frames, wall pockets, small tables and so on were also treated to burned-wood designs often enhanced with a watercolor wash to add a dash of color. An article appearing in the September 1896 issue of *Ladies' Home Journal* reported: "It will be easy for the reader in scanning the following list to imagine how readily it [burned-wood] may be adapted in the highest forms of interior decoration: Chimney panels, friezes, wall panels, wainscoting panels, set into sideboards and other heavy furniture, table tops, chair backs, hall benches and chests, book covers etc."[40] The majority of burned-wood projects completed by Victorian women at home were not so ambitious as those mentioned above, but many smaller objects were decorated with pyrography floral motifs, lettering, Indian maidens, Gibson Girl silhouettes, landscapes and other scenes. Depending upon one's artistic ability, kits could be purchased with or without a stamped design on the several hundred soft wood items available and waiting to be decorated. Like the other home crafts that women

*Middle-class women were expected to devote a certain amount of time to reading, not only for pleasure but self-improvement. As a leisure activity, exactly what women read (e.g., romantic novels) was often subject to controversy. This 1890 sketch from the book* The Home Manual *portrays the mistress of the house enjoying a quiet moment with her book.*

pursued, creating burned wood objects provided a way to productively pass time and economically beautify the home.

For middle-class Victorian women, snatches of time not devoted to their children, household concerns or social engagements were often spent reading. Popular weeklies such as *Harper's Weekly* and monthly periodicals such as *Peterson's, Godey's Lady's Book* or *Arthur's Home Magazine* were usually stacked near a comfortable chair in the sitting room. As enthusiastic readers, women made up the majority of those buying books and their preferences included poetry, educational works and popular novels.[41] One notable exception, however, was the Civil War era, when women in the South had to do without books and magazines because of blockades and paper shortages. In addition, despite the limited number of books that might have been available to them, they boycotted those by Northern authors, preferring instead to read works turned out by fellow Southerners.

Exactly what middle-class Victorian women should read was subject to strong opinion throughout the 19th century. Early on, many novels had a religious theme and were widely accepted as proper reading material. Also, the sentimental fiction that filled the pages of women's magazines was generally approved by the critics and moral guardians of the day because, as Richard L. Bushman notes in *The Refinement of America*, their theme revolved around "the war of fashion versus modesty, a plot that exposed and resolved the dilemmas of middle-class refinement."[42]

Ideally the Victorian woman would immerse herself in history books, biographies and poetry, which were promoted by critics and applauded for their lofty ideals and improving (or didactic) qualities. Books offering advice were themselves a popular genre, as should be clear from the many examples already cited, and the authors of such books did not hesitate to recommend yet more books as a source of edification and enjoyment. The following reading list, compiled by Richard A. Wells, was typical:

> *Books of Travel are both pleasing and healthful. Next, give attention to Bi-*
> *ography. Fiction, should have a place in our intellectual furnishing. Purity,*
> *beauty, breadth and power characterize Sir Walter Scott, and you will not*
> *err in placing him first. Read "Ivanhoe" or almost any other of his works.*
> *Dickens, Eliot and Bulwer will also come in for a share of your time. The*
> *works of master minds will afford as much pleasure and vastly more profit*
> *than the mass of mediocrities called "the latest novels." Now, to develop*
> *another set of intellectual muscles, we should change the exercise and read*
> *up on Science. Over against science put Poetry and the Drama in order to*

*preserve an intellectual equilibrium. Choose from among the poets such
ones as you find most congenial—Lowell, Whittier, Tennyson, Scott,
Longfellow—should be among your best friends. The poets are immortal;
they live because they deserve to, and because we need them for the softening
and beautifying of our lives.*[43]

Wells's recommendations for reading material are evidence of the emphasis
advice givers placed on high moral standards. Travel and science books
would educate; biographies would offer up good moral citizens Victorians
could emulate; and poetry and drama would balance weightier subject
materials with tributes to the beauty of nature, love, etc. Fiction by literary
giants such as Dickens could be read around the parlor table to the
enjoyment of all and then later discussed in polite society.

Women became avid readers during the Victorian era not only
because of an increase in leisure time and the affordability of books
(thanks to improved printing processes) but because reading was the
primary means of self-culture or self-improvement. Also, women were
largely responsible for educating their children and therefore continued
their own education, via books, as well. In many cases reading was not
so much a pleasure activity as it was a moral responsibility, and this
applied to both men and women.

Literary fiction was of course a special concern for critics and advice
givers. In looking at women as writers rather than as readers during the
midcentury period, the critics gave a nod of approval to such authors as
Louisa May Alcott and Harriet Beecher Stowe. Alcott's literary career began
with the publication of magazine articles followed by her books for young
people such as *A Modern Cinderella* and autobiographical works such as
*Little Women.* Her work as a Union nurse during the Civil War was the
subject of her memoirs, *Hospital Sketches.* Harriet Beecher Stowe also
authored several novels but is, of course, best known for her antislavery
novel *Uncle Tom's Cabin.* Works by other female writers, however, were often
strongly criticized. For example, watchdogs monitoring books opposed
Mrs. E. D. E. N. Southworth's 1859 novel *The Hidden Hand* in which the
assertive heroine forsakes her proper setting and role (in the home and as
domestic goddess) for adventure. Not only did the critics fear such romantic
novels would replace more cultured and learned reading, but as Louise L.
Stevenson points out, "From a Victorian perspective, the quality of women's
reading was crucial; if mothers read immoral books, they would teach their
children immoral lessons and ultimately jeopardize the future of society."[44]

By the late 19th century several female writers were recognized and widely read for their regional works or memoirs. Sarah Orne Jewett wrote extensively about village life in Maine in novels such as *The Country of the Pointed Firs* published in 1896; Lucy Larcom wrote *A New England Girlhood: Outlined from Memory*, which was published in 1889; Virginia Clay authored *A Belle of the Fifties: Memoirs of Mrs. Clay of Alabama*, which was popular during the early 1900s; and Elizabeth Cady Stanton recorded her memoirs in the 1898 *Eighty Years and More: Reminiscences, 1815–1897*. Perhaps best known, however, are the Civil War memoirs of South Carolinan Mary Chestnut.

In regard to what women should read, magazines also offered timely advice and kept women abreast of new books of merit with brief reviews of each. The qualities that *Godey's Lady's Book* admired in novels are evident in a May 1867 review of *The Claverings* by Anthony Trollope:

> *This is one of Mr. Trollope's happiest efforts. The aim of the story is to point out clearly not only the utter folly, but the great sinfulness of marrying for riches alone; while it illustrates, in perhaps more of a poetic than a strictly practical manner, how true love, having faith in itself, and a patience to wait, will at last meet its reward.*[45]

Reading was a significant part of middle-class life throughout the 19th century. It provided a road to self-culture, education and entertainment. As one advice manual succinctly put it: "Read we must and will, it is the passion of the present age."[46]

Gardening, both indoors and out, was another morally uplifting leisure activity during the Victorian age. Not only could it beautify the home and grounds, but cultivating flowers and greenery such as ferns was viewed by one advice giver as a means to "soften and refine the manners, make the heart innocently busy and happy, and encourage a love of home."[47]

It is not at all surprising Victorian middle-class women developed a keen interest in gardening; flowers were inextricably linked to the home in myriad ways. Rugs displayed large floral sprays, wallpapers depicted bouquets, blooms and petite blossoms, fabrics sported colorful floral and foliage motifs and decorative items throughout the house reinforced the floral theme. In *The Victorian Garden*, Allison Kyle Leopold tells us, "Nineteenth-century Americans turned to gardening with passion and fervor, and as with all their passions and pastimes, gardening played an important social role in their lives. Every activity, from cultivating a rose garden to creating a rockery . . . had symbolic associations."[48]

During the early Victorian period, women in both the North and South tended gardens of a different sort. The all-important kitchen garden fell under their care and provided the necessary fruits, vegetables and herbs that made their way to the dinner table and the medicine chest. Gardening purely for ornament was given little thought until the coffers of the middle class began to increase and women found the time to devote to concerns other than the basic needs of their families.

By the 1850s and 1860s architectural pattern books were extolling the virtues of the home's surroundings, paying special attention to the beauty in nature and planned landscape design. One of the most noted of such authors, Andrew Jackson Downing, served as editor of *The Horticulturist* magazine during the 1840s and early 1850s. Downing's first book, *A Treatise on the Theory and Practice of Landscape Gardening Adapted to North America*, was followed by his hugely popular architectural design books. Before long other such authors followed suit and landscaping became a common concern among the middle class. Women planted flower gardens big and small, and even urbanites reveled in the beauty of demure window boxes spilling over with colorful blooms that enhanced the home's appearance.

Looking from a different perspective, the Beecher sisters cited the health benefits of gardening in *The American Woman's Home*, telling mother that "occupations must be sought [for children] which exercise the muscles and interest the mind . . . Long and formal walks, merely for exercise, though they do some good . . . would be of triple benefit if changed to amusing sports, or to the cultivation of fruits and flowers, in which it is impossible to engage without acquiring a great interest."[49] In regard to young ladies, Catharine Beecher and Harriet Beecher Stowe professed, "One of the most useful and important [domestic amusements], is the cultivation of flowers and fruits. This, especially for the daughters of a family, is greatly promotive of health and amusement. . . . No father, who wishes to have his daughters grow up to be healthful women, can take a surer method to secure this end. Let him set apart a portion of his ground for fruits and flowers . . ."[50]

Not only was gardening applauded for its health benefits, but as the century progressed it was increasingly viewed as an outward display of gentility and womanly virtue. During the last quarter of the 19th century and on into the 20th century, cultivating a variety of flower gardens was common practice among middle-class women. Beautiful seed catalogs with chromolithographed images tempted them to plant assorted floral speci-

*Home gardening, a favorite leisure activity among middle-class women, was widely promoted as morally uplifting, physically beneficial and the ideal way to instruct small children regarding nature. By the late 1800s gardening had become big business, and numerous companies advertised in leading magazines. This particular advertisement by John Lewis Childs appeared in an 1896 Ladies' Home Journal.*

mens, many well suited to popular theme gardens of certain colors, oriental blooms, etc. Industry too responded by making available assorted factory-made garden tools, decorative items (such as containers and urns) and furnishings for outdoor areas. The number of books published for home gardeners increased and popular titles included *The American Gardener: A Treatise on the Situation, Soil and Laying Out of Gardens* by William Cobbett (1856), *The Art of Beautifying Suburban Home Grounds of Small Extent* by Frank Jesup Scott (1870), *Window Gardening* by Henry Williams (1873), *Every Woman Her Own Flower Garden* by Mrs. S. O. Johnson (1873), *A Garden in Pink* by Blanche Elizabeth Wade (1905) and *The Lure of the Garden* by Hildegarde Hawthorne (1911).

Regarding magazines, *The American Garden* was widely read (earlier in the century this publication had been known as *The Horticulturist*) and women's magazines included departments devoted to gardening concerns. The March 1890 issue of *The House Wife* reported the following on its "Flowers" page:

> *March is a peculiar month for the flower-lover; peculiar in that there is little work to do that shows satisfactory results. At this season of the year it is a good plan to consider what improvements in our work may be made over that of last year. If one has had a summer garden of geraniums, petunias, verbenas, coleus, ageratum and alyssum, suppose this summer we add to the above, lobelia, hydrangea, fuschias, and other plants of a similar nature, all of which will require about the same general care and culture as these we already have; we are thus above to improve our collection without detracting from the general effect. Look over the catalogues of the florist, seedmen and nurserymen and select your seeds, plants, or shrubs early that you may receive the cream of the stock.*[51]

Indoor gardening was also widely practiced during the Victorian era and went way beyond simply arranging fresh flowers and floral displays for the dining room or the parlor. During the 1860s and 1870s the Ward case, an enclosed terrarium with a glass dome or lid, was a popular means of cultivating ferns and other greenery indoors. In addition, beautiful ceramic jardinieres sporting large plants such as rubber trees, calla lilies or fuchsia, were carefully placed near windows in the parlor, and hanging plants such as ivy or flowering vines were suspended from window moldings. The long winter months also found women forcing bulbs indoors for cheerful blooms on long, gray days.

*Indoor gardens served not only to decorate the home, but provided the opportunity to garden all year round. A window garden, such as the one seen in this 1891 illustration, as well as larger conservatories, allowed women to force bulbs during winter months, get an early start on spring plantings and experiment with various types of flowers, foliage and ferns.*

During the 1890s and early 1900s architectural designs for middle-class homes often included large bay windows designed specifically for indoor gardening. *The Ladies' Home Journal* for September 1896 acknowledged this in "The Floral Bay Window" by Eben E. Rexford:

> *I would not advise the amateur to begin with a large miscellaneous collection, as she will be tempted to do. This is a good list for the beginner to choose from: Abutilon, Begonia, Calla, Chinese Primrose, Chrysanthemum, \*English Ivy, \*Ficus, Fuchsia, Geranium, \*Grevillea, Heliotrope, Lantana, Oleander, \*Palm, Primula Obconica and Streptosolen. Those marked with a star are grown for their foliage only.*[52]

While gardening as a leisure activity was considered morally uplifting, it also had the added benefit of creating a social climate middle-class women could actively participate in. Gardening clubs and competitions were established, and socializing often moved outdoors in the form of the "garden party." As the 19th century became more complex, gardening afforded the simple pleasure of getting back to basics—something Victorians were increasingly sentimental about as the 20th century approached.

# 6

# LIFE'S PASSAGES

Oh roses for the flush of youth,
And laurel for the perfect prime;
But pluck an ivy branch for me
Grown old before my time.

—Christina Georgina Rossetti

Victorian middle-class women faced numerous emotional and physical hardships during the course of their lives. As primary caregivers within the home, much of their adulthood was spent ministering to family members and friends when illness struck. In an era before modern medicine, sickness and disease were a constant threat and women had to be ever ready to dispense tonics, apply poultices and assist the doctor in bloodletting, applying leeches and other means to promote healing and recovery. Women, of course, were also subject to their own physical illnesses, and social reformers and doctors were quick in pointing to certain emotional conditions or maladies as the outcome of too much excitement or a less than ideal lifestyle.

Personal illness and caregiver responsibilities were not the only challenges facing women, however, as shorter life expectancy found them confronting old age in their 40s. If widowed, such women often encountered financial hardships and feelings that they had outlived their usefulness.

Many older women were dependent upon grown children for survival and emotional support.

Perhaps the greatest challenge of all, the rituals pertaining to death and mourning were generally considered woman's domain. Proper etiquette surrounding death and mourning customs became quite elaborate during the Victorian age, and by the late 1800s a specific dress code was in force. Also, the material culture entwined with death and mourning attire specified not only the proper black dress, but certain jewelry to be worn and special keepsakes for the home in order to remember and honor the dearly departed.

# SICKNESS AND HEALTH

Middle-class Victorian women were constantly concerned with their own health and the health of their family members. Health threats during the Victorian era included diseases such as yellow fever, whooping cough, cholera, diphtheria, influenza and tuberculosis. Other concerns, as reported in the 1859 book, *The Family and Householder's Guide*, included "scrofula, indigestion, bilious and liver complaints, lowness of spirits and nervous irritability and pulmonary consumption."[1] In many instances where doctors were unavailable, women had to be familiar with treatments for any number of life-threatening situations or sicknesses. One advice manual reported: "There is no point in which a woman needs more knowledge and discretion than in administering remedies for what seem slight attacks, which are not supposed to require the attention of a physician."[2]

Although hospitals were established in larger cities, they were viewed by the middle class as health-care institutions for the poor and working-class populations. Average families called upon physicians who made house calls, but due to time and distance the initial responsibility for treating illness and injury fell on women's shoulders.[3] In the antebellum South women had the added burden of caring for sick slaves, often turning a room in their home or a separate building on the plantation into an infirmary.

In addition to caring for the sick, women—especially in urban areas—paid calls on those who were ill. This became a structured part of their routine during the late 19th century, when paying "calls" was de rigueur among the middle class.

In the ongoing effort to safeguard themselves as well as beloved family members from sickness, Victorian women turned to medical guides, home manuals and magazine articles in order to learn means of preserving health. One advice tome told mothers and wives:

> *A healthy family, other things being equal, has a decided advantage, in the race of life, over one the health of whose members is feeble. Hence it is of the first importance to know, and to practice, the means for its preservation. Were proper attention given to this subject in our families, a vast sum of suffering and misery would be avoided, many valuable lives prolonged, and the anxieties, cares, loss of time and expense, resulting from unnecessary sickness would be saved.*[4]

Exactly what steps could the Victorian woman take to preserve her health and the health of her family? Fresh air was of primary concern in the home and especially in the bedrooms. They were to be aired daily, along with the bedding, to remove the "poisonous" vapors that accumulated during the night. In addition, many household authorities, including the Beecher sisters, were strong advocates of leaving a window cracked at night for a continual supply of fresh air. In 1869 *The American Woman's Home* commented:

> *There is a prevailing prejudice against night air as unhealthful to be admitted into sleeping-rooms, which is owing wholly to sheer ignorance. . . . When admitted from without into a sleeping-room it is colder, and therefore heavier, than the air within, so it sinks to the bottom of the room and forces out an equal quantity of the impure air, warmed and vitiated by passing through the lungs of inmates. Thus the question is, Shall we shut up a chamber and breathe night air vitiated with carbonic acid or night air that is pure? The only real difficulty about night air is, that usually it is damper . . . This is easily prevented by sufficient bed-clothing.*[5]

Women were also told to look to their cellars, fireplaces and stoves regarding proper ventilation and were advised not to burn kerosene lamps with long wicks that would fill a room with smoke. The more people occupying a house, the greater the need for fresh air.

While ventilation in the house was considered vital to good health, venturing outdoors at night in the cold air was dangerous, especially for women. Sore throats, coughs, rheumatism, consumption, asthmas, fevers and dysenteries resulted from leaving a seat in front of the parlor fireplace or crowded theaters or ballrooms and venturing forth into the chill and dampness of the night air. If it was indeed necessary to go out, women were cautioned to dress appropriately; their fancy evening attire was too thin and left shoulders uncovered against the change in temperature.

In contrast to the advice above, for those living in the South, near what one advice giver referred to as "the neighborhood of marshes," readers were told:

> *Health is best preserved in marshy districts by a regular and temperate life—exercise in the open air during the middle of the day, and by retiring, as soon as the sun sets, within the house, and closing all the doors and windows. The sleeping apartment should be in the upper story, and rendered perfectly dry by a fire, lit a few hours before going to bed, and then extinguished. Exposure to the open air should, if possible, not take place in the morning before the sun has had time to dispel the fog.*[6]

Exercise too was considered a powerful means of preventing illness and disease. Nineteenth-century advice givers recommended several hours of exercise each day as necessary to maintain good health—a suggestion very few women could follow. Between their heavy layers of restrictive clothing and the overwhelming variety of domestic duties that occupied their time, middle-class women were fortunate to be able to take a walk each day. Among exercises, walking, dancing (provided it was not carried to extremes) and horseback riding were considered ideal for women. From the early to mid-19th century, young women in the South were especially fond of horseback riding and actively pursued this pastime as a form of exercise.[7] By the late Victorian era, however, new modes of exercise in the form of leisure activities became available, and women increasingly participated in outdoor sports such as bicycling, croquet, tennis and swimming.

Personal cleanliness, as well as domestic cleanliness, was also viewed as important to good health. Warm baths, vital in preserving the skin and helping to keep it free from disease, were credited with allowing the stomach to function properly and creating general comfort. Likewise, a moderate diet and a sound, refreshing sleep each night were needed to restore energy. It is interesting to note that the scientific community of the mid-Victorian period viewed dreaming as an indication of imperfect sleep—of sleep that did not produce the refreshment essential to good health.

One last category the experts touched on in regard to preserving health was what they referred to as the "passion." The connection between mind and body was recognized as being important to a general well-being, and joy, hope and love were seen as positive influences while fear, grief and anger could be debilitating.

An exemplary lifestyle aside, Victorians were subject to numerous illnesses simply because of undeveloped sanitation measures, frequent epidemics and limited medications. During the first half of the 19th century home remedies and recipes, handed down from mothers to daughters, were the most frequent means to a cure; only later did household guides become popular. An example of the latter was *The Household Cyclopaedia of Practical Receipts and Daily Wants* (1873), which offered the following for treating ague (a fever with chills):

*The miasma of marshy ground, or stagnant water usually causes it. Vapour baths, hot fomentations, heat applied to the feet, and plenty of barley water, or gruel, may be administered during the cold stage. The remedy for the disease is quinine, and it is quite specific in its effects. Administered in doses from twenty to sixty grains shortly before the expected paroxysm, it checks it, and by continuing during the interval in smaller doses of from two to six grains, twice a day, the disease is usually cured. The patient should be very warmly dressed, and during the attacks, be covered with warm blankets. Persons subject to ague—or intermittent fever—should remove to a dry and bracing neighbourhood. The air of a city is more favourable than the air of the country to such persons. In chronic cases the administration of arsenic sometimes answers better than quinine, but a medicine so powerful must never be had recourse to except under proper medical advice.*[8]

The majority of medicinal concoctions were derived from plants, tree bark, roots, gum or oil. For instance, chamomile tea, made from the dried chamomile flower found in Europe, was used to treat fevers; Nightshade *(Atropa belladonna)* was used to create a narcotic; dandelion roots were an ingredient in medicinal extracts; quinine, an analgesic used to treat a variety of ailments, was a product of cinchona bark found in South America; and camphor, a crystalline compound, was created from the evaporation of oils found in the shoots of the laurel tree to serve as a painkiller and a main ingredient in liniments.[9]

Women kept these and many other ingredients on hand in a medicine chest or cupboard, and it was important that all vials, bottles, etc. be properly labeled for safety. Necessary ingredients or concoctions could be replenished as needed by paying a visit to the chemist or druggist. In 1890

Mrs. John A. Logan's book, *The Home Manual,* included a chapter called "The Mother's Medicine Chest." Readers were told:

*In traveling or for use at home, it is very desirable to have at hand a few remedies valuable in accidents or sudden sickness. A small box will hold the following articles:*

*Absorbent cotton*
*Sticking plaster*
*Bandages of muslin or flannel*
*Thread and needles*
*Pins*
*Vaseline*
*Aromatic spirits of Ammonia*
*Tincture of Assafoetida*
*Oil of Cloves*
*Hoffman's Anodyne*
*Syrup of Ipecac*
*Laudanum*
*Magnesia*
*Mustard*
*Paregoric*
*Spiced syrup of Rhubarb*
*Turpentine*

*To these may be added camphor-water, essence of ginger, lime-water, and sweet spirits of nitre.*[10]

While women generally played the role of caregiver, they were also subject to common physical afflictions. For example, dyspepsia (indigestion) was a frequent complaint and noted symptoms usually included a lack of appetite, stomach pains, heartburn and diarrhea. Early on, homemade tinctures or restoratives, along with moderation in eating, were recommended cures. In January 1856, *Godey's Lady's Book* included the following in their receipts column for the "Sick-Room and Nursery." To prepare a "Good Restorative" readers were instructed: "Bake two calves' feet in two pints of water, and the same quantity of new milk, in a jar closely covered, three hours and a half. When cold, remove the fat. Give a large teacupful the last and first thing. Whatever flavor is approved, give it by baking in it lemon-peel, cinnamon, or mace. Add sugar after." The recipe for a "Valu-

*This advertising trade card, featuring a healthy-looking young woman, was widely circulated during the late 1800s to extol the benefits of the patent medicine Burdock Blood Bitters. One of many such tonics or home remedies available from different companies, women were warned against the use of patent medicines due to their high alcohol content.*

able Stomach Tincture" required: "Cascarilla bark bruised, and orange-peel dried, of each one ounce; brandy, or proof spirit, one pint. Let the ingredients steep for a fortnight, and decant the clear liquor. Take two or three teaspoonfuls in a wineglass of water twice a day."[11]

During the late 1800s a variety of patent medicines were widely available and advertised as cure-alls for any number of ills, including dyspepsia. Hunt's Remedy Company of Providence, Rhode Island, advertised their product, Hunt's Remedy, as "the Best Kidney and Liver Medicine—Never Known to Fail." Attractive advertising trade cards designed to appeal to women reported Hunt's would cure everything from dyspepsia and nervous diseases to diabetes, dropsy and female weaknesses. Likewise, a charming trade card promoting Burdock Blood Bitters declared:

*What is it? A Powerful Restorative! Nature's True Renovator! A most successful combination for regulating the Bowels, for purifying the Blood, for toning up the Nerves, and imparting strength and vitality to the entire system. It acts powerfully upon the Liver and the Kidneys, and never fails to cure Indigestion and Dyspepsia. It is the best Family Medicine known. This is Burdock Blood Bitters.*

Other popular tonics included "Lydia Pinkham's Vegetable Compound," "Dr. Radway's Sarsaparillian Resolvent," "Ayer's Sarsaparilla" and "Baker's Stomach Bitters."

To Victorians facing numerous health complaints and illnesses, these patent medicines with their promises of a quick cure must have seemed like miracle drugs. The possibility that a single bottle held the key to all-around good health was too tempting to resist. As sales of such remedies, pills, blood tonics, potions etc., increased, medical experts became alarmed and spoke out to warn the public that among other hazards, alcohol was the major ingredient in patent medicines. For example, in 1905 Mary Wood-Allen, M.D., warned women:

*Never take patent medicines. Wonderful discoveries, favorite prescriptions and the like may be harmless, and they may not. And even if they are, how can you judge that they are suited to your special case? One very serious danger in the taking of patent medicines is the fact that they are so largely alcoholic in composition, and girls and women have all too often been led into the alcohol habit and become habitual drunkards through taking some advertised remedy.*[12]

Along with the physical complaints affecting Victorian women, Dr. Wood-Allen and others of the medical profession also viewed mental illnesses such as neurasthenia to be a direct result of narcotic use, a too leisurely lifestyle and boredom. Originally a condition associated with the frenzied lifestyle and mental pressures of upwardly mobile, middle-class, urban men, neurasthenia (symptoms included insomnia, dyspepsia, headaches, depression and other complaints) was viewed negatively when diagnosed in women. They were advised to refocus their energies on their assigned sphere—hearth and home—and to exercise more, as well as to avoid excitement and too much mental stimulation.[13]

"Health of the mind," as the Beecher sisters referred to it in *The American Woman's Home*, was of great concern to middle-class women. They noted that "the most frequent victims of this kind of predisposition [mental disease] are females of the middle and higher ranks, especially those of a nervous constitution and good natural abilities; but who, from an ill-directed education, possess nothing more solid than mere accomplishments, and have no materials for thought. . . . The liability of such persons to melancholy, hysteria . . . and other varieties of mental distress, really depends on a state of irritability of the brain."[14] Indeed hysteria, with its emotional outbursts, tearful scenes and fits of anger, was the most common "mental disease" plaguing Victorian women. One advice giver suggested the following cure:

*If the patient is of a strong constitution, she should live on a plain diet, take plenty of exercise, and take occasional doses of castor oil. If, as is mostly the case, the patient is weak and delicate, she will require a good nourishing diet, gentle exercise, cold baths, occasionally a dose of myrrh and aloes pills at night, and a dose of compound iron pills twice a day. In every case, amusing the mind, and avoiding all causes of over-excitement, are of great service in bringing about a permanent cure.*[15]

During the late 19th century, patent medicines were also promoted as a cure for the treatment of hysteria.

Constantly nursing the sick and dealing with their own bouts of illness, not to mention the risks associated with pregnancy (discussed in chapter 3), took their toll on Victorian women. Regardless of social rank, living the life prescribed them according to 19th-century culture and customs had a negative impact on their general well-being. Like hothouse flowers, women were frequently shut up in the too hot or too cold parlor with uncomfortable, restrictive and often injurious clothing (see chapter 4). Active exercise was limited to a few precious, acceptable activities. The advice of doctors and reformers who were opposed to harmful modes of dress and in favor of increased physical activity ran counter to the behavior and presentation expected of proper Victorian women. Attitudes were changing during the 1890s and early 1900s, but resolution of the conflict was slow to come. For example, an article appearing in the September 1897 *Ladies' Home Journal* addressed the new sport of bicycling, cautioning women that just because it was the latest rage it was not necessarily a proper pastime for them.[16] In contrast, by 1909 the advice offered in *Household Discoveries*, applauded bicycling as well as other forms of exercise, telling women that "walking and slow running are exceedingly important, especially if indulged in until they cause deep breathing. Of course outdoor exercise is best. Hill climbing is splendid. Tennis for the vigorous, golf and horseback riding and wheeling for the more mature, are excellent."[17]

Other notable changes at the turn of the century impacted on women not only in regard to their own well-being but in their capacity as caregivers. Comparing home manuals of the last quarter of the 19th century to those of the early 1900s, we find a shift in emphasis from diseases and nervous disorders to treatment of home injuries and accidents. Victorians relied on the growing medical community at the dawn of the new century—hospitals became acceptable centers for treatments and childbirth, and sanitoriums became commonplace for tuberculosis victims. Nervous disorders were cast aside with the restrictive clothing decreed proper for ladies, and a more comfortable attire better suited to outdoor activity was enjoyed by women in the name of good health.

# OLD AGE, DEATH AND THE AFTERLIFE

What the Victorians considered an old woman would be thought middle-aged today. If a 19th-century antebellum female survived childhood and her childbearing years, she had a good chance of living at least into her forties. This, however, was the exception rather than the rule. Even during the late 19th and early 20th centuries the odds had not yet vastly improved. According to *Length Of Life: A Study Of The Lifetable*, published in 1936, life expectancy for American women was only 37 years of age in 1800 and had risen to only 51 years of age by 1900.[18]

*This "old-age" Victorian woman is dressed appropriately for her age in dark, somber colors thought suitable for those women past "the bloom of youth."*

What was life like for the middle-class woman who did survive to old age? In *Victorian Women: A Documentary Account of Women's Lives in Nineteenth-Century England, France and The United States*, editors Erna Olafson Hellerstein, Leslie Parker Hume and Karen M. Offen note that while men could continue to work and to lead full lives as long as they were able, women were valued less (and compensated less) by society as they became older; ultimately, "their social status depended almost always on their fathers or husbands, less frequently on their children and only in very rare instances, on themselves."[19]

It was as if Victorian women who lived to what was then considered old age had outlived their usefulness. Advice literature of the 19th century recognized them only in passing, warning older women to act appropriately for their age, especially in manners of dress.[20] For example, *The Ladies' and Gentlemen's Etiquette*, published in 1877, reported:

> *Ladies will always dress according to their age. For an old person to assume the light colors and the simplicity of youth is no more incongruous than for the young to put on the richness of dress and abundant jewelry belonging to advanced life. We put bright colors upon our little children, we dress our young girls in light and delicate shades, the blooming matron is justified in adopting the warm, rich hues which we see in the autumn leaf, while black and neutral tints are declared appropriate to the old.*[21]

Similarly, the 1896 *The Glory of Woman* reported, "There should be fitness to the individual, as well as to the sex. We instinctively know that the young and old should not dress alike."[22] Regarding the change in appearance that accompanied the passing of years, especially hair color, one advice tome generously commented that "gray hair is a crown of glory, if it comes after a well-spent life."[23]

By the 1890s and early 1900s the medical community was addressing women in their "golden years" from the standpoint of the physical and mental changes associated with menopause. Citing it a "disease" peculiar to women, one late 1800s book stated:

> *The evening of her days approaches, and if she has observed the precepts of wisdom, she may look forward to a long and placid period of rest, blessed with health, honored, yes, loved with a purer flame than any which she inspired in the bloom of youth and beauty. But ere this haven of rest is reached, there is a crisis to pass, which is ever the subject of anxious solici-*

*tude. The more common and less scientific name for it is the change of life.*
*The age at which this occurs is variable. In this country, from forty to forty-*
*six years is the most common.*[24]

An advertisement for *What A Woman of Forty-Five Ought to Know* by Mrs. Emma F. A. Drake, M.D., listed topics such as the fears associated with the change of life, the physiological and mental aspects of the change, appropriate dress for a woman of advanced years, how to prolong the bloom of youth, guarding against becoming gloomy, lustful indulgence in patent medicines, holding a husband's affections, exercise of mind and soul, diet, physical exercise and the daily toilette.[25]

For older women, especially those who were widowed, their financial situation often left them little choice but to take up residence with a grown son or daughter and his/her family. As a grandmother, an older woman continued in a limited role to function for the good of others, helping care for children in the family and performing domestic chores as able. Multigenerational families under one roof were so common during the Victorian era that the 1879 book, *The Complete Home*, commented on this arrangement:

> *It is dangerous and disadvantageous, people say, for families to live together.*
> *Doubtless the rule is good, but Providence sometimes interferes with it.*
> *Thus, when it is needful in God's providential arrangings for us, that families should live together this may be a means of developing new graces in ourselves and our children. Therefore, people should not complain, and look on it as a great evil, that aged relatives must be received into their families; but rather feel thankful that they may repay past debts of love and tenderness. What should be more grateful to the feelings of every true heart than to be able to establish in one's home, and wait upon with affections and respect, an aged parent?*[26]

Another advice book, *The Voyage of Life*, suggested ways to preserve the self-respect of older persons:

> *Old age is honorable, and a multitude of years teach wisdom. Old age, however serene the conscience and well-spent the life, has its sadness. After all their care and toil they have a fear of being a burden. If you would make the aged happy, lead them to feel that there is still a place for them where they can be useful. Do not humiliate them by doing things after them. You may give them the best room in your house, you may garnish it with pic-*

This circa 1848 lithograph entitled "The Life & Age of Woman: Stages of Woman's Life from the Cradle to the Grave" by Jas. Baillie portrays Victorian attitudes about the lives of women, their assigned roles and the virtual uselessness of old age. (Courtesy Library of Congress, LC-USZ62-2853)

*tures, and flowers, you may yield them the best seat in your church-pew, the easiest chair in your parlor, the highest seat of honor at your table; but if you lead, or leave, them to feel they have passed their usefulness, you plant a thorn in their bosom that will rankle while their life lasts. If they are capable of nothing but preparing your kindlings, or darning your stockings, indulge them in those things, but never let them feel that it is because they can do nothing else; rather that they do it so well.*[27]

Concerning Victorian women and old age, the 1848 lithograph reproduced here reflects the 19th-century sentiment associated with a woman's life and her advancing years. Beneath the images depicting "The Life & Age of Woman" is the following verse:

In swaddling clothes
behold the bud,
Of sweet and gentle
womanhood.

Next she foreshews
with mimic plays,
The business of
her future days.

Now glorious as a
full-blown flower,
The heart of manhood
feels her power.
A husband now
her arms entwine
She clings around
him like the vine.

Now bearing fruit,
she rears her boys
And tastes a mother's
pains and joys.

Like sparkling fountain

gushing forth
She proves a blessing
to the earth.

A busy housewife
full of cares,
The daily food
her hand prepares.

As age creeps on
she seeks for grace,
Always to church
and in her place.

Now second childhood
loosens all her tongue,
She talks of love and
prattles with the young.

A useless cumberer
on the earth,
From house to house
they send her forth.

Chained to her chair
by weight of years,
She listless knits
till death appears.

For the Victorian woman, life—her own as well as that of her loved ones—was a fragile, precious commodity. Epidemics and illnesses could strike and cause the death of a family member or cherished friend in a matter of hours. As health care givers, women routinely stood the death watch, waiting and offering what comfort they could to those with little time left on earth. In coping with the devastation of death, their strong religious beliefs were often their saving grace. Christian faith as well as perceptions of death were refined throughout the Victorian era and no longer resembled

*Entitled "Journey of Life," this circa 1870s lithograph from the*
*book* The Complete Home *symbolizes the stages of life with*
*the ultimate goal being passage to the heavenly home above.*

the "hellfire and damnation" concept of religion and the afterlife as found in earlier centuries. Rather, the Victorians viewed death as a passing to a home in heaven. According to Henry Ward Beecher, noted 19th-century clergyman, author and lecturer (and brother of Catharine Beecher and Harriet Beecher Stowe), death was a "lifting up":

> *I love to think that what seems to be the mystery of the silence of death, which envelops so many that we loved on earth, is really not a mystery. Our friends are separated from us because they are lifted higher than our faculties can go. They have gone where they speak a higher language, and live in a higher sphere. Theirs is the glory; ours is the waiting for it. Theirs is the realization; ours is the hoping for it. Theirs is the perfection; ours is the immaturity striving to be ripe. And when the day comes that we shall disappear from these earthly scenes, we shall be joined to them again, but not as we were—for we shall not then be as we were—but as they are, with God.*[28]

Death as a journey to a heavenly home was the subject of countless poems that brought women comfort during the 19th-century. Short stories too focused on this topic. For example, a poem entitled "The Bliss of Heaven" begins with, "We're going home." Other popular 19th-century poems about death and heaven had titles such as "Going Home," "Home In View," "Home In Heaven," "The Future Home," "We Have No Home But Heaven" and "A Home Above." Women were reminded through such poems that dearly departed family members and friends would be waiting to greet them in the heavenly home; they would be reunited with children who died at a young age, and husbands would welcome them with open arms. This appealing picture of the afterlife helped many women cope with the profound losses brought about through death.

The death of a child was an especially hard burden to bear, but the death of a mother was also immortalized in many a tender poem. Among the more popular during the 19th century was "The Old Arm Chair" by Eliza Cook:

I love it—I love it, and who shall dare
To chide me for loving that old arm chair?
I've treasured it long as a sainted prize—

I've bedewed it with tears, and embalmed it with sighs;
'Tis bound by a thousand bands to my heart,
Not a tie will break, nor a link will start,
Would you learn the spell? A mother sat there;
And a sacred thing is that old arm chair.

In childhood's hour I lingered near
The hallowed seat with listening ear;
And gentle words that mother would give,
To fit me to die and teach me to live.
She told me shame would never betide,
With truth for my creed, and God for my guide;
She taught me to lisp my earliest prayer,
As I knelt beside that old arm chair.

I sat and watched her many a day,
When her eyes grew dim and her locks were gray,
And I almost worshipped her when she smiled
And turned from her Bible to bless her child.
Years rolled on, but the last one sped—
My idol was shattered—my earth star fled;
I learnt how much the heart can hear,
When I saw her die in that old arm chair.

'Tis past! 'tis past! but I gaze on it now
With quivering breath and throbbing brow;
'Twas there she nursed me—'twas there she died,
And memory flowed with lava tide—
Say it is folly, and deem me weak,
While the scalding tears run down my cheek.
But I love it—I love it, and cannot tear
My soul from my mother's old arm chair.[29]

Not only did sentimental poetry and idealistic visions of heaven and the afterlife with loved ones sustain Victorian women in some measure, large or small, during times of sorrow and great loss; they helped them to sustain others as well. Southerner Virginia Cary noted in her circa 1830s book *Letters on Female Character* that "this is the chief end of woman—to advance the cause of the Redeemer, by exerting quietly the influence she possesses as a *woman*, over the feelings, more than the understandings of her fellow beings."[30]

# MOURNING RITUALS

As perceptions of death and the afterlife were sentimentalized during the 19th century, so too were the rituals surrounding burial and the period of mourning that followed the loss of a loved one.

Simple 18th-century graveyards having plots marked with stone skeletons or crosses inscribed "Memento Mori" ("Remember you must die") evolved during the Victorian era into beautiful cemeteries where the dead were honored with elaborate headstones carved with images of angels or floral bouquets (lilies and roses were especially popular). Sentimental tributes or epitaphs graced Victorian headstones; common examples included "All is well," "We will meet again," "Gone home," "Gone, but not forgotten," "Dying is but going home" and "They are not dead." Poetry too was frequently inscribed on tombstones; popular verses included "A happier lot than ours, and larger light, surrounds thee there," and "Where immortal spirits reign, there we shall meet again."

As with many other areas of daily life, scientific advances, the progress associated with the industrial revolution, and the Victorian penchant for ceremony transformed the funeral, over the course of the century, from a quiet family affair held at the home of the deceased to a public display of mourning (often orchestrated by the mortician) in the church or funeral parlor.[31] Of course the social standing and the family of the deceased determined how elaborate the casket would be and the level ceremony associated with the burial, etc. Advice givers were constantly reminding the middle class that a tasteful, not showy, funeral was the mark of good breeding.

Funeral services were usually held at the deceased's house or in the church if an unusually large crowd was expected. A close friend of the family, a relative or the undertaker served as master of ceremonies. A procession to the cemetery followed the final viewing of the deceased and a short service. Although women were allowed to attend a burial, they were not required to do so.

Regarding the "House of Mourning," one advice giver suggested that "no calls of condolence should be made upon the bereaved family while the dead remains in the house, and members of the family may be excused from receiving any but their most intimate friends at that time. There should be no loud talking or confusion while the body remains in the house. The bell knob or door handle is draped with black crape, with a black ribbon tied on, if the deceased is married or advanced in years, and with a white ribbon, if young or unmarried."[32] Mourning rituals were primarily women's responsibility. They included creating tokens of remembrance—cherished mementos kept in a place of honor in the Victorian home or worn in the form of jewelry. For example, during the early 19th century, "mourning pictures" were a popular means of paying tribute to the dead. First embroidered, and then later created with watercolor paints, this type of memento was often completed by schoolgirls to develop artistic sensibilities and face the realities of a fragile existence.[33] According to C. Kurt Dewhurst, Betty MacDowell and Marsha MacDowell, mourning pictures were a very refined and genteel way of honoring the dead. Classic imagery was generally composed of landscapes, gravestones and weeping willow trees, and schoolgirls often embellished their mourning pictures with other motifs such as birds, flowers or angels. Each motif was, of course, symbolic, such as the female mourning figure "bowed in the classical posture of grief."[34]

During the 1840s several factors contributed to the decline of the mourning picture, including the fact that schools increasingly focused on solid learning rather than hand-crafted accomplishments for girls. In addition, the availability of lithographed memorial prints and "Family Records" served to record family deaths.[35] Eventually new styles and customs brought new ways of remembering the dead, including hairwork jewelry (see chapter 5), religious and symbolic handicrafts created at home and even photographs.

Paying tribute to the dead also meant honoring them with the customary period of mourning. Generally, Victorian etiquette dictated acceptable periods of mourning and mourning attire depending upon one's relation to the deceased. The prescribed period for wearing mourning attire was of course longer for a widow than for other relatives. One 1880s etiquette book gave the following specifications:

*The deepest mourning is that worn by a widow for her husband. It is worn two years, sometimes longer. Widow's mourning for the first year consists of*

*This circa 1880s chromolithographed family record by J. M. Vickroy & Co. was a popular means of recording Victorian family histories, with the dates that loved ones were "called away." Different vignettes depict the human life cycle, including "Our Last Resting Place" in the lower left-hand corner.* (Courtesy Library of Congress, LC-USZ62-98207)

*solid black woolen goods, collar and cuffs of folded untrimmed crape, a sim-*
*ple crape bonnet, and a long, thick, black crape veil. The second year, silk*
*trimmed with crape, black lace collar and cuffs, and a shorter veil may be*
*worn, and in the last six months gray, violet and white are permitted. A*
*widow should wear the hair perfectly plain if she does not wear a cap, and*
*should always wear a bonnet, never a hat.*[36]

Changing fashions meant advice such as the above could become outdated very quickly. For example, another 1880s etiquette book remarked on the mourning attire for a widow, "The custom of wearing purple the second year is now obsolete; mourning is only lightened by leaving off crape, wearing white ruches, illusion, etc."[37]

Quickly acquiring the proper mourning wardrobe could prove costly, especially for a widow. The 1883 *Collier's Cyclopedia of Social and Commercial Information* recognized this, telling readers "to write to some well-known house for patterns; good mourning establishments can afford to sell better materials at cheaper rates than small, inferior houses. Mourning has generally to be purchased hurriedly, and too often a dressmaker gets carte blanche almost to furnish the mourning. No wonder mourning is considered expensive." *Collier's* goes on to offer a listing of mourning attire required by a widow:

*One best dress of Paramatta covered entirely with crape.*
*One dress, either a costume of Cyprus crape, or an old black dress covered*
   *with rainproof crape.*
*One Paramatta mantle lined with silk and deeply trimmed with crape.*
*One warmer jacket of cloth lined, trimmed with crape.*
*One bonnet of best silk crape, with long veil.*
*One bonnet of rainproof crape, with crape veil.*
*Twelve collars and cuffs of muslim or lawn, with deep hems.*
*One black petticoat.*
*Four pairs of black hose, either silk, cashmere, or spun silk.*
*Twelve handkerchiefs with black borders for ordinary use, cambric.*
*Caps, either of lisse, tulle, or tarlatan, shape depending very much on the age.*
*If in summer a parasol should be required, it should be of silk deeply*
   *trimmed with crape, almost covered with it, but no lace or fringe for the*
   *first year.*
*A muff, if required, would be made of Paramatta, and trimmed with*
   *crape.*[38]

*From the 1883* Collier's Cyclopedia of Social and Commercial Information, *a chapter heading, the "Etiquette of Mourning." The majority of etiquette manuals published during the late 19th and early 20th centuries included such chapters for the middle class, as funerals and mourning rituals became sentimentalized and ritualized.*

Mourning attire for a father, mother or child was worn for one year. Solid black was required during the first six months, followed by three months of black with white trim (on collars and cuffs) and the last three months gray, purple and violet were acceptable colors for clothings. According to *Godey's Lady's Book* of March 1855, mourning clothes worn by a daughter—specifically her walking dress—included a "Dress of black silk and an over skirt of crape; crape collar and sleeves, crape and silk bonnet with fall, entirely black inside; black parasol; jet brooch and chain; black kid gloves."[39] If a woman was wearing mourning for a child under the age of 12, proper etiquette called for her to wear white during the summer months and gray with black trim during the winter. Mourning for a grandparent, brother or sister was worn for six months and for an aunt, uncle, nephew or niece, three months. In all cases, however, the transition from black to colors was to be made gradually.

Etiquette books published during the last quarter of the 19th century as well as the early 20th century usually included chapters devoted to funerals and mourning rituals and attire. Most authors agreed that "deep" mourning prohibited wearing kid gloves. Rather, cloth or silk gloves were an acceptable substitute. Also, no jewelry was to be worn during the first month, and trim work (embroidery, puffs, plaits on dresses) was not allowed. Mourning handkerchiefs of fine linen were required to have a black border, as were mourning cards.

The advice books and etiquette tomes agreed that mourning attire was a necessary, outward show of respect for the dead. As old customs were slowly eroding with the approach of the 20th century, one author implored, "We sincerely trust the old custom of wearing decent mourning for those taken away from us, will never be really discontinued in America, for it is one of those proofs of our home affections which can never be done away with without a loss of national respect."[40]

# APPENDIX A
# SELECT RULES OF ETIQUETTE FOR VICTORIAN WOMEN

The following is a sampling of the rules of etiquette and deportment that influenced the lives of Victorian women. Taken from various 19th-century behavior manuals, these laws of etiquette were a vital link to acceptable social standing and middle-class daily life.

"Familiarity—No girl should permit a boy to be so familiar as to toy with her hands, or play with her rings; to handle her curls or encircle her waist with his arm. Such impudent intimacy should never be tolerated for a moment. No gentleman will attempt it; no lady will permit it."

—*Good Morals and Gentle Manners*, 1873

"Introductions—The proper form of introduction is to present the gentleman to the lady, the younger to the older, the inferior to the superior."

"The Lover's Kiss—It is hardly necessary to say that the lover's kiss is never paraded in public."

"Conversation—The very first requisite of a good conversationalist is to be a good listener. The second is to know what not to say. The third is to have ideas and be able to express them concisely, intelligently and agreeably."

"Improper Attitudes—Never loll, fidget, yawn, bite the nails or be guilty of any other like gaucherie in the presence of others."

—*Complete Etiquette*, 1877

"Dinners and Dining—To give a formal dinner with ease and grace it is necessary first to establish a home habit of observing the simple customs that make the table so charming. Nothing is such a test of good breeding as behavior at the table. In every house, great or small, the dining-room should be as bright, neat and cosey as possible, and at the table the mistress, particularly, should wear her brightest smile. Trials and troubles should never be allowed to shadow the table. They impair digestion, and send people away glum and gloomy, instead of refreshed and strengthened."

"Dinners and Dining—One should not sit too near the table, or too far from it, or drum with the fingers, or make diagrams with his knife and fork, or twirl his goblet, or play with his salt-cellar, or suck or pick his teeth, or cough or sneeze, or smack his lips, or draw soup into his mouth with a gurgling sound, or put elbows on the table, fidget in the chair, blow soup to cool it, or soak up gravy with bread."

"Ladies' Calls and Cards—Good taste never touches extremes, and the card of the well-bred lady will be neither too large nor too small; its quality and texture will be unexceptionable, and the name will appear engraved in plain, medium-sized script, clear, without flourish, and with the prefix of 'Mrs.' or 'Miss' in every case, except when the lady herself has earned a title."

"Dressing to Make Calls—Ladies in making calls dress much more elegantly than for walking or shopping as a compliment to those visited."

—*The Manners That Win*, 1880

"Kissing in Public—The custom which has become quite prevalent of women kissing each other whenever they meet in public is regarded as vulgar, and by ladies of delicacy and refinement is entirely avoided."

"Prudery—Avoid an affectation of excessive modesty. Do not use the word 'limb' for 'leg.' If legs are really improper, then let us, on no account, mention them. But having found it necessary to mention them, let us by all means give them their appropriate name."

"General Rules for Balls—Young ladies must be careful how they refuse to dance, for unless a good reason is given, a gentleman is apt to take it as evidence of personal dislike. After a lady refuses, the gentleman should not urge her to dance, nor should the lady accept another invitation for the same dance."

"Shopping Etiquette—In inquiring for goods at a store or shop, do not say to the clerk or salesman, 'I want' such an article, but, 'Please show me' such an article, or some other polite form of address."

"Singing and Playing in Society—A lady in company should never exhibit any anxiety to sing or play: but being requested to do so, if she intends to comply, she should do so at once, without waiting to be urged. Having complied, she should not monopolize the evening with her performances."

—*Our Deportment*, 1882

"Conversation—Remember in conversation that a voice 'gentle and low' is, above all other extraneous acquirements, 'an excellent thing in a woman.' There is a certain distinct but subdued tone of voice which is peculiar to only well-bred persons. A loud voice is both disagreeable and vulgar. It is better to err by the use of too low rather than too loud a tone."

"Dress—To dress well requires something more than a full purse and a pretty figure. It needs taste, good sense, and refinement. Dress may almost be classed as one of the fine arts."

"Dress—There is as much propriety to be observed in the wearing of jewelry as in the wearing of dresses. Diamonds, pearls, rubies, and all transparent precious stones, belong to evening dress, and should on no account be worn before dinner. In the morning let your rings be of the more simple and massive kind; wear no bracelets; and limit your jewelry to a good brooch, gold chain, and watch. It is well to remember in the choice of jewelry that mere costliness is not always the test of value. Of all precious stones, the opal is one of the most lovely and least common-place. No vulgar woman purchases an opal. She invariably prefers the more showy ruby, emerald, or sapphire."

"Dress—Never be seen in the street without gloves. Your gloves should fit to the last degree of perfection."

"Dress—Your shoes and gloves should always be faultless."

—*Collier's Cyclopedia*, 1883

"How to Address Others—Husbands and wives indicate pleasant conjugal relation existing where they address each other in the family circle by their Christian names, though the terms of respect 'Mr.' and 'Mrs.' may be applied to each among strangers. When speaking of each other among near and intimate relatives, they will also use the Christian name; but among general acquaintances and strangers, the surname."

"What Should Be Avoided When Calling—

Do not stare around the room.
Do not take a dog or small child.
Do not linger at the dinner hour.
Do not lay aside the bonnet at a formal call.
Do not fidget with your parasol.
Do not make a call of ceremony on a wet day.
Do not turn your back to one seated near you.
Do not touch the piano, unless invited to do so.
Do not handle ornaments or furniture in the room.
Do not remove the gloves when making a formal call.
Do not open or shut doors or windows or alter the
    arrangement of the room.
Do not, if a lady, call upon a gentleman, except officially or
    professionally, unless he may be a confirmed invalid."

"Etiquette of Traveling—Avoid wearing laces, velvets, or any articles that naturally accumulate and hold dust. Excessive finery or a lavish display of jewelry are in bad taste on extended journeys. Before commencing a journey, consider carefully what will be most suitable to wear, and study how little baggage may be taken."

"Attractive Personal Appearance—In the cultivation of beauty in dress, it will become necessary to discriminate between ornament as displayed by the savage, and the science of beauty as observed in a more highly civilized life. Ornament is one thing; beauty quite another."

*—Hill's Manual of Social and Business Forms*, 1888

"Selecting Company—A young man or woman upon first entering into society should select those persons who are most celebrated for the propriety and elegance of their manners."

"Demanding Attentions—A lady never demands attentions and favors from a gentleman, but always accepts them gratefully and graciously and with expressed thanks."

*—Manners, Culture and Dress of The Best American Society*, 1891

"Beauty—How to be beautiful, and consequently, powerful, is a question of far greater importance to the feminine mind than predestination or any other abstract subject. If women are to govern, control, manage, influence, and retain the adoration of husbands, fathers, brothers, lovers, or even cousins, they must look their prettiest at all times."

—*Polite Life and Etiquette*, 1891

"How to Dress in the Evening—We have translated the French *en toilette* into 'Full Dress' but we still lack some equivalent for their expressive phrase, *demi-toilette*. Full dress for a woman means merely a gown, made with low neck and short sleeves, and it is worn at balls, dinners, dances, at the opera, and at any entertainment after six o'clock given at private houses. The 'half-toilet' consists of a gown cut low, but filled in at the neck with lace, chiffon, or other gauzy material. This costume is worn at little dinners and informal evening gatherings."

—*Correct Social Usage*, 1907

# APPENDIX B

# NINETEENTH-CENTURY ADVICE AND RECIPES FOR THE TOILETTE

The art of being beautiful was serious business for Victorian women. Advice givers offered guidance in how to be lovely and many such books included recipes for homemade beauty products, toilet waters, creams, lotions and hair washes. Included here are a select sampling of recipes and helpful advice the Victorian woman turned to in her quest to be beautiful.

"Exquisite neatness of person is inseparable from genteel breeding. It is a matter of principle as well as pride with the true gentleman and lady not only to seem, but to be, scrupulously clean. Untidiness not only puts friends to blush, but obscures the brightest talents. The gentleman who offers a lady his escort to a public place of amusement, has a right to expect that she will not appear with frowsy hair, badly-fitting or ill-chosen dress, and redolent of cheap perfumes."

— *The Manners That Win,* 1880

## REGARDING TOILET WATERS:

"Perfumes are a necessary appendage to the toilet; let them be delicate, not powerful; the attar of roses is the most elegant; the Heduesmia is at once fragrant and delicate. Many others may be names . . . but recollect that none must be patronized which are so obtrusive as to give the idea that they are not indulged in as a luxury but used from necessity."

— *True Politeness, The Ladies' Book of Etiquette,* 1878

"Lavender Water—Essence of ambergris two drachms, oil of cinnamon six drops, oil of geranium two drachms, oil of lavender three drachms, essence of musk two drachms, spirit of wine ten ounces. Put the various oils and essences into a clean glass bottle that will hold three-quarters of a pint, and pour the spirit of wine upon them. Shake the whole for a few minutes until the ingredients are thoroughly incorporated, and keep the perfume tightly corked."

*—Godey's Lady's Book,* April, 1867

"Tincture of Roses—Take the leaves of the common rose and place, without pressing them, in a common bottle; pour some good spirits of wine upon them, close the bottle, and let it stand till required for use. This tincture will keep for years, and yield a perfume little inferior to attar of roses; a few drops of it will suffice to impregnate the atmosphere of a room with a delicious odor."

*—The Manners That Win,* 1880

"Rose Water—Half an ounce powdered white sugar and two drachms of magnesia; with these mix twelve drops of attar of roses, add a quart of water and two ounces of alcohol, mixed in a gradual manner, and filter through blotting paper."

*—The Manners That Win,* 1880

"Cologne—Take one gallon of spirits of wine and add of the oil of lemon, orange and bergamot each a spoonful, also add extract of vanilla forty drops. Shake until the oils are cut, then add a pint and a half of soft water."

*—Manners, Culture and Dress of The Best American Society,* 1891

"Geranium Perfume—A perfume which is very agreeable to many may be made from the leaves of any of the sweet-smelling geraniums. The tincture, obtained by packing the leaves in a fruit jar, filling it with alcohol and allowing it to stand for a few weeks, is perhaps the easiest to prepare. The leaves may be renewed, if desired, to strengthen the perfume."

*—Household Discoveries,* 1909

# REGARDING COMPLEXION AND SKIN CARE:

"Cold Cream—Oil of almonds, one pound; white wax, four ounces. Melt together gently in an earthen vessel, and when nearly cold stir in gradually twelve ounces of rosewater."

*—Godey's Lady's Book,* October 1855

"Cure for Chapped Hands—Take some prepared chalk, scrape it fine; have some fresh lard; blend both together to the consistency of salve. Rub the hands with it before going to bed, and sleep in old kid gloves with the palms cut out. This preparation will also whiten the hands considerably."

*—Godey's Lady's Book,* December 1867

"The beauty of the eyes is independent of all arts of the toilet. The soul looks out of them, and those who would preserve their beauty should take care there is beauty of character behind them. Nothing is more vulgar than painting or coloring the lids or lashes."

*—The Manners That Win,* 1880

"The best beautifier is health, and one-half the attention which fine ladies give to decorating themselves, and one-half the time wasted in frivolous gossip and the furbelows of dress which detract from simplicity and real artistic beauty, given to exercise in the open air, bathing, and care of the health, would make paints and powders superfluous."

*—The Manners That Win,* 1880

"Face Powders—If ladies resort to artificial means to make up complexions, they should be artistically applied, and not as one would apply whitewash to a rough fence. Nothing is more vulgar and disgusting than a face on which the powder is plainly visible, and which looks as if dipped in a flour barrel. The best and cheapest powder is little pellets of refined chalk."

*—The Manners That Win,* 1880

"To Remove Freckles—At night wash the skin with elder-flower water, and apply an ointment made by simmering gently one ounce of venice soap, quarter of an ounce of deliquated oil of tartar, and ditto of oil of bitter almonds. When it acquires consistency, three drops of oil of rhodium may be added. Wash the ointment off in the morning with rose-water."

—*Manners, Culture and Dress of The Best American Society,* 1891

"The Face—It is no longer considered vulgar to aid nature when the good old lady withholds some of her gifts, though good form does not permit that such tiny artifices shall be noticeable. The woman who feels the crying need of a bit of color in her lips or cheeks must apply it with infinite care. A good rouge is made of: Lavender vinegar 100 grams, spermaceti ten grams, rouge six grams, powdered talcum fifteen grams. Mix and filter."

—*Correct Social Usage,* 1907

## REGARDING THE HAIR:

"Elder Flower oil for the Hair—Take of the best almond or olive oil, one pound; elder flowers two ounces; place the flowers in the oil in a jar or wide-mouthed bottle; let them remain forty-eight hours; then strain. The oil must now stand in a quiet and cool place for at least a month, in order to clear itself. The bright part being poured off, is fit for use."

—*Godey's Lady's Book,* July 1855

"To Cleanse Long Hair—Beat up the yolk of an egg with a pint of soft water. Apply it warm, and afterwards wash it out with warm water."

—*Godey's Lady's Book,* April 1867

"A Nice, Economical Hair Wash—Black Tea—If you want to have a good head of hair, never apply to cosmetics; use nothing else to clean it but strong, cold black tea. I generally use it, and recommend it to all ladies desirous of having a voluminous head of hair."

—*Godey's Lady's Book,* September 1867

"Tonic for the Hair—Ounce best castor oil, two ounces each French brandy and bay rum, scent with rose geranium."

—*The Manners That Win,* 1880

"Hair Dye—In the list of hair dyes one agent has long been overlooked which is found in the humblest household. It is too common and humble, indeed, to excite confidence at first; but it is said that the water in which potatoes have been boiled with the skins on forms a speedy and harmless dye for the hair and eyebrows. No hesitation need be felt about using this, for potato-water is a safe article used in the household pharmacopoeia in a variety of ways."

—*The Manners That Win*, 1880

"Hair-Curling Fluid—One of the fluids in use is made by dissolving a small portion of beeswax in an ounce of olive oil and adding scent according to fancy."

—*Manners, Culture and Dress of The Best American Society*, 1891

"The Hair and Scalp—The essential thing in shampooing hair is to rinse it thoroughly. Light hair is much improved if, after the final rinsing, it is washed once more in a strong solution of chamomile flowers. Allow them to steep a few minutes, strain and use hot. This is the famous wash which keeps the Swiss peasant girl's hair so light far into middle age."

—*Correct Social Usage*, 1907

# A SELECT LISTING OF POPULAR NAMES FOR WOMEN DURING THE VICTORIAN ERA

| | | | | |
|---|---|---|---|---|
| Abigail | Ada | Adaline | Adelia | Adeline |
| Adora | Agatha | Agnes | Alethea | Alexandra |
| Alice | Almira | Althea | Amanda | Amelia |
| Angelica | Angeline | Ann | Anna | Annabel |
| Arabella | Athena | Augusta | Aurelia | Aurora |
| Barbara | Beatrice | Belinda | Bertha | Bessie |
| Beulah | Blanch | Bridget | Camilla | Caroline |
| Cassandra | Catharine | Cecilia | Celeste | Charity |
| Charlotte | Chloe | Christina | Clara | Clarice |
| Clarissa | Claudia | Clementine | Constance | Cora |
| Cordelia | Cornelia | Deborah | Delia | Della |
| Diana | Dora | Dorinda | Dorothy | Doxie |
| Edith | Edna | Eleanor | Electra | Elisabeth |
| Eliza | Ella | Ellen | Ellie | Elsie |
| Emeline | Emily | Emma | Ernestine | Esmerelda |
| Esther | Eudora | Eugenia | Eunice | Eva |
| Evangeline | Fanny | Fatima | Faustina | Felicia |
| Flora | Florence | Frances | Francelia | Fredrica |
| Gabriella | Geneva | Genevieve | Georgiana | Geraldine |
| Gertie | Gertrude | Hannah | Harriet | Hattie |
| Helen | Hessa | Hester | Hilda | Hortensia |
| Ida | Imogene | Ionia | Irene | Isabel |
| Isadora | Jane | Janet | Jean | Jeannette |

| | | | | |
|---|---|---|---|---|
| Jemima | Jennie | Jenny | Jessie | Joan |
| Joanna | Josepha | Josephine | Judith | Julia |
| Juliet | Junietta | Katharine | Katie | Katrina |
| Kittie | Laura | Laurietta | Lavinia | Lena |
| Letitia | Libbie | Lillian | Lilly | Lorana |
| Louisa | Lucinda | Lucy | Lurella | Lydia |
| Mabel | Madeline | Maggie | Mahala | Margaret |
| Marie | Marietta | Marilla | Martha | Mary |
| Mathilda | Maud | May | Meggie | Melicent |
| Melissa | Metta | Mildred | Minnie | Miranda |
| Morella | Nancy | Naomi | Nellie | Nettie |
| Nina | Nora | Octavia | Olive | Olivia |
| Olympia | Ophelia | Orlinda | Othalia | Pansy |
| Pauline | Penelope | Phoebe | Phyllis | Polly |
| Porcia | Priscilla | Rachel | Rebecca | Rena |
| Rhoda | Rosa | Rosabel | Rosalie | Rosalind |
| Rosamond | Rose | Rosetta | Roxana | Ruth |
| Samantha | Sara | Selina | Sibyl | Sophia |
| Stella | Susanna | Sylvia | Theodora | Theresa |
| Tilda | Tillie | Uretta | Ursula | Valeria |
| Victoria | Viola | Violet | Virginia | Vivian |
| Welthy | Wincie | Winnie | Zella | Zenobia |

—*Hill's Manual of Social and Business Forms,* 1888

# ENDNOTES

## INTRODUCTION

1. Carl Bode, *Midcentury America: Life in the 1850s*. Carbondale, Ill.: Southern Illinois University Press, 1972, p. 91.

## CHAPTER ONE

1. John F. Kasson, *Rudeness & Civility: Manners in Nineteenth Century Urban America*. New York: The Noonday Press, 1991, p. 41.
2. Ibid., p. 44.
3. Daniel Wise, *The Young Lady's Counsellor*. New York: Carlton & Porter, 1851, Preface pp. v–vi.
4. Mrs. L. H. Sigourney, *Letters To Young Ladies*. New York: Harper & Brothers, Publishers, 1854, p. 20.
5. Richard L. Bushman, *The Refinement of America: Persons, Houses, Cities*. New York: Vintage Books, 1992, p. 313.
6. Ibid., pp. 327–328.
7. Thomas J. Schlereth, *Victorian America: Transformations in Everyday Life*. New York: HarperPerennial, 1991, p. 264.
8. Mrs. L. H. Sigourney, *Letters To Young Ladies*. New York: Harper & Brothers, Publishers, 1854, pp. 45–46.
9. Louise L. Stevenson, *The Victorian Homefront*. New York: Twayne Publishers, 1991, pp. 121–122.
10. Mrs. L. H. Sigourney, *Letters To Young Ladies*. New York: Harper & Brothers, Publishers, 1854, p. 46.
11. George W. Burnap, *The Sphere and Duties of Woman*. Baltimore: Printed & Published by John Murphy, 1848, pp. 130–139.
12. Ibid., pp. 145–146.
13. Sarah J. Hale, "What Should Be Done," *Godey's Lady's Book*, July 1855, p. 83.

14. Daniel Wise, *The Young Lady's Counsellor*. New York: Carlton & Porter, 1851, pp. 206–209.

15. Virginia DeForrest, "Anna, or Cottage Devotion," *Godey's Lady's Book*, August 1855, pp. 205–206.

16. *Correct Social Usage: A Course of Instruction in Good Form, Style and Deportment by Eighteen Distinguished Authors*. New York: The New York Society of Self Culture, 1907, pp. 9–16.

17. Catherine Clinton, *The Plantation Mistress: Woman's World in the Old South*. New York: Pantheon Books, 1982, pp. 137–138.

18. G. S. Weaver, *The Heart of the World: or Home and Its Wide Work*. Columbus, Ohio: Potts, Leech & Co., Publisher, 1883, p. 209.

19. George W. Burnap, *The Sphere and Duties of Woman*. Baltimore: John Murphy, 1848, p. 99.

20. Daniel Wise, *The Young Lady's Counsellor*. New York: Carlton & Porter, 1851, pp. 235–237.

21. Lee M. Edwards, *Domestic Bliss: Family Life in American Painting 1840–1910*. Yonkers, N.Y.: The Hudson River Museum, 1986, p. 21.

22. Thos. E. Hill, *Hill's Manual of Social and Business Forms: Guide to Correct Writing*. Chicago: Hill Standard Book Co., Publishers, 1888, p. 164.

23. Ibid., p. 165.

24. G. S. Weaver, *The Heart of the World: or Home and Its Wide Work*. Columbus, Ohio: Potts, Leech & Co., Publisher, 1883, pp. 222–231.

25. John H. Young, A.M., *Our Deportment or the Manners, Conduct and Dress of The Most Refined Society*. Detroit: F. B. Dickerson & Co., 1882, p. 411.

26. Thos. E. Hill, *Hill's Manual of Social and Business Forms*. Chicago: Hill Standard Book Co., Publishers, 1888, p. 136.

27. Mrs. John A. Logan, *The Home Manual*. Chicago: The Royal Publishing House, 1890, pp. 334–335.

28. Richard A. Wells, A.M., *Manners, Culture and Dress of The Best American Society*. Springfield, Mass.: King, Richardson & Co., 1891, p. 225.

29. Ibid., p. 226.

30. Mrs. Stickney Parks, "Girl's Affairs," *The Ladies' Home Journal*, June 1912, p. 24.

31. Richard A. Wells, A.M., *Manners, Culture and Dress of The Best American Society*. Springfield, Mass.: King, Richardson & Co., 1891, p. 234.

32. Mrs. E. B. Duffey, *The Ladies' and Gentlemen's Etiquette: A Complete Manual of the Manners and Dress of American Society*. Philadelphia: Henry T. Coates & Co., 1877, p. 290.

33. Mlle. Bon Ton, "Fashions," *Godey's Lady's Book*, February 1885, p. 229.

34. John H. Young, A.M., *Our Deportment*. Detroit: F. B. Dickerson & Co., 1882, p. 194.

35. Ibid., p. 207.

36. Erna Olafson Hellerstein, Leslie Parker Hume and Karen M. Offen, *Victorian Women: A Documentary Account of Women's Lives in Nineteenth-Century England, France, and the United States*. Stanford, Calif.: Stanford University Press, 1981, p. 122.

37. Thos. E. Hill, *Hill's Manual of Social and Business Forms*. Chicago: Hill Standard Book Co., Publishers, 1888, p. 167.

38. *Collier's Cyclopedia of Social and Commercial Information*. New York: Collier Publishing Co., 1883, p. 626.

39. Thos. E. Hill, *Hill's Manual of Social and Business Forms*. Chicago: Hill Standard Book Co., Publishers, 1888, p. 167.

40. Jenni Calder, *Women and Marriage in Victorian Fiction*. New York: Oxford University Press, 1976, p. 9.

41. Lucy Ellen Guernsey, "The Other Side—A Tale of Buttons," *Godey's Lady's Book*, July 1855, pp. 55–60.

42. G. S. Weaver, *The Heart of the World*. Columbus, Ohio: Potts, Leech & Co., Publisher, 1883, pp. 36–37.

43. Mrs. Mary Wood-Allen, M.D., *What A Young Woman Ought to Know*. Philadelphia: The Vir Publishing Co., 1905, p. 266.

44. G. S. Weaver, *The Heart of the World*. Columbus, Ohio: Potts, Leech & Co., Publisher, 1883, p. 391.

45. Catherine Clinton, editor, *Half Sisters of History: Southern Women and the American Past*. Durham, N.C.: Duke University Press, 1994, see pp. 77–92, essay "Women's Perspective on the Patriarchy in the 1850s" by Anne Firor Scott.

46. Catherine Clinton, *Tara Revisited: Women, War, & The Plantation Legend*. New York: Abbeville Press, 1995, p. 42.

47. Richard A. Wells, A.M., *Manners, Culture and Dress of The Best American Society*. Springfield, Mass.: King, Richardson & Co., 1891, p. 264.

48. Ibid., p. 268.

## CHAPTER TWO

1. Catherine Clinton, *The Plantation Mistress*. New York: Pantheon Books, 1982, p. 9.

2. Ibid., p. 8.

3. Anna Fergurson, *The Young Lady's Guide to Knowledge and Virtue*. New York: G. W. Cottrell & Co., 1848, pp. 19–20.

4. Daniel Wise, *The Young Lady's Counsellor*. New York: Carlton & Porter, 1851, pp. 88–90.

5. Mrs. E. Oakes Smith, "Woman and her Needs," (circa 1851), appears in the book *Midcentury America: Life in the 1850s* edited by Carl Bode. Carbondale, Ill.: Southern Illinois University Press, 1972, pp. 80–84.

6. Catharine E. Beecher and Harriet Beecher Stowe, *The American Woman's Home*. Hartford, Conn.: The Stowe-Day Foundation, 1987 reprint of the 1869 original, p. 22.

7. Marion Harland, "Entirely at Home," *Godey's Lady's Book*, January and February 1867, pp. 29–39, 133–140.

8. Catharine E. Beecher and Harriet Beecher Stowe, *The American Woman's Home*. Hartford, Conn.: The Stowe-Day Foundation, 1987 reprint of the 1869 original, p. 17.

9. Richard Bushman, *The Refinement of America: Persons, Houses, Cities*. New York: Vintage Books, 1993, p. 444.

10. Sheila M. Rothman, *Woman's Proper Place*. New York: Basic Books, Inc., 1978, p. 14.

11. John H. Young, A.M., *Our Deportment: or the Manners, Conduct and Dress of The Most Refined Society*. Detroit: F. B. Dickerson & Co., 1882, p. 208.

12. G. S. Weaver, *The Heart of the World: or Home and Its Wide Work*. Columbus, Ohio: Potts, Leech & Co., Publisher, 1883, p. 36.

13. Sheila M. Rothman, *Woman's Proper Place*. New York: Basic Books, Inc., 1978, p. 103.

14. Erna Olafson Hellerstein, Leslie Parker Hume and Karen M. Offen, *Victorian Women: A Documentary Account of Women's Lives in Nineteenth-Century England, France, and the United States*. Stanford, Calif.: Stanford University Press, 1981, p. 119.

15. David P. Handlin, *The American Home: Architecture and Society 1815–1915*. Boston: Little, Brown and Company, 1979, p. 16.

16. Catharine E. Beecher and Harriet Beecher Stowe, *The American Woman's Home*. Hartford, Conn.: The Stowe-Day Foundation, 1987 reprint of the 1869 original, pp. 23–24.

17. Colleen McDannell, "Parlor Piety: The Home as Sacred Space in Protestant America," included in the book *American Home Life, 1880–1930* edited by Jessica Foy and Thomas J. Schlereth. Knoxville, Tenn.: The University of Tennessee Press, 192, pp. 162–189.

18. Palliser, Palliser & Co., *American Victorian Cottage Homes*. Mineola, N.Y.: Dover Publications, Inc., 1990 reprint of the 1878 *Palliser's American Cottage Homes*, p. 1.

19. Catharine E. Beecher and Harriet Beecher Stowe, *The New Housekeeper's Manual: Embracing a New Revised Edition of The American Woman's Home; or, Principles of Domestic Science*. New York: J. B. Ford and Company, 1873, pp. 13–14.

20. Susan Lasdun, *Victorians at Home*. New York: The Viking Press, 1891, see Introduction by Mark Girouard, p. 8.

21. Louis A. Godey, "Godey's Arm Chair," *Godey's Lady's Book*, July 1855, p. 90.

22. Colleen McDannell, "Parlor Piety," included in the book *American Home Life, 1880–1930*, edited by Jessica Foy and Thomas J. Schlereth. Knoxville, Tenn.: The University of Tennessee Press, 1992, p. 184.

23. Sidney Morse, *Household Discoveries and Mrs. Curtis's Cook Book*. Toledo, Ohio: The Success Co., 1909, p. 51.

24. Katherine C. Grier, "The Decline of The Memory Palace: The Parlor after 1890," included in the book *American Home Life, 1880–1930* edited by Jessica Foy and Thomas J. Schlereth. Knoxville, Tenn.: The University of Tennessee Press, 1992, p. 63.

25. Kenneth L. Ames, *Death in the Dining Room & Other Tales of Victorian Culture*. Philadelphia: Temple University Press, 1992, p. 67.

26. Henry Hudson Holly, *Holly's Country Seats*. Mineola, N.Y.: Dover Publications, Inc., 1993 reprint of the 1863 original, p. 76.

27. Ibid., pp. 44–49.

28. David P. Handlin, *The American Home: Architecture and Society 1815–1915*. Boston: Little, Brown and Company, 1979, p. 344.

29. Ibid., pp. 344–345.

30. Catharine E. Beecher and Harriet Beecher Stowe, *The American Woman's Home*. Hartford, Conn.: The Stowe-Day Foundation, 1987 reprint of the 1869 original, p. 84.

31. Alexander V. Hamilton, *The Household Cyclopaedia of Practical Receipts and Daily Wants.* Springfield: W. J. Holland & Co., 1873, p. 17.

32. Katherine C. Grier, "The Decline of the Memory Palace," included in the book *American Home Life, 1880–1930* edited by Jessica Foy and Thomas J. Schlereth. Knoxville, Tenn.: The University of Tennessee Press, 1992, p. 54.

33. Charles L. Eastlake, *Hints on Household Taste.* Mineola, N.Y.: Dover Publications, Inc., 1986 republication of the 1878 fourth edition, p. 159.

34. Richard A. Wells, A.M., *Manners, Culture and Dress of The Best American Society.* Springfield, Mass.: King, Richardson & Co., 1891, p. 463.

35. Louis A. Godey, "Godey's Arm Chair," *Godey's Lady's Book,* July 1855, p. 182.

36. Lydia Maria Child, *The American Frugal Housewife.* Worthington, Ohio: Worthington Historical Society, 1980 reprint of the 1832 12th edition, p. 90.

37. Richard L. Bushman, *The Refinement of America: Persons, Houses, Cities.* New York: Vintage Books, 1992, p. 270.

38. Ellen M. Plante, *The Victorian Home.* Philadelphia: Running Press, 1995, p. 28.

39. Richard A. Wells, A.M., *Manners, Culture and Dress of The Best American Society.* Springfield, Mass.: King, Richardson & Co., Publisher, 1891, pp. 465–467.

40. Allison Kyle Leopold, *Victorian Splendor.* New York: Stewart, Tabori and Chang, 1986, pp. 113–114.

41. Elan and Susan Zingman-Leith, *The Secret Life of Victorian Houses.* Washington, D.C.: Elliott & Clark Publishing, 1993, p. 36.

42. Kenneth L. Ames, *Death in the Dining Room & Other Tales of Victorian Culture.* Philadelphia: Temple University Press, 1992, p. 71.

43. Harvey Green, *The Light of the Home: An Intimate View of the Lives of Women in Victorian America.* New York: Pantheon Books, 1983, pp. 93–94.

## CHAPTER THREE

1. George W. Burnap, *The Sphere and Duties of Woman.* Baltimore: John Murphy, 1848, pp. 109–110.

2. "A Mother's Love," *Godey's Lady's Book,* January 1867, p. 39.

3. William Graham, "A Tribute to My Mother," *The Ladies' Repository: A Monthly Periodical, Devoted to Literature, Art and Religion,* December 1876, pp. 493–495.

4. Anne C. Rose, *Victorian America and the Civil War.* New York: Cambridge University Press, 1992, p. 170.

5. Monfort B. Allen, M.D. and Amelia C. McGregor, M.D., *The Glory of Woman or Love, Marriage and Maternity.* Chicago: John E. Hoham & Co., 1896, p. 127.

6. Ibid., p. 170.

7. Elisabeth Donaghy Garrett, *At Home: The American Family 1750–1870.* New York: Harry N. Abrams, Inc., Publishers, 1990, p. 230.

8. Ibid., pp. 230–231.

9. Thomas J. Schlereth, *Victorian America: Transformations in Everyday Life.* New York: HarperPerennial, 1991, pp. 272–273.

10. Ibid., pp. 273–274.

11. Harvey Green, *The Light of the Home*. New York: Pantheon Books, 1983, p. 30.

12. Anne Firor Scott, "Women's Perspective on the Patriarchy in the 1850s," included in the book *Half Sisters of History: Southern Women and the American Past* edited by Catherine Clinton, Durham, N.C.: Duke University Press, 1994, pp. 76–92.

13. Monfort B. Allen, M.D. and Amelia C. McGregor, M.D., *The Glory of Woman*. Chicago: John E. Hoham & Co., 1896, p. 104.

14. Karin Calvert, "Children in the House, 1890–1930," included in the book *American Home Life, 1880–1930*, edited by Jessica Foy and Thomas J. Schlereth. Knoxville, Tenn.: The University of Tennessee Press, 1992, p. 77.

15. Sharon Bloemendaal, "Is She Or Isn't He? Identifying Gender in Portraits," *The New York-Pennsylvania Collector*, June 1995, p. 14.

16. "Little Children," *Godey's Lady's Book*, June 1867, p. 531.

17. Harvey Green, *The Light of the Home*. New York: Pantheon Books, 1983, p. 35.

18. Thomas J. Schlereth, *Victorian America: Transformations in Everyday Life*. HarperPerennial, 1991, p. 277.

19. Karin Calvert, "Children in the House, 1890–1930," included in the book *American Home Life*, edited by Jessica Foy and Thomas J. Schlereth. Knoxville, Tenn.: The University of Tennessee Press, 1992, p. 82.

20. Virginia DeForrest, "Ellen Goodwin; or a Sense of Duty," *Godey's Lady's Book*, December 1855, pp. 535–537.

21. Mrs. Julia McNair Wright, *The Complete Home: An Encyclopaedia of Domestic Life and Affairs*. Philadelphia: J. C. McCurdy & Co., Publishers, 1879, pp. 87–117.

22. Anne Scott MacLeod, "The Caddie Woodlawn Syndrome: American Girlhood in the Nineteenth Century," included in the book *A Century of Childhood 1820–1920*. Rochester, N.Y.: The Margaret Woodbury Strong Museum, 1984, pp. 99–100.

23. Catherine Clinton, *The Plantation Mistress*. New York: Pantheon Books, 1982, p. 155.

24. Alexander V. Hamilton, *The Household Cyclopaedia of Practical Receipts and Daily Wants*. Springfield: W. J. Holland & Co., 1873, p. 362.

25. Ibid., pp. 160–161.

26. Lydia Maria Child, *The Mother's Book*. Boston: Carter & Hendee, 1831, pp. 1–2.

27. Ibid., pp. 3–4.

28. John H. Young, A.M., *Our Deportment*. Detroit: F. B. Dickerson & Co., 1882, p. 224.

29. Ibid., pp. 224–225.

30. *The Manners That Win. Compiled from the Latest Authorities*. Minneapolis, Minn.: Buckeye Publishing Co., 1880, pp. 22–34.

31. Ibid., pp. 22–34.

32. Catharine E. Beecher and Harriet Beecher Stowe, *The American Woman's Home*. Hartford, Conn.: The Stowe-Day Foundation, 1987 reprint of the 1869 original, pp. 276–277.

33. Barbara Finkelstein and Kathy Vandell, "The Schooling of American Childhood: The Emergence of Learning Communities, 1820–1920," in the book *A Century of Childhood 1820–1920*. Rochester, N.Y.: The Margaret Woodbury Strong Museum, 1984, p. 75.

34. Ibid., p. 66.

35. Ibid., p. 87.

36. Catharine E. Beecher and Harriet Beecher Stowe, *The American Woman's Home*. Hartford, Conn.: The Stowe-Day Foundation, 1987 reprint of the 1869 original, p. 19.

37. Catherine Clinton, *The Plantation Mistress*. New York: Pantheon Books, 1982, pp. 36–37.

38. Anne C. Rose, *Victorian America and the Civil War*. New York: Cambridge University Press, 1992, pp. 164–166.

39. Ibid., p. 170.

40. "Golden Maxims For Families," *Godey's Lady's Book*, March 1867, p. 270.

41. Prof. J. W. Van Dervoort, *The Voyage of Life: A Journey From the Cradle to the Grave*. New York: Union Publishing House, 1882, pp. 387–397.

42. G. S. Weaver, D.D., *The Heart of the World*. Columbus, Ohio: Potts, Leech & Co., Publisher, 1883, pp. 71–72.

43. Thomas J. Schlereth, *Victorian America*. New York: HarperPerennial, 1991, p. 277.

44. Thos. E. Hill, *Hill's Manual of Social and Business Forms*. Chicago: Hill Standard Book Co., Publishers, 1888, p. 175.

45. John H. Young, *Our Deportment*. Detroit: F. B. Dickerson & Co., 1882, pp. 406–407.

46. Donna R. Braden, "The Family That Plays Together Stays Together: Family Pastimes and Indoor Amusements, 1890–1930," included in the book *American Home Life, 1880–1930* edited by Jessica Foy and Thomas J. Schlereth. Knoxville, Tenn.: The University of Tennessee Press, 1992, pp. 146–148.

47. Mrs. John A. Logan, *The Home Manual*. Philadelphia: The Royal Publishing House, 1890, p. 116.

# CHAPTER FOUR

1. Lydia E. White, *Success in Society*. Boston: James H. Earle, 1889, p. 8.

2. John F. Kasson, *Rudeness & Civility: Manners in Nineteenth-Century Urban America*. New York: The Noonday Press, 1991, p. 60.

3. Mrs. E. B. Duffey, *The Ladies' and Gentlemen's Etiquette*. Philadelphia: Henry T. Coates & Co., 1877, p. 81.

4. John H. Young, A.M., *Our Deportment*. Detroit: F. B. Dickerson & Co., 1882, pp. 145–146.

5. Thos. E. Hill, *Hill's Manual of Social and Business Forms*. Chicago: Hill Standard Book Co., Publishers, 1888, p. 182.

6. John F. Kasson, *Rudeness & Civility: Manners in Nineteenth-Century Urban America*. New York: The Noonday Press, 1991, p. 133.

7. *Correct Social Usage: A Course of Instruction in Good Form, Style and Deportment by Eighteen Distinguished Authors*. New York: The New York Society of Self Culture, 1903, pp. 246–273.

8. Richard L. Bushman, *The Refinement of America: Persons, Houses, Cities*. New York: Vintage Books, 1993, p. 399.

9. John H. Young, A.M., *Our Deportment*. Detroit: F. B. Dickerson & Co., 1882, p. 153.

10. Charles Dudley Warner, "A Little Journey in the World," *Harper's New Monthly Magazine*, July 1889, pp. 214–225.

11. John F. Kasson, *Rudeness & Civility: Manners in Nineteenth-Century Urban America*. New York: The Noonday Press, 1991, p. 257.

12. Catharine E. Beecher, *Miss Beecher's Domestic Receipt Book: Designed as a Supplement to Her Treatise on Domestic Economy*. New York: Harper & Brothers, Publishers, third edition, 1860, p. v.

13. Ibid., pp. 234–235.

14. Ibid., pp. 235–237.

15. "Practical Hints for the Household," *Godey's Lady's Book*, September 1885, p. 293.

16. *Smiley's Cook Book and New and Complete Guide for Housekeepers*. Chicago: Smiley Publishing Company, 1898, p. 663.

17. Ibid., p. 659.

18. John H. Young, A.M., *Our Deportment*. Detroit: F. B. Dickerson & Co., 1882, p. 111.

19. *Collier's Cyclopedia of Social and Commercial Information*. New York: Collier Publishing Co., 1883, p. 595.

20. Ibid., p. 593.

21. Ruth Ashmore, "Side-Talks With Girls," *The Ladies' Home Journal*, March 1897, p. 31.

22. Dr. J. H. Hanaferd, "Hints About Health-Dancing as an Exercise for Girls," *Godey's Lady's Book*, September 1867, p. 265.

23. Mrs. Mary Wood-Allen, M.D., *What A Young Woman Ought To Know*. Philadelphia: The Vir Publishing Co., 1905, pp. 74–75.

24. *The Manners That Win. Compiled from the Latest Authorities*. Minneapolis, Minn.: Buckeye Publishing Co., 1880, pp. 149–150.

25. Ibid., p. 131.

26. "Fashions," *Peterson's Ladies Magazine*, September 1874, p. 94.

27. Louisa May Alcott, *Little Women*. New York: Books, Inc., Publishers, 1941, pp. 247–249.

28. *The Manners That Win. Compiled from the Latest Authorities*. Minneapolis, Minn.: Buckeye Publishing Co., 1880, pp. 94–95.

29. Alexander V. Hamilton, *The Household Cyclopaedia of Practical Receipts and Daily Wants*. Springfield: W. J. Holland & Co., 1873, p. 309.

30. Mrs. John A. Logan, *The Home Manual*. Philadelphia: The Royal Publishing House, 1890, p. 11.

31. Lynn Schnurnberger, *Let There Be Clothes*. New York: Workman Publishing, 1991, p. 258.

32. George W. Burnap, *The Sphere and Duties of Woman*. Baltimore: John Murphy, 1848, pp. 163–164.

33. Mrs. L. H. Sigourney, *Letters to Young Ladies*. New York: Harper & Brothers, Publishers, 1854, pp. 97–98.

34. Harvey Green, *The Light of the Home*. New York: Pantheon Books, 1983, p. 130.

35. "A Series of Papers on the Hair," *Godey's Lady's Book*, May 1855, p. 531.

36. Clarence Poe, editor, *True Tales of the South at War*. Chapel Hill, N.C.: University of North Carolina Press, 1961, p. 55.

37. Jerry June, "Practical Dress," *The House Wife*, March 1890, p. 9.

38. "The Young Lady's Toilet," *Godey's Lady's Book*, January 1856, p. 78.

39. Mrs. Merrifield, "How Far Should the Fashions Be Followed?" *Godey's Lady's Book*, January 1856, p. 30.

40. Alexander V. Hamilton, *The Household Cyclopaedia of Practical Receipts and Daily Wants*. Springfield: W. J. Holland & Co., 1873, pp. 127–128.

41. Ibid., p. 127.

42. "Receipts," *Godey's Lady's Book*, July 1855, p. 79.

43. Mrs. E. B. Duffey, *The Ladies' and Gentlemen's Etiquette*. Philadelphia: Henry T. Coates & Co., 1877, p. 299.

44. Monfort B. Allen, M.D. and Amelia C. McGregor, M.D., *The Glory of Woman or Love, Marriage and Maternity*. Chicago: John E. Hoham & Co., 1896, p. 376.

45. Emma E. Waker, M.D., "Pretty Girl Questions," *The Ladies' Home Journal*, June 1912, p. 18.

46. Allison Kyle Leopold, "The Changing Face of Victorian Beauty Part IV," *Victorian Homes*, Summer 1991, pp. 22–23.

# CHAPTER FIVE

1. Faye Dudden, *Serving Women: Household Service in Nineteenth-Century America*. Hanover, N.H.: University Press of New England, 1983, p. 44.

2. Catherine Clinton, *The Plantation Mistress*. New York: Pantheon Books, 1982, p. 25.

3. Eliza Leslie, *The House Book; or A Manual of Domestic Economy, for Town and Country*. Philadelphia: 1849 10th edition, pp. 3–5.

4. Joseph B. and Laura E. Lyman, *The Philosophy of Housekeeping*. Hartford, Conn.: S. M. Betts & Company, 1869, p. 304.

5. Ellen M. Plante, *The American Kitchen 1700 to the Present: From Hearth to Highrise*. New York: Facts On File, Inc., 1995, p. 66.

6. Catharine E. Beecher and Harriet Beecher Stowe, *The American Woman's Home*. Hartford, Conn.: The Stowe-Day Foundation, 1987 reprint of the 1869 original, pp. 226–227.

7. Miss E. Neil, *The Everyday Cookbook and Family Compendium*. Chicago: M. A. Donohue & Co., circa 1880s, p. 284.

8. Mrs. F. L. Gillette and Hugo Ziemann, *The White House CookBook*. Akron, Ohio: Saalfield Publishing Company, 1915 revised edition, pp. 589–590.

9. D. Sturgis, "The Planning and Furnishing of the Kitchen in the Modern Residence," *Architectural Record*, no. 16, 1904, p. 391.

10. Mrs. John A. Logan, *The Home Manual*. Philadelphia: The Royal Publishing House, 1889, pp. 282–283.

11. Marion Harland, *Breakfast, Luncheon and Tea*. New York: Charles Scribner's Sons, 1875, pp. 5–15.

12. C. Kurt Dewhurst, Betty MacDowell and Marsha MacDowell, *Artists In Aprons*. New York: E. P. Dutton in Association with the Museum of American Folk Art, 1979, p. 14.

13. Ibid., p. 20.

14. Mrs. L. H. Sigourney, *Letters To Young Ladies.* New York: Harper & Brothers, Publishers, 16th edition, 1854, p. 78.

15. Catharine E. Beecher and Harriet Beecher Stowe, *The American Woman's Home.* Hartford, Conn.: The Stowe-Day Foundation, 1987 reprint of the 1869 original, pp. 298–299.

16. Ibid., p. 353.

17. Louis A. Godey, "Godey's Arm-Chair," *Godey's Lady's Book,* August 1855, p. 185.

18. Sarah J. Hale, "Editor's Table," *Godey's Lady's Book,* February 1867, p. 192.

19. "Chitchat Upon New York and Philadelphia Fashions For September," *Godey's Lady's Book,* September 1855, p. 288.

20. "Chitchat Upon New York and Philadelphia Fashions For February," *Godey's Lady's Book,* February 1867, p. 203.

21. Mrs. Julia McNair Wright, *The Complete Home.* Philadelphia: J. C. McCurdy & Co., 1879, pp. 28–29.

22. Alexander V. Hamilton, *The Household Cyclopaedia of Practical Receipts and Daily Wants.* Springfield: W. J. Holland & Co., 1873, p. 196.

23. *Bloomingdale's Illustrated 1886 Catalog.* Mineola, N.Y.: Dover Publications, Inc., 1988 abridged republication of the Spring & Summer 1886 catalog. See the Introduction by Nancy Villa Bryk, p. 3.

24. Ibid., Introduction page.

25. C. Kurt Dewhurst, Betty MacDowell and Marsha MacDowell, *Artists In Aprons.* New York: E. P. Dutton in Association with the Museum of American Folk Art, 1979, p. 47.

26. Ibid., p. 53.

27. Alexander V. Hamilton, *The Household Cyclopaedia of Practical Receipts and Daily Wants.* Springfield: W. J. Holland & Co., 1873, p. 320.

28. Kenneth L. Ames, *Death in the Dining Room & Other Tales of Victorian Culture.* Philadelphia: Temple University Press, 1992, p. 143.

29. "Work Department," *Godey's Lady's Book,* August 1885, p. 188.

30. Francine Kirch, "The Ladies' Work Table," *Victorian Homes,* Spring 1989, pp. 32–35.

31. Francine Kirch, "Shellcraft: Creating Summer's Souvenirs," *Victorian Homes,* Summer 1990, pp. 16–18.

32. Catharine E. Beecher and Harriet Beecher Stowe, *The American Woman's Home.* Hartford, Conn.: The Stowe-Day Foundation, 1987 reprint of the 1869 original, p. 91.

33. Ibid., pp. 91–92.

34. *Smiley's Cook Book and New and Complete Guide for Housekeepers.* Chicago: Smiley Publishing Company, 1898, p. 733.

35. "Work Department," *Godey's Lady's Book,* June 1867, pp. 549–550.

36. Alexander V. Hamilton, *The Household Cyclopaedia of Practical Receipts and Daily Wants,* Springfield: W. J. Holland & Co., 1873, pp. 337–338.

37. *Godey's Lady's Book,* May 1855, p. 562.

38. C. Jeanenne Bell, *Answers To Questions About Old Jewelry 1840–1950.* Florence, Ala.: Books Americana, 1996, p. 8.

39. *Godey's Lady's Book,* December 1850, p. 568.

40. F. William Fosdick, "The Fire Etcher and His Art," *The Ladies' Home Journal*, September 1896, p. 3.

41. Louise L. Stevenson, *The Victorian Homefront*. New York: Twayne Publishers, 1991, p. 36.

42. Richard L. Bushman, *The Refinement of America: Persons, Houses, Cities*. New York: Vintage Books, 1993, p. 302.

43. Richard A. Wells, A.M., *Manners, Culture and Dress of The Best American Society*. Springfield, Mass.: King, Richardson & Co., 1891, pp. 476–478.

44. Louise L. Stevenson, *The Victorian Homefront*. New York: Twayne Publishers, 1991, p. 37.

45. "Literary Notices," *Godey's Lady's Book*, May 1867, p. 471.

46. Mrs. Julia McNair Wright, *The Complete Home*. Philadelphia: J. C. McCurdy & Co., 1879, p. 199.

47. Ibid., p. 168.

48. Allison Kyle Leopold, *The Victorian Garden*. New York: Clarkson Potter/Publishers, 1995, p. 15.

49. Catharine E. Beecher and Harriet Beecher Stowe, *The American Woman's Home*. Hartford, Conn.: The Stowe-Day Foundation, 1987 reprint of the 1869 original, p. 117.

50. Ibid., pp. 294–295.

51. "Flowers," *The House Wife*, March 1890, p. 12.

52. "The Floral Bay Window," *The Ladies' Home Journal*, September 1896, p. 18.

## CHAPTER SIX

1. E. G. Storke, *The Family and Householder's Guide*. Auburn, N.Y.: The Auburn Publishing Company, 1859, p. 119.

2. Catharine E. Beecher and Harriet Beecher Stowe, *The American Woman's Home*. Hartford, Conn.: The Stowe-Day Foundation, 1987 reprint of the 1869 original, pp. 337–338.

3. Thomas J. Schlereth, *Victorian America: Transformations in Everyday Life 1876–1915*. New York: HarperPerennial, 1991, pp. 286–287.

4. E. G. Storke, *The Family and Householder's Guide*. Auburn, N.Y.: The Auburn Publishing Company, 1859, pp. 106–107.

5. Catharine E. Beecher and Harriet Beecher Stowe, *The American Woman's Home*. Hartford, Conn.: The Stowe-Day Foundation, 1987 reprint of the 1869 original, p. 56.

6. E. G. Storke, *The Family and Householder's Guide*. Auburn, N.Y.: The Auburn Publishing Company, 1859, p. 109.

7. Catherine Clinton, *The Plantation Mistress*. New York: Pantheon Books, 1982, p. 140.

8. Alexander V. Hamilton, *The Household Cyclopaedia of Practical Receipts and Daily Wants*. Springfield: W. J. Holland & Co., 1873, pp. 157–158.

9. Ibid., pp. 180–185.

10. Mrs. John A. Logan, *The Home Manual*. Philadelphia: The Royal Publishing House, 1890, p. 221.

11. "Receipts, Etc.-Sick-Room and Nursery," *Godey's Lady's Book*, January 1856, p. 75.

12. Mrs. Mary Wood-Allen, M.D., *What A Young Woman Ought To Know*. Philadelphia: The Vir Publishing Company, 1905, p. 137.

13. Harvey Green, *The Light of the Home*. New York: Pantheon Books, 1983, pp. 138–141.

14. Catharine E. Beecher and Harriet Beecher Stowe, *The American Woman's Home*. Hartford, Conn.: The Stowe-Day Foundation, 1987 reprint of the 1869 original, p. 260.

15. Alexander V. Hamilton, *The Household Cyclopaedia of Practical Receipts and Daily Wants*. Springfield: W. J. Holland & Co., 1873, p. 179.

16. "On Being Old-Fashioned," *The Ladies' Home Journal*, September 1897, p. 14.

17. Sidney Morse, *Household Discoveries*. Toledo, Ohio: The Success Co., 1909, p. 646.

18. Louis I. Dublin and Alfred J. Lotka, *Length of Life: A Study of the Life Table*. New York: 1936, pp. 47–57.

19. Erna Olafson Hellerstein, Leslie Parker Hume and Karen M. Offen, *Victorian Women: A Documentary Account of Women's Lives in Nineteenth-Century England, France, and the United States*. Stanford, Calif.: Stanford University Press, 1981, p. 453.

20. Ibid., p. 454.

21. Mrs. E. B. Duffey, *The Ladies' and Gentlemen's Etiquette*. Philadelphia: Henry T. Coates & Co., 1877, pp. 260–261.

22. Monfort B. Allen, M.D. and Amelia C. McGregor, M.D., *The Glory of Woman or Love, Marriage and Maternity*. Chicago: John E. Hoham & Co., 1896, p. 436.

23. *The Manners That Win. Compiled from the Latest Authorities*. Minneapolis, Minn.: Buckeye Publishing Co., 1880, p. 399.

24. Monfort B. Allen, M.D. and Amelia C. McGregor, M.D., *The Glory of Woman*. Chicago: John E. Hoham & Co., 1896, pp. 251–252.

25. Mrs. Mary Wood-Allen, M.D., *What A Young Woman Ought To Know*. Philadelphia: The Vir Publishing Co., 1905, p. 278.

26. Mrs. Julia McNair Wright, *The Complete Home*. Philadelphia: J. C. McCurdy & Co., 1879, pp. 370–371.

27. Prof. J. W. Van Dervoort, *The Voyage of Life. A Journey from the Cradle to the Grave*. Chicago: Acme Publishing House, 1883, pp. 402–403.

28. Madison C. Peters, D.D., *The Great Hereafter or Glimpses of The Coming World*. New York: J. A. Wilmore & Co., 1897, p. 73.

29. Ibid., pp. 216–217.

30. Virginia Cary, *Letters on Female Character*. Richmond, Va.: A. Works, 1830, p. 50.

31. Thomas J. Schlereth, *Victorian America: Transformations in Everyday Life 1876–1915*. New York: HarperPerennial, 1991, pp. 290–293.

32. John H. Young, A.M., *Our Deportment*. Detroit: F. B. Dickerson & Co., 1882, pp. 297–299.

33. C. Kurt Dewhurst, Betty MacDowell and Marsha MacDowell, *Artists In Aprons*. New York: E. P. Dutton in association with the Museum of American Folk Art, 1979, p. 66.

34. Ibid., pp. 59–62.

35. Ibid., p. 76.

36. John H. Young, A.M., *Our Deportment*. Detroit: F. B. Dickerson & Co., 1882, p. 338.

37. *The Manners That Win. Compiled from the Latest Authorities.* Minneapolis, Minn.: Buckeye Publishing Co., 1880, p. 248.

38. *Collier's Cyclopedia of Social and Commercial Information.* New York: Collier Publishing Co., 1883, p. 628.

39. *Godey's Lady's Book,* March 1855, p. 143.

40. *Collier's Cyclopedia of Social and Commercial Information.* New York: Collier Publishing Co., 1883, p. 630.

# BIBLIOGRAPHY

Allen, Monfort B., and Amelia C. McGregor, M.D. *The Glory of Woman or Love, Marriage and Maternity.* Chicago: John E. Hoham & Co., 1896. An advice tome pertaining to marriage, maternity, child rearing and beauty.

Ames, Kenneth L. *Death in the Dining Room & Other Tales of Victorian Culture.* Philadelphia: Temple University Press, 1992. Explores the social history and material culture of specific aspects of everyday Victorian life.

Beecher, Catharine E. *Miss Beecher's Domestic Receipt-Book: Designed as a Supplement to Her Treatise on Domestic Economy.* New York: Harper & Brothers, Publishers, 3rd edition, 1860. Primarily a recipe book with limited information on housekeeping.

———. *The New Housekeeper's Manual.* New York: J. B. Ford & Company, 1873. Actually a revised and expanded edition of *The American Woman's Home*, published in 1869.

Beecher, Catharine E., and Harriet Beecher Stowe, *The American Woman's Home or, Principles of Domestic Science; Being a Guide to the Formation and Maintenance of Economical, Healthful, Beautiful, and Christian Homes.* Hartford, Conn.: The Stowe-Day Foundation, 1987 reprint of the 1869 original. The most noted of all 19th-century household manuals, with information pertaining to housekeeping, etiquette, child rearing, home decoration, sewing, etc.

Bell, Jeanenne. *Answers To Questions About Old Jewelry 1840–1950.* Florence, Ala.: Books Americana, 1996. A price guide for collectors with detailed historical information on jewelry and Victorian fashions.

Bode, Carl. *The Anatomy of American Popular Culture, 1840–1861.* Berkeley, Calif.: University of California Press, 1960. Explores the social history of various aspects of midcentury life.

———. *Midcentury America: Life in the 1850s.* Carbondale, Ill.: Southern Illinois University Press, 1972. A close-up look at typical mid-19th-century life.

Brownstone, Douglas L. *A Field Guide to America's History.* New York: Facts On File, Inc., 1984. Explores early American industrial structures, modes of transportation, architecture and artifacts and shows the reader how to recognize their long-ago sites of existence.

Burnap, George W. *The Sphere and Duties of Woman.* Baltimore: John Murphy, 1848. An instructional manual for young women with information on character building, the domestic world and proper etiquette.

Bushman, Richard L. *The Refinement of America: Persons, Houses, Cities.* New York: Vintage Books, 1993. Explores the development of genteel American society.

Calder, Jenni. *Women and Marriage in Victorian Fiction.* New York: Oxford University Press, 1976. Examines the works of several British authors and shows how Victorian attitudes affected the moral and artistic development of authors such as Dickens, Tolstoy, etc.

Clinton, Catherine. *The Plantation Mistress: Woman's World in the Old South.* New York: Pantheon Books, 1982. A detailed look at the lives of late 18th and early 19th-century Southern women of the plantation class.

———. *Half Sisters of History: Southern Women and the American Past.* Durham, N.C.: Duke University Press, 1994. Explores various aspects of the lives of Southern women during the 19th century.

———. *Tara Revisited: Women, War, & The Plantation Legend.* New York: Abbeville Press, 1995. Examines Civil War–era lives of Southern women and the myths surrounding plantation life.

*Collier's Cyclopedia of Social and Commercial Information.* New York: Collier Publishing Company, 1883. An all-purpose home manual with information on etiquette, business matters, letter writing, etc.

*Correct Social Usage: A Course of Instruction in Good Form, Style and Deportment by Eighteen Distinguished Authors.* New York: The New York Society of Self Culture, 1907. An early 20th-century etiquette manual.

Dewhurst, Kurt C., Betty MacDowell and Marsha MacDowell. *Artists In Aprons: Folk Art by American Women.* New York: E. P. Dutton in Association with the Museum of American Folk Art, 1979. Explores the everyday handiwork of American schoolgirls and women with emphasis on their folk-art qualities.

Dudden, Faye. *Serving Women: Household Service in Nineteenth-Century America.* Hanover, N.H.: University Press of New England, 1983. A close-up look at domestic servitude in Victorian America.

Duffey, Mrs. E. B. *The Ladies' and Gentlemen's Etiquette: A Complete Manual of The Manners and Dress of American Society.* Philadelphia: Henry T. Coates & Company, 1877. A deportment manual addressing proper conduct, manner of dress, table etiquette, etc.

Eastlake, Charles L. *Hints On Household Taste.* Mineola, N.Y.: Dover Publications, Inc., 1969 unabridged republication of the 1878 4th edition. Noted interior design and household guide that influenced furniture styles, interior decoration, etc., during late 1900s.

Edwards, Lee M. with contributions by Jan Seidler Ramirez and Timothy Anglin Burgard. *Domestic Bliss: Family Life in American Painting 1840–1910.* Yonkers, N.Y.: The Hudson River Museum, 1986. Examines 19th-century genre paintings and was published to coincide with a major exhibit held at both The Hudson River Museum and The Margaret Woodbury Strong Museum during 1986.

Fergurson, Anna. *The Young Lady's Guide to Knowledge and Virtue.* New York: G. W. Cottrell & Company, 1848. A midcentury behavior book for young women.

Foy, Jessica and Thomas J. Schlereth. *American Home Life, 1880–1930: A Social History of Spaces and Services.* Knoxville, Tenn.: The University of Tennessee Press, 1992. Examines social aspects of everyday life during the late Victorian era and early 20th century with chapters devoted to parlor life, kitchens, etc.

Garrett, Elisabeth Donaghy. *At Home: The American Family 1750–1870.* New York: Harry N. Abrams, Inc., 1990. A room-by-room look at family life with beautiful artwork of the period depicting same.

Green, Harvey. *The Light of the Home: An Intimate View of the Lives of Women in Victorian America.* New York: Pantheon Books, 1983. Explores the material culture surrounding the lives of middle-class women in the Northeast during the late 19th-century period.

Hamilton, Alexander V. *The Household Cyclopaedia of Practical Receipts and Daily Wants.* Springfield: W. J. Holland & Co., 1873. An all-purpose household manual complete with recipes.

Handlin, David P. *The American Home: Architecture and Society 1815–1915.* Boston: Little, Brown and Co., 1979. Explores how Americans built and lived in their homes between the early 19th-century period and the First World War.

Hellerstein, Erna Olafson, Leslie Parker Hume and Karen M. Offen, *Victorian Women: A Documentary Account of Women's Lives in Nineteenth-Century England, France, and the United States.* Stanford, Calif.: Stanford University Press, 1981. Includes a collection of historical documents by and about 19th-century women.

Hill, Thos. E. *Hill's Manual of Social and Business Forms.* Chicago: Hill Standard Book Co., Publishers, 1888. A large, all-purpose home manual addressing etiquette, fashionable dress, business matters, letter writing, social engagements, polite conversation and so on.

Holly, Henry Hudson. *Holly's Picturesque Country Seats.* Mineola, N.Y.: Dover Publications, Inc., 1993. Unabridged republication of the 1863 original. Contains architectural designs for cottages, villas, mansions, churches, etc.

Howard, Hugh. *How Old Is This House?* New York: Farrar, Straus and Giroux, 1989. Contains information on various architectural styles throughout the history of America and offers clues to identification.

Kasson, John F. *Rudeness & Civility: Manners in Nineteenth Century Urban America.* New York: The Noonday Press, 1991. Explores the social history surrounding the development and practice of polite etiquette in Victorian America.

Klein, Marilyn W. and David P. Fogle. *Clues to American Architecture.* Washington, D.C.: Starrhill Press, 1985. A pocket-size handy reference to identifying American architectural styles complete with drawings.

Lasdun, Susan. *Victorians at Home.* New York: The Viking Press, 1981. Examines interior design, customs and social life in 19th-century England.

Leopold, Allison Kyle. *The Victorian Garden.* New York: Clarkson Potter/Publishers, 1995. Looks at the various types of gardens, flowers and greenery popular in Victorian America.

———. *Victorian Keepsake.* New York: Doubleday, 1991. Offers primary source material on love, courtship and marriage, accompanied by vintage ephemera for illustration.

Logan, Mrs. John A. *The Home Manual.* Chicago: The Royal Publishing House, 1890. This all-purpose home manual was sold by subscription only. Contains advice on all home-related topics.

Mace, O. Henry. *Collector's Guide to Victoriana.* A price guide for the collector with detailed information on the material culture of the Victorian age.

*The Manners That Win. Compiled from the Latest Authorities.* Minneapolis, Minn.: Buckeye Publishing Co., 1880. An etiquette and deportment manual with extensive information on dress, beauty, the art of polite conversation, etc.

Morse, Sidney. *Household Discoveries and Mrs. Curtis's Cook Book.* Toledo, Ohio: The Success Company, 1909. Actually two books in one, this large tome includes extensive household advice and numerous recipes.

Moss, Roger W. and Gail Caskey Winkler. *Victorian Interior Decoration: American Interiors 1830–1900.* New York: Henry Holt and Company, 1986. Explores the furnishings, interior design, etc. popular during the Victorian era.

Palliser, Palliser & Co. *American Victorian Cottage Homes.* Mineola, N.Y.: Dover Publications, Inc., 1990 unabridged republication of the 1878 Palliser's American Cottage Homes. An architectural plan book offering a wide variety of 19th-century-style homes in different price ranges.

Peters, Madison C. *The Great Hereafter or Glimpses of The Coming World.* New York: J. A. Wilmore & Company, 1897. Contains essays about death and the afterlife as well as numerous poems on the same topics.

Plante, Ellen M. *The American Kitchen 1700 to the Present: From Hearth to Highrise.* New York: Facts On File, Inc., 1995. Explores the history of the American kitchen and women's changing roles from the colonial era through present day.

———. *The Victorian Home.* Philadelphia: Running Press Book Publishers, 1995. A coffee-table size decorating book with advice on how to create a Victorian revival interior. Offers information on 19th-century interior design, social customs, etc. Illustrated with beautiful color photos.

Rose, Anne C. *Victorian America and the Civil War.* New York: Cambridge University Press, 1992. Explores American life, social customs, family life, etc. during the Civil War years in the 1860s.

Schlereth, Thomas J. *Victorian America: Transformations in Everyday Life 1876–1915.* New York: HarperPerennial, 1991. Explores the social history and various facets/changes of daily life during the late Victorian era.

Schnurnberger, Lynn. *Let There Be Clothes.* New York: Workman Publishing, 1991. Examines the history of clothing and fashions including specific attire, accessories, undergarments, etc.

Sigourney, Mrs. L. H. *Letters To Young Ladies.* New York: Harper & Brothers, Publishers, 1854. A behavior/conduct book for young Victorian women with chapters devoted to character, family life, the domestic sphere, chores, solid learning, etc.

*Smiley's Cook Book and New and Complete Guide for Housekeepers.* Chicago: Smiley Publishing Company, 1898. A household guide complete with advice and recipes.

Stevenson, Louise L. *The Victorian Homefront: American Thought and Culture 1860–1880.* New York: Twayne Publishers, 1991. Examines a 20-year period of Victorian culture with chapters devoted to the home, forms of entertainment, the arts, etc.

Storke, E. G. *The Family and Householder's Guide.* Auburn, N.Y.: The Auburn Publishing Company, 1859. An all-purpose household guide with information on etiquette, cleaning, cooking, child rearing, sickness, etc.

Thurer, Shari L. *The Myths of Motherhood.* New York: Penguin Books, 1995. Examines motherhood through the ages.

Van Dervoort, Prof. J. W. *The Voyage of Life. A Journey from the Cradle to the Grave.* Chicago: Acme Publishing House, 1883. A sentimental narrative about life and death.

Weaver, G. S. *The Heart of the World: or Home and Its Wide Work.* Columbus, Ohio: Potts, Leech & Co., 1883. Instructional narrative exploring the home as the center of all that was good in Victorian society, women's role as domestic goddess, etc.

Wells, Richard A. *Manners, Culture and Dress of The Best American Society.* Springfield, Mass.: King, Richardson & Co., Publisher, 1891. An etiquette and deportment manual containing the rules of society and advice on dress, manners, social functions, etc.

Wise, Daniel. *The Young Lady's Counsellor: or, Outlines and Illustrations of The Sphere, The Duties, and The Dangers of Young Women.* New York: Carlton & Porter, 1851. An instructional/behavior manual for young women with chapters devoted to domestic roles, duties toward others, the pitfalls of fashion and leisure, etc.

Wood-Allen, Mary, M.D. *What A Young Woman Ought To Know.* Philadelphia: The Vir Publishing Co., 1905. Female anatomy, womanhood, fashions, love and marriage are discussed in this advice book for young women.

Wright, Mrs. Julia McNair. *The Complete Home: An Encyclopaedia of Domestic Life and Affairs.* Philadelphia: J. C. McCurdy & Co. Publishers, 1879. An uplifting tome praising the benefits of domestic life and the value of woman's work.

Young, John A. *Our Deportment or The Manners, Conduct and Dress of The Most Refined Society.* Detroit: F. B. Dickerson & Co., 1882. A typical late 19th-century etiquette book with chapters on dress, social situations, funerals, beauty, table etiquette, home decoration, etc.

Zingman-Leith, Elan and Susan. *The Secret Life of Victorian Houses.* Washington, D.C.: Elliott & Clark Publishing, 1993. Beautiful color photos of Victorian revival interiors (many of bed and breakfasts in Cape May, N.J.) accompany this text exploring various rooms, artifacts, etc., found in the typical Victorian home of the 19th century.

# INDEX